PRAISE FOR
THE WRONG ENEMY

"A valuable contribution to a hefty body of work on the American war in Afghanistan that has become stale and somewhat hackneyed. It provides a raw, unvarnished and important look at one of the darkest and least understood parts of the Afghan war . . . Ms. Gall, a reporter for the *New York Times* in Afghanistan and Pakistan for more than a decade, beginning shortly after 9/11, is in an extraordinary position to write this important and long-overdue book."   — *New York Times*

"Gall's long years of reporting for the *New York Times* from the front lines of the war are clear in this book, particularly in her vivid reconstruction of how things went rapidly downhill after the easy U.S.-led victories over the Taliban at the end of 2001."   — *Wall Street Journal*

"[An] important work . . . Tracing the arc of the conflict from the days after the 9/11 attacks until the recent past, Gall's narrative unfolds on both sides of the Afghanistan-Pakistan border, employing both sweep and dexterity as she weaves seemingly disparate events into a coherent whole."   — *Los Angeles Times*

"If you have never visited Afghanistan, *The Wrong Enemy* will take you there."   — *Washington Post*

"The author offers a compelling account of the attack on bin Laden's compound, the repercussions of which are still being felt. Gall admirably never loses sight of the human element in this tragedy."
— *Kirkus Reviews*

Books by Carlotta Gall

Chechnya: Calamity in the Caucasus
(co-authored with Thomas de Waal)

The Wrong Enemy:
America in Afghanistan, 2001–2014

· THE ·
WRONG
ENEMY

AMERICA IN AFGHANISTAN, 2001–2014

CARLOTTA GALL

MARINER BOOKS
HOUGHTON MIFFLIN HARCOURT
BOSTON · NEW YORK

*For my father, Sandy Gall, who showed me the way in
Afghanistan and encouraged me to write this book, and for
my mother, Eleanor Gall, who gave me the spirit of adventure.*

*And in memory of Sultan Munadi (1975–2009),
best of friends and colleagues, kidnapped by the Taliban
and killed in a rescue attempt.*

First Mariner Books edition 2015

www.hmhco.com

Library of Congress Cataloging-in-Publication Data
Gall, Carlotta, author.
The wrong enemy : America in Afghanistan, 2001–2014 / Carlotta Gall.
pages; cm
Includes bibliographical references and index.
ISBN 978-0-544-04669-6 (hardback)   ISBN 978-0-544-53856-6 (pbk.)
1. Taliban. 2. Afghan War, 2001– 3. Pakistan — Politics and government.
4. Afghanistan — Politics and government. 5. Pakistan. Inter Services Intelligence.
6. Qaida (Organization) 7. United States — Foreign relations — Pakistan.
8. Pakistan — Foreign relations — United States. 9. United States — Foreign relations —
Afghanistan. 10. Afghanistan — Foreign relation — United States. I. Title.
DS371.412.G35 2014
958.104'7 — dc23   2013044257

Book design by Brian Moore

Printed in the United States of America
DOC 10 9 8 7 6 5 4 3 2 1

CONTENTS

"We may be fighting the wrong enemy in the wrong country."

— *The late Richard C. Holbrooke, U.S. special representative to Afghanistan and Pakistan*

FOREWORD

I arrived in the town of Mazar-i-Sharif in northern Afghanistan on a cold evening in November 2001, just days after the Taliban had fled. Two months had passed since the attacks of 9/11 and one month since America had gone to war in Afghanistan. The U.S. Air Force had been bombing Afghanistan since October 7, set on chasing down al Qaeda and toppling the Taliban government that harbored its leaders. I had crossed the strictly controlled border from Uzbekistan thanks to an Afghan friend. I had not seen him for six years, but he had helped my father travel into Afghanistan during the Soviet occupation and decided to help his friend's daughter cover this war. It was one of the reasons I came to love the Afghans. Friendship and loyalty mattered.

I had visited Mazar-i-Sharif several times in the 1990s and knew it as a busy trading town, its streets spanning out from the glorious turquoise dome and tiled walls of the Shrine of Hazrat Ali in its central square. I was shocked at how impoverished the city and its inhabitants had become. They had suffered two terrible massacres in four years under the Taliban and lived under virtual blockade. Thousands of families, displaced by the war and Afghanistan's worst drought in decades, had moved to the city in search of work and food. The streets were clogged with horsecarts, street stalls, and laborers pulling loads through the potholes. Families carrying children in their arms stepped through the mud to the central hospital. Scores of women begged on the mud-slicked streets, their faces hidden behind the lattice screen of the burqa, the head-to-toe pleated veil that turned women into soulless beings. The only part of their body visible was a calloused hand stretched out to passersby. Everyone was cold and hungry. The restaurants and tea shops were empty because of Ramadan. Street stalls sold imported fruit juice and stale biscuits, but there was not an egg to be had in the whole city.

I was reporting for the *New York Times,* one of two dozen correspondents scrambled and sent to the region in the weeks after 9/11. I would end up staying for over a decade, engrossed in America's struggle in Afghanistan. The Afghans would overthrow the Taliban and embrace peace, only to falter and slip back, dragged into a fight that few of them wanted. I packed up and left my previous post in the Balkans and went to live in Kabul, staying with the story even as the world's attention was drawn away to Iraq. For me, Afghanistan was always the most important news story of the time. It was where 9/11 began and would finally be answered. It was where my reporting life had started, and from where rose this great wave of Islamism that has powered many of today's wars.

By 2001, I had been reporting on wars for nearly eight years: five in Russia where I covered the war in Chechnya closely, and three in the Balkans, chronicling the war in Kosovo and the fall of Slobodan Milošević for the *New York Times.* At the time of 9/11, I was reporting on NATO's most pressing concern, an incipient guerrilla movement in Macedonia on the border with Kosovo. I watched the attack on the twin towers with fellow journalists in a hotel bar in Skopje. I knew immediately that Osama bin Laden was behind the attacks. I knew the story would lead back to Afghanistan, and I felt dread for the Afghans.

Afghanistan had featured large in my life for nearly twenty years, ever since the early days of the Soviet invasion. As a Russian language student, I had met drunken Red Army soldiers back from Afghanistan in a Soviet bar. The war was never officially acknowledged, but those conscripts told hair-raising stories of Afghan guerrillas mutilating soldiers caught on the battlefield. I heard the other side of the story from my father, a British television journalist who was in Afghanistan with the mujahideen, and brought back pictures of refugees pouring out of the country along donkey trails, villagers taking up arms against Soviet jets and helicopters, and Russian prisoners talking about drug-taking and hazing in the ranks. It was the Soviet Union's Vietnam — I was fascinated. In the 1990s, I traveled to Pakistan and Afghanistan and saw for myself the harsh mountains and emerald valleys of the Hindu Kush, and met the Afghans, resilient and gracious even in the destitution of the refugee camps.

I came across international jihadis in the Pakistani city of Peshawar then, too. We called them Wahhabis, after the fundamentalist Islamic sect that has its roots in Saudi Arabia. They were rough fighters, Arabs and North Africans who would run us off the roads, and Egyptian and Kuwaiti doctors who showed a hostile arrogance to us Westerners. We did not realize then, but they were the beginnings of bin Laden's al Qaeda. They were often a menace to the Afghans with their militaristic ambitions. After the Soviet withdrawal from Afghanistan, they were looking for a cause.

I saw Wahhabis turn up in Chechnya in 1995 and watched how they transformed the Chechens' deserving cause for self-determination into an extremist Islamist struggle. Determined to spark a greater conflagration across the Muslim North Caucasus, the Arabs set Chechens against each other and helped provoke the second war in the republic in 1999, bringing more disaster and destruction down on the small territory. They wrought even greater havoc in Afghanistan and Pakistan. They dreamed of creating an Islamic caliphate stretching across South and Central Asia, home to some 500 million Muslims. Pakistan, the first nuclear-armed Muslim state, would be at its core. Some of us saw and wrote about the extremist trend as it unfolded, but no Western government seemed concerned.

Now, by going to war in 2001, the United States was walking into the Islamists' trap. It was just what al Qaeda wanted: for Afghanistan again to serve as a battleground for Muslim fighters against a superpower. The Afghans once more were their unlucky pawns.

It would become America's longest overt war. Thirteen years later, there is no swift resolution in sight, and support at home has waned.

Few Americans seem to care anymore about Afghanistan, and I decided I owed it to all those caught up in the maelstrom of Afghanistan to put down a record of events as I had seen them from the ground.

The war has been a tragedy costing untold thousands of lives and lasting far too long. The Afghans were never advocates of terrorism yet they bore the brunt of the punishment for 9/11. Pakistan, supposedly an ally, has proved to be perfidious, driving the violence in Afghanistan for its own cynical, hegemonic reasons. Pakistan's generals and mullahs have done great harm to their own people as well as their Afghan neighbors and NATO allies. Pakistan, not Afghanistan, has been the true enemy.

The U.S. and NATO response has always been behind the curve, "trailing" the insurgency, as the military terms it, and ignoring it to wage war in Iraq. It was a fatal error to allow the insurgency to grow so strong that defeating it would be brought into question and cost so many lives. Politicians and diplomats, barring the exceptional few, were mealymouthed, pleading that they had no leverage over Pakistan, and downright negligent.

I watched the resurgence of the Taliban with mounting alarm and, ultimately, great sorrow since it could have been prevented. I witnessed many of the scenes in this book, met most of the participants, and heard their accounts firsthand. In retelling these events, I am offering a first brush of history. It is a partial record, as war reporting always is, but it is as I and many Afghans saw it. I lived in Kabul, with a foothold in Islamabad, from 2001 to 2011, traveling all over Afghanistan and through much of Pakistan too. I returned for nine months, from 2012 to 2013, to write this book. Over twelve years, I lost friends and acquaintances in suicide bombings and shootings, and saw others close to me savagely maimed. I do not pretend to be objective in this war. I am on the side of the victims. The human suffering has been far too great, and we have a duty to ponder the reasons for such a calamity.

Kabul, Afghanistan

May 2013

PROLOGUE

"I'm in trouble here."

— *Photographer colleague in Quetta*

December 2006. After five days of reporting in and around Quetta, Pakistan, I had somehow irritated the secretive but powerful Directorate for Inter-Services Intelligence, the ISI. I had been following the trail of several suicide bombers, calling on their families, visiting the madrassas they had attended, and interviewing government officials, Taliban sympathizers, and opposition politicians. I had been working with a Pakistani photographer and several different local reporters. We were followed over several days of reporting in Quetta by plainclothes intelligence men who were posted at our respective hotels and trailed us on motorbikes. That is not unusual in Pakistan, where accredited journalists are free to travel and report, but their movements, phone calls, and interviews are often monitored. But the Pakistani military has its own red lines. There are some subjects it does not want reported, and it has used intimidation to suppress the truth.

On our fifth and last day in Quetta, four plainclothes men detained my photographer colleague at his hotel downtown. They seized his computer and photo equipment and brought him to the parking lot of my hotel. There they made him call me and ask me to come down to talk to them. "I'm in trouble here," he told me. It was after dark. I did not want to go down to meet a bunch of ISI men, but I told my colleague I would get help. I alerted my editor in New York.

Before I could reach any Pakistani officials, the agents raided my hotel room. I had earlier refused to admit them, but now they got the hotel staff to open the door with a key card, and then they broke through the door chain. The lintel splintered. They burst in in a rush, snatching my laptop from my hands. They were plainclothes intelligence, I realized. Among them was an English-speaking officer wearing a smart new khaki-colored fleece. The other three were the muscle, in bulky winter jackets over dark-colored shalwar kamize, loose-fitting shirt and pants. One of them had the photographer in tow.

They went through my clothes and seized my computer, notebooks, and a cell phone. When one of the muscle men grabbed my handbag from me, I protested. He punched me twice, hard, in the face and temple, knocking me over. I fell back onto the coffee table, smashing the cups there, grabbing at the officer's fleece to break my fall and nearly pulling him down on top of me. For a moment it was funny. I remember thinking it was just like a hotel-room bust-up in the movies.

But then I flew into a rage and berated them for barging into a woman's bedroom and using physical violence. The English-speaking officer who appeared to be in charge told me that I was not permitted to visit the neighborhood of Pashtunabad (as we had), and that it was forbidden to interview members of the Taliban (as we had tried to). He refused to show me any ID or say who they were — but he said we could apply to the Special Branch of the police for our belongings the next day. As they were leaving, I told them that the photographer should stay with me. The officer refused. "He is Pakistani, we can do with him whatever we want." That was chilling. I knew they were capable of torture and murder, especially in Quetta, where the security services were a law unto themselves.

They drove off in a white jeep. I took down the license number and later found it belonged to the Special Branch police service. The car was just a cover. In fact, the men were military intelligence. They drove to the Military Intelligence building in Quetta, the town's most dreaded institution, which was behind a campaign of ruthless suppression of Baluch nationalists since 2006. Baluchistan is one of the poorest regions of Pakistan, and the indigenous Baluch tribes have fought repeated insurgencies demanding greater political autonomy and rights over the province's rich natural resources.

My foreign editor, Susan Chira, had been working the phones and had reached the minister of state for information and broadcasting, Tariq Azim. He was dining with Prime Minister Shaukat Aziz at the time and was able to tap him for the cell phone numbers of security officials in Quetta. With his intervention, my belongings were returned several hours later. The photographer was released after more than five hours in detention and ordered to leave town.

It became clear later that intelligence agents had copied data from our computers, notebooks, and cell phones, and tracked down our contacts and acquaintances in Quetta. Most of the people I interviewed, I learned, were subsequently visited by intelligence agents, and some of the local journalists who had helped me were warned by Pakistan's intelligence services not to work with foreign journalists again. Afghans were at most risk, and several had to leave town to avoid arrest. I was later told by a diplomat that the rough treatment was ordered by the head of the ISPR, the Inter-Services Public Relations, the press department of the Pakistani military, in order to discourage me in my reporting. Our photographer was severely threatened and told not to work with the *New York Times* in the future. The intimidation continued for months, and eventually he was forced to cut all ties with the paper.

One Quetta journalist who had worked a couple of days with us came home late that night and saw a strange car parked near his house. It was a red Vigo SUV, with tinted windows and a special license plate with white writing on a black background. It looked like an intelligence agency car. "We journalists can smell their cars," he told me years later. He remembered a message from me earlier in the evening, advising caution, so he walked straight past his house and went to stay with a friend. He turned his phone off for a week and stayed away from work for a day until he heard things had calmed down.

Another journalist did not wait for anyone to call on his home. When he heard from a friend what had happened to us, he turned off his cell phone and removed the battery and SIM card. Pakistani journalists have learned that is the first thing they should do in times of trouble, since cell phone companies, and therefore intelligence agents, can track your location through the GPS in your phone, even when it is switched off. Then he left home, arranging with his father to relay a signal to him the next morning if there was trouble. He drove all night, heading hundreds of miles first south, then north, then east of the provincial capital without stopping. Any risk of breakdown or encounter with thieves on the roads was minor compared to being picked up by intelligence agents. At 9 a.m. the next morning, he came back into Quetta and looked for the signal from his father. All was quiet, so he returned home.

The extreme caution of the two journalists was indicative of the pressures under which Pakistani journalists work. Few dared talk about it, but after several years working in Pakistan, I was learning that journalists who reported on taboo subjects, including the presence of the Taliban in Pakistan, ISI covert operations, Pakistan's nuclear program, or issues within the military, risked intimidation and often physical abuse. In the worst cases, journalists had been killed.

In Baluchistan, where the Pakistani military was waging a dirty war against Baluch nationalist rebels, disappearances of journalists and political activists were common. Hundreds of Baluch were missing or detained. Many turned up dead. Cases of extrajudicial killings by Pakistani security forces became so frequent from 2006 to 2013 that human rights organizations described the practice as "kill and dump."

The ISI in particular was responsible for picking up and threatening local journalists all over the country. Reporters were usually hustled into a car by plainclothes intelligence agents and disappeared for two or three days. Family and friends did not know where they were. There was never any judicial process. When they were released, they usually refused to talk about where they had been or what had happened, yet their colleagues noticed they were changed: they were quieter and their journalism became more cautious, avoiding controversial issues. During their disappearance they had, in fact, been beaten, strung up, and often sexually abused. They and their families were threatened, and they were warned to conform in their reporting or suffer terrible consequences.

In the worst cases, these journalists died at the hands of their tormentors. The tribal-areas journalist Hayatullah Khan Dawar was killed in 2006 after being the first reporter to identify a U.S. drone strike in Pakistan, which was an embarrassing revelation for the military. The government of Pervez Musharraf cooperated with the United States on the secret drone program but lied to its own people, denying that it was doing so. Hayatullah was detained for six months and then summarily executed. Saleem Shahzad, who wrote extensively about militancy and the ISI, was found dead in 2012 after being detained by intelligence agency personnel. He was killed on the orders of Pakistan's most senior generals.[1] At least forty-two journalists have been killed in the past decade, twenty-three of them murdered, in direct relation to their work in Pakistan, according to the Committee to Protect Journalists.[2] Not one of these cases has been put to a credible trial.

Those who survived were warned before their release not to tell anyone what had happened and not to talk to the media. This has proved an effective method of control. Quetta-based journalists could long ago have exposed the presence of the Taliban leadership in their city and the close relationship between the ISI and the militants. The reporters were entirely capable of tracking down the Taliban leader Mullah Mohammad Omar and Osama bin Laden, yet they did not dare relate the things they saw and heard.

Three days after his all-night drive, the Quetta reporter received an anonymous phone call. "I am from the cantonment," the caller said. He refused to give his name. He spoke Urdu with a Punjabi accent, indicating he was not native to Quetta. "Cantonment" meant the protected military quarter, and the reporter understood that the man was from the intelligence services. The caller warned the reporter not to work with any foreign journalists again. "If you do, you will be responsible for the consequences," he said. With those few words he accomplished what he intended. The journalist ceased working with foreign reporters from then on.

Pakistan has always exercised a strong level of control over journalists and the institutions of the media. Journalists had been imprisoned, beaten, and corrupted by previous governments, both military and civilian. General Musharraf's period of rule, from 1999 to 2008, was not generally considered a fearsome dictatorship. Still, certain sections of society came to fear brutal detentions and interrogations at the hands of Musharraf's security services, in particular Baluch and other separatists, and journalists who broke the rules. Then and now, people writing or talking about events in the tribal areas that challenge the military narrative of events are silenced.

A schoolteacher from South Waziristan who is a writer and poet was noted for the eloquent articles he composed for local newspapers. Then one day he fell silent. He told an acquaintance that he had been called in by an army officer heading the ISI chapter in Wana and told to cease writing articles. "If you don't, it will be very bad for you," he was told. The army officer said that it was his job to shut the writer up, and he did not care how he accomplished it, by warning the writer or by killing him. "Even if we kill you we will still get paid [our salaries]. Are you sure you want to write anymore?" the officer asked.

After years of working in Pakistan and Afghanistan, I came to understand the depth of the ISI's control over journalists and society at large. Journalists were not only warned off covering certain subjects, but hundreds of reporters and editors were kept on the government payroll to publish articles favorable to the military and in support of the policies it espoused. Military press officials would also write articles themselves, and then place them with a newspaper under a fictitious name. I learned this over time when I tried to follow up on interesting stories in the papers and discovered that the reporters often did not exist and the stories were bogus.

A retired editor explained to me how the system worked. He was once commissioned to write an article by an official in the main military press office, the ISPR. The ISPR edited the piece and placed it with two newspapers, after which the editor received official remuneration for his work from the Ministry of Information and Broadcasting. The ISPR's influence was such that it was able to order up an article, have it published, and arrange payment with evident ease. The civilian governments acted similarly but had nothing like the same reach or clout of the generals. Farahnaz Ispahani, media advisor to President Asif Ali Zardari from 2008 to 2013, told me that the ISPR would draft the press releases for the foreign ministry, and the head of the ISPR, a major general, would sit in on meetings at the information ministry to direct coverage on state radio and television.

In addition to the ISPR, there was another whole media wing of the ISI, known as the "M" wing, that worked to manipulate the media and control the discourse inside and outside of the country. Its officials drove campaigns in the press, whipping up support for jihad in Kashmir or Afghanistan, stirring criticism against civilian governments or political parties, and driving sentiment against the United States. Its aims were grand: to build national morale and maintain leverage in international relations. It also sought to manipulate public opinion away from issues that the military deemed sensitive, and encourage society to vent in a direction that did not hurt Pakistan. America was fair game for attacks even though the countries were supposed to be allies.

For more than two decades, the Pakistani military has been manipulating the media to hide the truth from its own people and its allies about the depth of its support for Islamist terrorism. This account tries to tell at least some of the stories that it sought to suppress.

· 1 ·

The Taliban Surrender

"We should not wash blood with blood."

— *General Abdul Rashid Dostum on the surrender of Mullah Fazel,
the Taliban commander in the north*

November 2001. Even in defeat the Taliban were ferocious. They came fast out of the darkness, in a convoy of muddy pickups and SUVs, hurtling through the old fortress gatehouse and skidding to a halt at the headquarters building. Black-turbaned guards armed with rifles and rocket launchers leapt from the backs of their vehicles and flanked their leader's car, a white Land Cruiser with blackened windows. They carried their weapons with the ease of long practice, and moved with an arrogance and sense of purpose that made us onlookers scatter. Two guards stayed atop their vehicles, manning antiaircraft guns. The remainder formed a perimeter, marking the opposition. It was 10 o'clock, a cold November night. The Taliban had driven into the heart of the enemy camp, inside the high walls and inner courtyards of the Qala-i-Janghi, the House of War.

The nineteenth-century fort lies southwest of the city of Mazar-i-Sharif in northern Afghanistan. Its massive earth embankments, battlements, and mud-brick walls, twenty feet thick, were built by Amir Abdul Rahman, the creator of the modern state of Afghanistan. Until recently the fort had been a Taliban military base, but for the last month, U.S. bombers had been striking military targets in Afghanistan, and the

Taliban had abandoned the fort and its arsenal of weapons. Now it was in the hands of their opponents, the American-backed fighters of the United Front, who had swept down from their mountain hideouts and seized power.

The men on guard were a mixed crowd. The United Front was a coalition of ethnic groups from northern and central Afghanistan. There were stocky Uzbeks with Asiatic features in long corduroy tunics and Uzbek police commanders in Communist-era uniforms, who wore mustaches rather than beards; small, wiry Hazaras wearing checkered headscarves, members of a Shiite group that had fought ferocious battles against the Taliban; and Tajik commandos of the Northern Alliance, in combat fatigues and army boots, the best-trained men of the anti-Taliban forces. The United Front was brought together by the late legendary resistance commander Ahmed Shah Massoud.[1] His own faction, the mostly Tajik Northern Alliance, made up the backbone of the fighting force, but he had sought to broaden the resistance to the Taliban with support from other ethnic and regional groups. The fighters were mostly illiterate farmers and laborers, hardened men from mountain villages who had fought for ten years as mujahideen, resistance fighters against the Soviet occupation, and then through another decade of Afghan civil war and Taliban offensives.

The United Front hated the Taliban. The Uzbeks, Hazaras, and Tajiks had been driven deep into the mountains over the last few years where they had struggled to survive. The Taliban were a predominantly ethnic Pashtun movement, whose fighters were mostly from southern Afghanistan and spoke Pashtu, a different language from the Persian-dialect Dari of the northerners. The northern fighters watched the Taliban warily but with weapons shouldered. Their leaders were inside the building, and the Taliban were expected.

The door of the Land Cruiser opened and a thickset, bearded man in loose white clothes appeared. Mullah Fazel Mazloom, deputy defense minister in the Taliban regime and commander of all Taliban forces in northern Afghanistan, scowled out from under his heavy black turban. He was a man with a fearful reputation for cruelty and for sweeping military offensives that spared no one. Behind him was Mullah Noorullah Noori, a slighter, younger man who served as the Taliban governor of Balkh and was the senior political figure in the north. The two men had led the Taliban's offensive across northern Afghanistan, conducting bloody reprisals against communities that resisted. They were feared across the region. Just the sight of their convoy speeding through the darkened streets of Mazar-i-Sharif on their way to the fort that night had started a rumor that the Taliban were returning to recapture the town.

I was among a group of Western journalists who jostled forward as the car door opened. A television cameraman switched on his camera light, illuminating the scene and momentarily blinding everyone. The Taliban leader drew back into his car and slammed the door. There was a short silence as everyone looked around, confused. Then the order came: "No lights! No lights!" Television was banned under the Taliban government, and its officials usually refused to be filmed. They were still insisting on this rule, even in defeat, so the cameraman turned off his light. The cleric emerged a second time, his face obscured by a woolen shawl wrapped round his head and shoulders. He stepped down into the crowd, hurrying into the building and up the stairs, followed closely by a coterie of commanders and guards. The jostling eased once they were gone. The journalists spread out, talking among themselves, switching on satellite telephones to report the arrival of the Taliban for talks. The Taliban guards turned their attention to the foreigners. They advanced on me and another female reporter with curious stares until the guards shooed them away.

Upstairs, in a long, low-ceilinged meeting room, Mullah Fazel was confronting his deadliest enemies. Assembled on dilapidated sofas and armchairs along the sides of the room were men who, in the last week, with U.S. air support, had smashed his dominion and grasped control of northern Afghanistan: General Abdul Rashid Dostum, the growling Soviet-trained Uzbek militia leader who had often played kingmaker in the wars of the last twenty-five years, switching sides at critical moments and precipitating coups; Atta Mohammad Noor, the tall, lean leader of the Northern Alliance fighters, a bitter rival of Dostum for control of the north when they were not fighting the Taliban; and Mohammad Mohaqiq, the leader of the Shiite Hazara forces in the north, whose people had suffered some of the worst sectarian violence at the hands of the predominantly Sunni Taliban.

Each of these men had been fighting for the last quarter century, ever since the Soviet invasion of Afghanistan, sometimes on opposing sides. They had come together in recent months to stem the Taliban advance across northern Afghanistan. Since its formation seven years earlier, the Taliban had sought to gain control over the whole country and establish a fundamentalist Islamist regime, the Islamic Emirate of Afghanistan. By 2001, they had come close to achieving that aim. Then came the attacks of 9/11 against the World Trade Center in New York and the Pentagon in Washington, D.C., and everything changed.

As we waited outside in the courtyard with the guards, we watched some of the United Front's new American allies enter the meeting room that night: a tall, broad-shouldered CIA operative who used the name Dave — or Daoud to the Afghans — wore a long Afghan tunic and hiking boots and spoke the local languages; and several bearded men in the plain fatigues of the U.S. special forces, who had been dropped in weeks earlier to assist the different groups of the anti-Taliban coalition. Several dozen Afghan elders and commanders had gathered too, among them a former Taliban commander, Amir Jan Naseri. An influential Pashtun mujahideen figure from the ancient city of Balkh, Amir Jan had fallen out with the Taliban and defected to the United Front six months earlier. His contacts on both sides allowed him to serve as an intermediary in bringing Mullah Fazel to negotiate.

The meeting was a severe turn of fortune for Mullah Fazel. He had commanded over ten thousand Taliban fighters along with hundreds more al Qaeda and other foreign fighters across several battlefronts in northern Afghanistan. He had come close to annihilating the men with whom he now negotiated. When two al Qaeda members posing as journalists assassinated Ahmed Shah Massoud on September 9, 2001, they removed the most important opposition figure standing in the way of the Taliban advance. The United Front had seemed bound to collapse. Mullah Fazel was poised to overrun the last northern districts and complete the Taliban plan to conquer all of Afghanistan.

That was just two days before the attacks of 9/11. Within a month, U.S. missiles began demolishing Taliban frontline positions and military camps with a pinpoint accuracy that shook the Islamist fighters and awed ordinary Afghans. American special forces personnel in the mountains with the United Front called in strikes on Taliban positions. Afghans on horseback raced in after the strikes to seize villages and hilltops, and finish off stragglers. The Taliban were forced to abandon their command posts and take cover in civilian buildings. They smeared mud over their trucks and cars, covering every bit of glinting chrome in a vain attempt at camouflage. It was no protection against modern guided missiles. Even in the cities, missiles were finding the Taliban, guided by Afghan informers working undercover and equipped with GPS locators and satellite telephones. It took just over a month for Taliban rule to collapse in the north. The first major town, Mazar-i-Sharif, fell to United Front troops on November 9. Two other northern towns, Taloqan and Bamiyan, fell on November 11, and Herat, the main city in western Afghanistan, on November 12. The Taliban were suddenly on the run.

Mullah Fazel's forces fell back to the town of Kunduz, under fire from American missiles. Afterward we saw the detritus of their retreat: their vehicles, shredded into fist-sized pieces of metal, littered the desert from Mazar-i-Sharif. Farming villages were dotted with yellow canisters, lethal cluster bombs that had decimated the Taliban foot soldiers. In Kunduz, a market town of low, walled houses and horsecarts, the retreating fighters were quickly surrounded by advancing United Front forces. The Taliban were cut off from the rest of their army hundreds of miles away in southern Afghanistan with no chance of reinforcements. Among them were thousands of Afghans, mostly Pashtuns whose homes were in the south, and hundreds of al Qaeda and foreign fighters—Arabs; North Africans; Muslims from Central Asia, Russia, and China; and a few men from Western countries, including several British Pakistanis and the American Muslim convert John Walker Lindh. They had nowhere to go and were dependent on their Afghan hosts. There were also hundreds of Pakistanis: scores of military advisors and trainers, members of Pakistan's Inter-Services Intelligence, which was secretly assisting the Taliban; trained fighting men from Pakistan's militant groups, which had long used Kunduz as a base in northern Afghanistan to train recruits and support the Taliban campaign; and hundreds of illiterate villagers and religious students who had rushed to support the Taliban on the urging of their religious leaders when the United States began bombing.

The collapse in the north rippled through the country. Taliban soldiers, police, and government officials began deserting their posts and escaping south to their home base in Kandahar — or east into Pakistan. On the night of November 13, the Taliban withdrew from the capital, Kabul, slipping away under cover of darkness. United Front forces drove into the city with barely a fight the next day. Their fighters claimed Jalalabad, the main city in the east, on the same day.

Trapped in Kunduz, Mullah Fazel faced being overrun or, worse, massacred by Northern Alliance troops who had surrounded the town and were set on avenging the death of their leader, Ahmed Shah Massoud. Their commanders threatened daily to storm the town and slaughter the Taliban and al Qaeda forces unless they surrendered.

Mullah Fazel's forces were depleted and badly shaken by the bombing raids. Dozens had been wounded. His units were struggling to hold the outskirts of Kunduz. Those who could were escaping the besieged town, bribing opposition fighters or using tribal contacts to smuggle themselves out. Most were ready to surrender, said one fighter who had been captured trying to escape Kunduz and who stood chained up in an underground pit guarded by Northern Alliance fighters when I interviewed him. "It is the bombing, there is no defense against it," he told me, shivering in his muddy hole.

As the Taliban lines disintegrated, Pakistan's leader, General Pervez Musharraf, put three telephone calls through to General Dostum, asking him to broker a surrender with the Taliban trapped in Kunduz.[2] Musharraf did not want to approach the Northern Alliance, the followers of Massoud who had long opposed Pakistan's attempts to dominate Afghanistan. The Taliban, for their part, did not want to surrender to the Shiite Hazaras, fearing revenge for the two thousand Hazaras whom they had slaughtered in Mazar-i-Sharif three years earlier.

So Musharraf approached Dostum, a most treacherous and untrustworthy leader but an opportunist who could be expected to do a deal. Dostum was already cooperating with the United States, and he had an American special forces team at his side. Musharraf confided to Dostum that he had been wrong to support just one group in Afghanistan — the Taliban — and said he wanted to rectify that. It suited Dostum to be the dealmaker who ended the war in northern Afghanistan. It would let him emerge once again as an important power broker.

Musharraf's intervention came just in time for Mullah Fazel. Dostum sent Pashtun emissaries to Kunduz, men with tribal contacts who were able to approach the Taliban leaders. They offered the Taliban a straightforward way out: surrender your weapons and you will be allowed to go home. Most of the Taliban were from the south and wanted above all to get away from the north where they had vengeful enemies and feared a slaughter. The tribal leaders in Kunduz urged the Taliban to spare the town from American bombing, which was already causing heavy destruction in outlying villages.

Yet the Taliban despised Dostum. He had been trained by the KGB and had fought on the side of the Communists during the ten-year Soviet invasion of Afghanistan in the 1980s. His militias were notorious for their ruthless pogroms around the country, just as he himself was notorious for repeated betrayals of alliances. Mullah Fazel ultimately had no other choice. He was receiving orders from his leaders in the southern capital, Kandahar, and from his Pakistani mentors to make a tactical retreat and conserve forces for the future.

In testimony he later gave before a military tribunal in Guantánamo Bay, Mullah Fazel denied receiving any orders and said it was his own decision to surrender to Dostum. The deal, he said, was that his forces would give up their weapons and then be allowed to go home.[3] Yet according to American military prosecutors, he received orders from the

Taliban defense minister to surrender. The Taliban leadership maintained command and control throughout their retreat.

That leadership, under the direction of Mullah Omar and his defense minister, Mullah Obaidullah Akhund, had crucial support from Pakistan. During the Kunduz siege, Pakistan began evacuating its own people on secret military flights from the airfield on the edge of town. According to Afghan intelligence officials, there were two to three thousand Pakistanis trapped there, including trained military operatives. Pakistan had long boosted the Taliban's military campaign with its own troops and advisors but had always kept them hidden from international scrutiny, using retired officers on contract, civilians, and only occasionally active soldiers, never in uniform.

For ten to fifteen days in the second half of November, one or two Pakistani military flights had flown into Kunduz airfield every evening, airlifting a total of approximately two thousand people as well as weapons and communications systems, according to Afghans who were monitoring Taliban radio communications.[4] Two battalions of Pakistanis, including special forces, artillery units, and hundreds of snipers, had controlled the airport and strengthened the Taliban frontlines in the north. Neither they nor their equipment were found when the town was finally captured by the Northern Alliance. Not everyone was so lucky. Hundreds of Central Asian fighters were killed in the U.S. bombing or drowned trying to ford the river north into Tajikistan. Nearly a thousand low-level Pakistani fighters were left behind to fend for themselves, ending up as prisoners of Dostum's troops. Pakistan was bowing to the superior might of the United States, pulling out of the fight in Afghanistan and advising the Taliban to change tactics to a guerrilla campaign.

As the Taliban retreat accelerated across the country and the vise around Kunduz tightened, Mullah Fazel took up Dostum's offer of negotiations. Dostum guaranteed Mullah Fazel safe passage from American bombs if he undertook the five-hour drive across the desert to Qala-i-Janghi. It was the holy month of Ramadan, when Muslims fast during the daylight hours, so after breaking his fast at sunset, Mullah Fazel gathered some of his toughest commanders in a convoy of twenty vehicles and set out westward across the desert, journeying deep behind enemy lines.

One of the thorniest issues Mullah Fazel had to negotiate was what to do with the hundreds of foreign fighters, which included some diehard al Qaeda members, under his command. Some of them were demanding safe passage overland to Pakistan. Others were vowing to fight to the death. The Taliban had already approached the United Nations to assist with the repatriation of the foreigners to their home countries, but the UN was quick to decline. Pakistan, for its part, called for the protection of the foreigners not least because there were still hundreds of Pakistanis among them. Afghan leaders wanted them expelled from Afghanistan. The United States, with only small military teams on the ground, was in no position to manage a mass surrender of foreign fighters. It would take a month for the Pentagon to send in a force to screen the prisoners and transfer them out of the country.

The air at the meeting was redolent with hostility. Atta Mohammad distrusted Dostum and disagreed with any deal that was not complete surrender of the Taliban. The Hazara leader, Mohammad Mohaqiq, did not speak during the two hours of discussions. "I was there to bear witness because I hate them because they killed so many Hazaras," Mohaqiq told me later. "I was not happy to be there. Looking at their faces they were a strange type of species," he said. The American bombing had forced them to surrender, he said. "They looked tired and humbled. They were almost finished."[5]

The talk focused on arranging a ceasefire and guarantees for the Taliban to surrender peacefully and give up their weapons. Close to midnight, General Dostum called in the reporters who had been waiting outside to hear Mullah Fazel announce his surrender. As we crowded in, I had to climb onto a sofa for a view. The elders and commanders were ranged on sofas and armchairs, Dostum and Mullah Fazel at the center. I recognized two of the mediators, Pashtun tribal commanders, wearing stiffly tied, long-tailed silk turbans to honor the occasion, on a couch between the two parties. One or two of the American special forces team stood against the wall, watching. Dostum prompted the camera-shy mullah to answer questions for the cameras. Mullah Fazel said they had reached an agreement to end the fighting, and the two men shook hands. The settlement included all foreign fighters. "They are all under my command and they will all surrender," he said. "They will accept my word."

Dostum spoke of the twenty-five years of war that had pitted men against each other in every village, city, province, and tribe. "We should not wash blood with blood, we should wash blood with water," Dostum said. "We must stop the interference of foreign people in our country. We must rebuild our country after so much strife." That was a reference to both al Qaeda and Pakistan.

The journalists were dismissed, and the discussions among the leaders continued until dawn. The stakes were high. One of Dostum's rivals claimed that Mullah Fazel had offered Dostum half a million dollars to help him and his closest commanders get away safely. For his troops Mullah Fazel wanted an amnesty, and in return for surrendering their weapons and vehicles, safe passage to southern Afghanistan. He was also pragmatic enough to offer to cooperate with the Americans. According to one of the mediators, he agreed to help catch bin Laden if he was given his freedom to return to southern Afghanistan. Mullah Fazel said he knew two of bin Laden's aides well and could track him down through them. He swore he would catch the "rat" for destroying Afghanistan. He also offered to negotiate a peaceful surrender of the last southern provinces.[6] Distrust ran high. No one took him up on the offer.

As dawn broke, Mullah Fazel drove back across the desert to Kunduz and did as he had promised. He made a speech to his followers and told them the fight was over. They were to hand over their weapons and would be allowed to go home. A group of Arabs refused to accept Mullah Fazel's orders and began to argue. Some of the foreign fighters, Muslims from Central Asia, Russia, and China, were escaping persecution or arrest and did not want to risk being captured and deported back to their home countries. The Pakistanis feared retribution from Dostum's militias and the Northern Alliance. The Arabs, from Saudi Arabia, Qatar, Yemen, and Iraq, were the most ideologically committed jihadists and wanted to fight to the death. Above all, they did not want to be handed over to the Americans. The argument escalated, and as they leveled threats at Mullah Fazel, his bodyguards drew their weapons and shot some of the Arabs dead.[7]

That ended the discussion. In the days that followed, Mullah Fazel kept his word and delivered thousands of Taliban and foreign fighters into the hands of the United Front. The mechanics of the surrender, the logistics of disarming and transporting a force of thousands of fighters, proved fatefully difficult and dangerous.

Two days after the meeting, a colleague and I were driving out of Mazar-i-Sharif when we ran into a mass of black turbans. Hundreds of armed fighters were sitting on their haunches in the desert, at the city gates. They were foreign fighters: Arabs, Pakistanis, and Central Asians, dressed like the Taliban, with heavy black silk turbans and eyes ringed with kohl. Their eyes followed us as we turned around and beat a retreat. They had pitched up at dawn on foot, without warning, the Northern Alliance guards told us. They said they had walked through the night and had come to give themselves up to the chief mediator, the Pashtun tribal elder Amir Jan Naseri. They had been told to hand in their weapons and that they would be allowed to continue on to Kandahar, so they sat down in ranks in the desert to wait. The fighters' arrival caught the United Front by surprise and made them and their American allies suspect a plot to retake the city.

Just a day earlier, the United Front had received intelligence that Mullah Omar had announced his forces would soon retake one of Afghanistan's cities. One of the most powerful Taliban commanders, Mullah Dadullah, had already split away from Mullah Fazel's convoy and was lodging at Amir Jan's home northwest of the city. The United Front was on alert for an attack.

The fighters sat silent in the desert most of the day as Dostum's forces worked out what to do with them. Extra troops arrived to stand guard.

An American special forces team came to watch. It was midafternoon when Dostum turned up, and his guards began disarming the foreign fighters and taking them off in trucks to the fort of Qala-i-Janghi, the only place nearby secure enough to hold so many people. At this point, it became clear to the foreigners that they were being treated as prisoners. As Dostum's men searched the foreign fighters, they found and confiscated large sums of money, credit cards, and cell phones. The fighters gave up their weapons and climbed into cattle trucks, but their faces were sullen as they looked out at a growing crowd of northern fighters.

I approached one of the trucks and talked to a Pakistani Talib, looking down unhappily at the crowd. "We did not come to surrender," he said to me in English. They had been told they would be sent home, he said. It was nearing the end of the day by the time the last ones were loaded and driven away. Everyone was weary from fasting all day.

When they arrived at the fort, one of the prisoners rushed at the police chief supervising the operation and set off a grenade in a suicide attack, killing the police chief and two others. Then a group of Arabs blew themselves up in an outbuilding. It was growing dark, and the police were rushing to finish the job, so they locked the prisoners in the basement of a concrete building for the night. The next morning they began a more thorough search of the prisoners, bringing them up one by one from the basement, removing their black turbans, and tying their arms with the long material of the turbans. An intelligence official filmed the process as the police placed the prisoners on their knees in rows, in the grassy area of the inner courtyard. Several hundred Taliban prisoners — Pakistanis, Arabs, North Africans, and some with embroidered caps from Central Asia — were led out. An American agent, Johnny Micheal Spann, and his tall colleague Dave crouched on the grass over to one side, interviewing a prisoner. The cameraman was filming General Dostum's officials questioning prisoners at the entrance to the building when several prisoners burst up the stairs and charged the guards. Within seconds, they had seized weapons and gunned down several guards, along with Agent Spann. His colleague

Dave fought off his attackers, shooting one man who jumped on him, and fell back with Dostum's guards as they sprayed automatic gunfire across the yard.

A running battle spread. Prisoners rushed the gatehouse and headquarters building where Red Cross officials were meeting with Dostum's officials. Dave burst onto the roof of the building and borrowed a German journalist's satellite telephone to call for help. In those first moments, Dostum's men nearly lost control of the fort as prisoners ransacked the arsenal and took up firing positions on rooftops and walls. Over thirty prisoners were killed where they knelt in the grass. Several days later we found them lying on the open ground, their arms still tied behind their backs.

The battle raged for five days and left hundreds dead. Every day, we reporters would drive out to the fort and dash across the fields to the base of the mud walls where we hunkered down with Dostum's soldiers listening to bullets zinging overhead. Dostum rushed in reinforcements. British and American special forces joined in the fight, pumping machine-gun fire down from the battlements into the inner courtyards where the Taliban fighters took cover in ditches and outbuildings. The Taliban fired mortars and rockets over the fortress walls into the surrounding fields. American troops called in airstrikes — hitting their own side, killing two American soldiers and a number of Afghans and leaving a gaping hole in the fortress wall. The Taliban dug foxholes and hid in basements and stables, while Dostum's men, cut off from their arms store, ran out of ammunition and had to beg other commanders in the United Front to come to their aid.

A steady stream of dead and wounded United Front soldiers were carried away from the fort. During a lull, Dostum's soldiers ventured over the walls and down a sloping ramp into the inner courtyard, only to get caught and nearly surrounded by Taliban fighters in foxholes. "They are fighting with every kind of weapon," said one soldier. "When we shouted at them, they would not listen. They said, 'You are Americans, and we will not surrender to you.'"

• • •

On the fifth day, Dostum's men drove their only tank into the fort, blasted several buildings at point-blank range, and claimed victory. As they cleared the buildings, they let journalists in to see the damage. The shell-pocked fort was still smoldering from the battle. The air smelt of brick dust, cordite, and decomposing bodies. Dead and wounded horses, part of Dostum's cavalry, created a scene of medieval carnage. Afghans were stepping over dozens of unexploded mortars. I counted 150 Taliban lying dead inside the compound. A large number seemed to be Pakistanis, poorly dressed in the national attire of baggy pants and long shirts, cheap jackets and tennis shoes. They were young and bearded, their faces blank in death. Soldiers searched their pockets — one had a small plastic bag of rice. A dozen foreigners with wispy beards and smooth cheeks lay dead near the bombed-out kitchen buildings. They wore military fatigues under their Pakistani baggy pants, and good quality fleeces and sweatshirts. One had a Dolce & Gabbana black fleece top, another a San Francisco 49ers sweatshirt. Some had bullets in their pockets and small cotton sachets of gunpowder filings.

Another group of fighters, probably killed in one of the American airstrikes, lay hurled around a crater in the ground. Trees were splintered by shrapnel, and several more dead lay beside a battery of rockets. Inside an outbuilding, which turned out to be a stable, I found a group of Arabs dead in a circle. It looked like the group suicide bombing that happened the first night. Others had died by the gatehouse, trying to escape. They carried books in Arabic. "Trust in Islam and there will be life after death," read one small pocket prayer book. "There was no way to make them surrender," said a plainclothes policeman as he walked through the wreckage. "And if we could have made them surrender, they would have started another fight."

Dostum arrived to survey the battle damage that afternoon. He explained the high number of dead in his usual monosyllabic growl: "It was war." At his headquarters, sitting on the balcony amid rubble and brick dust, he said he had lost three of his best commanders and thirty men in the five days of fighting. Three of the dead came from one family. More than two hundred United Front soldiers were wounded. "We tried to treat the prisoners humanely, and they took advantage," he said. "I gave orders for them to be allowed to wash and pray, but they attacked us." Later he brought along the two Taliban leaders, Mullah Fazel and Mullah Noori, who had negotiated the surrender. The two men made no comment as they looked upon the carnage. Mullah Noori moved his lips in prayer. Mullah Fazel's face was impassive under his heavy black turban.

Yet even then, after nearly a week, the battle was not over. There were survivors still alive in the basement, shooting at anyone who ventured down the stairs. The commander at the scene, Haji Din Mohammad, said he thought there were maybe just one or two left alive down there, so he tried to smoke them out. Then he fired rockets into the basement. Finally, he diverted icy water from an irrigation channel down upon them. As the water crept up to their waists and the dead floated among them, some of the remaining fighters realized they would not survive the cold if they stayed in the flooded bunker. Others still argued against surrendering, but at 10 o'clock that night, a dozen Pakistanis and one Afghan crept up the stairs and called out to Dostum's guards, who let the group out and locked them in a metal container for the night.

A colleague of mine from *The Guardian* was shown the thirteen prisoners early in the morning. They begged for blankets and water. One man, shivering uncontrollably, had a cardboard box on his head in an apparent attempt to find some warmth. Another lay shaking on the floor, part of his face shot away. At 8 o'clock that morning, wounded, starving, and close to collapse, the remainder of the fighters surrendered. We watched them emerge from the basement like cavemen, soaking wet, with blackened faces and matted hair. There were dozens of them. At least twenty were carried out by stretcher. "We gave up because there was nothing left, we had no ammunition, no weapons, no food," said one, who had been shot through the foot. He told

me his name was Abdul Jabar, age twenty-six, from Tashkent in Uzbekistan. "Our commander made the decision to surrender, and we
all agreed."

In the end, eighty-five men came out of the basement alive, although
not all of them survived their wounds and the onset of hypothermia.
We called out to them as they were led out. One Arab spoke some
English and said he was born in the United States, in Baton Rouge,
Louisiana. A large number, with long black curly locks, said they were
from Yemen. One who remained silent would turn out to be John
Walker Lindh, the "American Talib," who had gone to study Islam in
a madrassa in Pakistan and ended up being trained by al Qaeda and
fighting in northern Afghanistan.

  The wounded lay in the mud, asking for food and water as Dostum's
fighters backed in two trucks to take them away. Red Cross officials arrived with dressings, and fed bananas, oranges, and water to the prisoners, whose hands were bound. One prisoner, Mohammad, said that
they had wanted to surrender two days ago but that a group of seven
Arab fighters had refused to let them. A thin Pakistani boy, Ijaz Latif,
said he was sixteen or seventeen and had been in Afghanistan only two
months.

Abdul Jabar, who was from Uzbekistan, spoke to me in Russian, and
told me the Uzbek fighters had begun the jail uprising. They belonged
to the Islamic Movement of Uzbekistan, a group that opposed the re-
pressive regime of President Islam Karimov, the longtime Communist
leader of Uzbekistan, and had sought refuge in neighboring Afghanistan. The group had allied itself with the Taliban and al Qaeda in return
for a safe haven. They had genuine grievances. Karimov's government
was notorious for its religious and political repression and the use of
torture in its prisons. In one documented case, a prisoner had been
placed in a vat of scalding water and boiled alive. The Uzbeks had been
sucked in by the aggressive proselytizing of Pakistani religious groups,
which began missionary work in Central Asia in the 1980s and drew
recruits to religious schools in Pakistan. Uzbek students went looking

for an Islamic education and freedom to practice their religion and emerged as militant jihadists. Those networks are still active today and continue to attract young men from Central Asia toward violent jihad.

The Uzbeks started the uprising in the fort that day because they feared deportation above all. Going back to Uzbekistan would mean almost certain execution, Abdul Jabar said. They had lost their charismatic leader, Juma Namangani, in the bombing, and facing an uncertain fate, presented the most unpredictable element of the foreign fighters. They had been told that if they gave up their weapons they would be allowed to go free and would be sent to the southern Taliban stronghold of Kandahar. But when they were locked up in the fort as prisoners of Dostum, who was known to be ruthless and to have close relations with the government of Uzbekistan, some of their group decided to put up a last fight. "Our commander began it," Abdul Jabar said. "He told us: 'It is better to die a martyr than be in prison.'"

Abdul Jabar was educated and had been working in the political office of the movement in Kabul. He accepted apples and water gratefully from Red Cross workers. "I am not against Americans," he said, adding that he thought the attacks of 9/11 in New York were wrong because they targeted civilians. "Only God knows what will happen, but if they send us back to Uzbekistan that will be the end."

The survivors of the battle at Qala-i-Janghi were transferred to a prison in the nearby town of Shiberghan and the wounded to the government hospital there. After a few weeks, they were removed by American forces of the 10th Mountain Division and were among the first contingent to be transferred to the Guantánamo Bay prison in Cuba for indefinite detention. Most were to remain there for the best part of a decade. The six Uzbeks were eventually freed and allowed to settle in other countries.

Even as the battle at Qala-i-Janghi was unfolding, thousands of other Taliban fighters were surrendering at Kunduz under the agreement between General Dostum and Mullah Fazel. They drove out in a long column, stirring up a trail of dust across the plain to Erganak, a low pass to the west of Kunduz. There, they were disarmed and loaded onto trucks for the ten-hour journey west to the prison in Shiberghan. After the prisoner uprising at Qala-i-Janghi, the mood of their captors was far from friendly. Wary of further suicide bombings, Dostum's men bound the prisoners' arms so tightly they could not move. The troops overloaded the trucks, and even locked some prisoners into airtight shipping containers for the journey. Hundreds died from asphyxiation on the way and were buried in mass graves in the desert. It would be the worst mass killing of the war. Dostum's commanders admitted that forty prisoners died from war wounds during the journey but denied any massacre. Scores more went down with dysentery, tuberculosis, and malnutrition in Dostum's prison in the months that followed. Within the year, the Red Cross had to intervene with an emergency feeding program to prevent yet more deaths.

As the surrender progressed, Mullah Fazel and Mullah Noori drove out of Kunduz and gave themselves up to Dostum. The general escorted them back to his fancy guesthouse in the town of Shiberghan. There, they lived under guard but in the relative luxury of satin-covered beds, en suite bathrooms, and a terrace that overlooked fountains and a rose garden. They remained in the guesthouse for several weeks until one day when American forces came and arrested them. Whatever amnesty Dostum had offered them he did not deliver. Members of the Northern Alliance told me they had urged the American military to arrest the mullahs before they could escape.

They were flown out of Afghanistan and held in prison cells onboard the battleship USS *Bataan,* and then they, too, were transferred to Guantánamo Bay prison. Eleven years later, they were still in prison, the longest serving inmates among a diminishing number of Afghan detainees, when their names reappeared in the news. As the Obama administration began exploring peace talks with the Taliban leadership, one of the first demands of the insurgent group was the release of the last five senior members of the Taliban still imprisoned in Guantánamo, among them Mullah Fazel and Mullah Noori.

• • •

By the end of 2001, the Taliban's grand scheme to establish an Islamic emirate in Afghanistan had come to an ignominious end. Whatever the intention of the foreign fighters at Qala-i-Janghi, the Taliban surrender at Kunduz was genuine. It was the only formal surrender of Taliban forces in the war, and the signal moment of their defeat. For the band of mullah-commanders who had swept all before them since 1994 and come close to ruling all of Afghanistan, it was an astounding collapse. It had happened in just weeks under the overwhelming force of American airpower and a vengeful opposition on the ground. The military weaknesses of the Taliban movement were suddenly exposed, as were the miscalculations of their Pakistani and al Qaeda advisors.

They had misjudged the strength of the American attack. They had been greatly overextended in northern Afghanistan when the U.S. bombing began and were not able to retreat in good order. The Taliban also misread the strength of their standing with the Afghan population. They had ruled Afghanistan through a relatively small but oppressive force of commanders and officials, and had only temporarily co-opted influential regional and religious figures to help ensure the loyalty of the population. They mistook this command for popularity. They had expected the population to rally to their side in the event of an American attack, but instead, when the bombing began, local leaders urged them to negotiate to avoid further destruction. As the bombing smashed their bases and forced them into retreat, the Taliban found the population turning away. Just when the whole of Afghanistan had seemed within reach, their power evaporated.

December 2001. In the Pakistani frontier town of Peshawar, which had long been a center for Afghan mujahideen in exile, Taliban commanders convened a council of war. Unbeknownst to the West, this meeting foreshadowed a grim road ahead. A former militant commander who was present told me about the gathering a decade later. Over sixty men were present, including Afghan Taliban commanders, their Pakistani allies from the Pashtun borderlands, and Pakistani militant and religious leaders who had been active in Afghanistan. They gathered in a large meeting hall to discuss what they should do next.

Watching from the sidelines were several well-known figures from the Pakistani military and intelligence services. Among them was the late Major General Zaheer ul-Islam Abbasi, a former military and intelligence officer who served on the Afghan desk of the Inter-Services Intelligence in the 1980s, when he had helped run the Afghan resistance against the Soviet Army. He had also assisted the Kashmiri militants and was imprisoned for an attempted coup against the then-government of Benazir Bhutto in 1995. Abbasi was one of the most active supporters of the militant groups in the years after 2001. Mir Ali, a town in North Waziristan, would become the central headquarters of the resistance, and Abbasi would visit the place at least twice in the months that followed, according to the former militant commander who attended the meeting.

Another figure at the meeting, well known and liked by generations of jihadi fighters, was the master trainer Colonel Imam. His real name was Brigadier Sultan Amir, a Pakistani special forces officer. Once a promising protégé of the United States, he underwent special forces training at Fort Bragg, North Carolina, in 1974, learning in particular the use of sabotage and explosives, and completed a master parachutist course with the 82nd Airborne Division. Imam had overseen the training of thousands of Afghan mujahideen during the 1980s and closely mentored the Taliban when they first formed. Mullah Omar had been one of his trainees, as had many members of the Taliban. Retired from the military in the mid-1990s, he had been posted as a diplomat to run the Pakistani consulate in Herat during the Taliban period. From there he helped direct their advance up through the country. He was in his post, confident of the Taliban's overall victory, when 9/11 happened. He told me that he was recalled to Pakistan immediately afterward but returned to Kandahar to see Mullah Omar. The Taliban leader was refusing to hand over bin Laden and Imam advised Omar to resist the American campaign by retreating to the mountains and waging what the Afghans did best, a guerrilla war.[8] Now the planning for that guerrilla war was underway.

The Taliban ambassador to Pakistan, Abdul Salam Zaeef, was also present at the Peshawar meeting. A former fighter in his thirties, Mullah Zaeef became the face of the Taliban regime after 9/11, a short, stocky figure with black turban and spectacles who denounced the United States bombing campaign to the world's media at press conferences in the embassy garden. A few weeks after the Peshawar war council, he would be detained by Pakistani police and transported to a cell on the USS *Bataan,* and then to Guantánamo Bay.

Also attending the meeting was Mohammad Haqqani, a son of the powerful Taliban commander and minister Jalaluddin Haqqani. The presence of a representative of the well-connected Haqqani family was a signal to all that the fight would go on. Jalaluddin was one of the stalwart fighters of the anti-Soviet jihad in the 1980s. He was a favorite of Pakistani intelligence and Arab donors, because he controlled large swathes of southeastern Afghanistan and had hosted militant training camps for groups of foreign fighters, including bin Laden. His preeminence in the border region led him to be named the minister for tribal affairs in the mujahideen and Taliban governments. His continuing support for the Taliban would be vital.

For two decades, Pakistan had used proxy forces, Afghan mujahideen and Taliban in Afghanistan, and Kashmiri militants against India, to project its influence beyond its borders. General Abbasi and Colonel Imam were among the main players in executing this policy. The Peshawar meeting was as much a confirmation of longstanding policy as it was the start of a new chapter of war in Afghanistan.

The meeting lasted several hours. Discussion focused on how to confront the American military in Afghanistan and their Afghan partners. The Taliban leaders divided Afghanistan into separate areas of operations, assigning command of each geographical region to different men who would direct an insurgency. The plan, they were told, was to "trip up America." The Taliban comeback was underway.

2

The People Turn

"You let Mazar-i-Sharif go, and you let Kabul go, and you
surrendered all the other places, and now you cannot let
Kandahar go and save it from destruction?"

— *senior Taliban commander Haji Bashar Noorzai to Mullah Omar*

October 2001. High in a mountain hamlet, surrounded by the brown jagged peaks of southern Afghanistan, a family of mujahideen fighters prepared for battle. Veterans of the ten-year war against the Soviet Army, the men were Pashtuns, the same tribal group as the Taliban, and lived in Uruzgan, a stronghold of the movement. Yet they had chafed under Taliban rule, and now, as the first American bombs fell, they were taking their weapons out of hiding and preparing a rebellion. The patriarch of the family, Mohammad Lal, had pledged to work against the Taliban two years earlier. The time for action had come. The Americans were threatening to topple the government, the United Front was regrouping in the north, and an old tribal associate, Hamid Karzai, was on his way.

Karzai was a minor tribal politician from Kandahar in southern Afghanistan who had for several years been working on an alternative to Taliban rule. He had minimal military experience, yet two days after the U.S. bombing commenced, he left his home in Quetta, Pakistan, and slipped into southern Afghanistan on a secret mission to rally the Pashtun tribes to rise up against the Taliban. He had a promise of

American support, and he knew many Pashtuns were weary of Taliban rule, but his first days in the country were proving difficult and
dangerous.

Karzai had traveled by motorbike into Kandahar on October 9, 2001,
with a former mujahideen commander, Hafizullah Khan. They stayed
two nights in and near the city, listening to the first heavy bombing by
American jets on the military barracks and the airport. Their hosts
were frightened and urged them to leave. When two other commanders joined them, they decided to head for the mountains. The four set
off together by car, wearing local clothes and turbans, passing Taliban
checkpoints on the edge of town at lunchtime when the guards were
usually inside eating or taking naps.[1]

The group stayed with a longtime tribal associate of Karzai's father
in the provincial town of Tarin Kot and began gathering supporters
and weapons. But there, also, the elder soon told them it was too dangerous to stay longer. There were warnings the Taliban were looking
for them, so they moved to another house on the edge of town. This
was the Taliban heartland, and since the American bombs had started
to fall, the mood was ugly. Anyone suspected of siding with the Americans or harboring an opposition leader such as Karzai could expect
imprisonment or execution.

Knowing his position was growing precarious, Karzai sent a message to Mohammad Lal, who offered him shelter in his mountain
hamlet of Durji. The valley was so remote that the Russians had never
occupied it during their ten-year invasion of Afghanistan. Mohammad Lal was the only one of their hosts who was not scared of the
Taliban, Hafizullah Khan explained to me.

Karzai came on foot, walking five hours through the mountains
from Tarin Kot. He was plainly worried. When his host invited him
to sit down to eat, he insisted on talking first in private. The two men
knew each other from the resistance against the Soviets, but they were
not close. Karzai, forty-three, had worked in politics in Pakistan; Mohammad Lal, forty-six, had been a fighter in Uruzgan. Over the last
two years, they had started working together to build support for an
alternative to Taliban rule. Karzai had advocated convening a loya

jirga, a traditional tribal assembly, which would form a broadly representative government under the former king, Mohammad Zahir Shah.
Tribal leaders and landowners, such as Mohammad Lal, supported the
idea; after over two decades of war, their role as the traditional leaders
of Afghan society had been steadily eroded. First the Communists,
then the warlords, and then the mullahs had usurped their position.
"Since the Communists, the leading tribal families have suffered and
that is why we supported Karzai, to bring people of intelligence and
talent back into power," Mohammad Lal told me.[2]

Karzai's father had been politically active until he was assassinated
in July 1999, almost certainly by members of the Taliban. It only made
the son more determined to resist the mullahs. He traveled in the
months before 9/11 to consult with Ahmed Shah Massoud about starting a resistance movement in the southern mountains. The experienced guerrilla commander advised caution, warning Karzai that it
would be extremely hard to fight the Taliban in their own heartland.
Massoud told Karzai he needed to find an impregnable valley that he
could defend and establish a sure supply route, which would be difficult since the Taliban and Pakistan between them maintained a strong
grip over the south.

Now, however, Karzai had U.S. support. He was carrying large sums of
cash from the Americans and a satellite telephone with which he could
call in weapons and supplies. This was the time to take up arms against
the Taliban, he urged. The Americans would not let the Taliban government stay in power after the 9/11 attacks, he said. Mohammad Lal
did not hesitate. He told Karzai that he and his sons were ready to fight.
Finally, Karzai agreed to sit down and eat.

Mohammad Lal set to work to gather other commanders and fighters in the region. He could count on twenty-six men from his own
family — uncles, brothers, cousins, and three of his eldest sons. But
they needed more. He sent word to former mujahideen commanders whom they both knew. Tribal allegiances are everything to the
Pashtuns. When these men received a message to gather at Moham-

mad Lal's house, they came. Over the next two nights, Karzai sat on the floor of Mohammad Lal's farmhouse meeting with fifteen commanders. They wore the traditional turbans of the region, with shawls wrapped around their shoulders against the cold.

One of those present was Mohammad Rahim, a burly former soldier who had fought the Russians from these same mountains. He now relished a chance to fight the Taliban who had destroyed his poppy crop earlier that year. Yet not all the men gathered at that meeting were convinced. They said the Taliban were too strong and that a small group of fifteen commanders could not stand up to them. Of the group, only four commanders agreed to join Karzai, with some thirty or forty followers.[3] The others took the cash and departed. Some of them went to the Taliban to report what had happened. Nevertheless, Karzai was encouraged. Mohammad Lal's son took him back to Tarin Kot by motorbike to fetch eighty additional fighters. They pitched camp at Kharnai, an upper valley with a spring, deeper in the mountains above Durji.

Karzai had been in Afghanistan for two weeks, and already reports had begun to filter in that the Taliban were mobilizing a force of seven hundred men against them. Hafizullah Khan warned Karzai the men could not fight if attacked. They had no food, few weapons, and only two magazines of bullets each. It was cold in the mountains, and some of the men were just wearing sandals. He sent men off to buy shoes and urged Karzai to call his American contacts for an arms drop. That night they lit fires on the mountainside. They heard planes overhead but nothing came. Hafizullah Khan's mood darkened. He knew they could not fend off a large force. "Karzai did not know how to make plans to fight, he was just acting on emotions," he recalled.

As more reports came in of Taliban approaching, men drifted away. Some of Mohammad Lal's commanders went down into the valley to find out more news. Another group of fighters left in another direction, promising to return with more friends. In fact they were spies who gave the Taliban details of Karzai's position. On the second night, American planes dropped three hundred Kalashnikov rifles, rockets, machine guns, and grenades. "I was very happy," Hafizullah Khan recalled, laughing. They collected the weapons, armed everyone, and spread out in positions throughout the two valleys. It was just in time. On the third night, the Taliban attacked.

Mohammad Lal had posted his twenty-two-year-old son, Abdul Wali, as a lookout watching the lower approaches of the camp. It was his group who first heard the Taliban approaching in the night. He challenged them, and the Taliban opened fire. The defenders poured machine-gun and rocket fire down on the Taliban in the dark. Up in the camp, Mohammad Lal rushed out to steady his men. "I was trying to explain that this man, Karzai, had come to our village, and we had to protect him," he recalled later. "It was night, it was very difficult fighting," he said. As the battle raged, two Taliban fighters broke through and reached close enough to fire on the camp. "Bullets were hitting our turbans they were so close," Rahim recalled. A mortar landed among them but by fluke did not explode.

In the next valley, Hafizullah Khan and his men were nearly overrun. The Taliban attacked the arms dump and firefights broke out all over the mountainside. A group whisked Karzai up to safety in a cave in the mountainside. At morning light, Taliban reinforcements arrived and the attacks intensified. The fighting raged for twelve hours but the defenders managed to hold the two valleys. By afternoon the Taliban had pulled back. American military officials had been monitoring the battle from the air but had not intervened. They later congratulated the Afghans on how they had resisted the attack.

Although the group had beaten off the Taliban, they remained in a precarious position with little food. Karzai announced he wanted to move on to another district to build more support, but his commanders were reluctant. Mohammad Lal insisted that they were safest remaining where they were, since the valley had good natural defenses. Hafizullah Khan warned that they should ready themselves for another attack or ask the Americans to pick them up. Yet Karzai was determined to move on. Finally, they sent most of their fighters back to their homes, and a small core of ten commanders hiked north with

Karzai. They headed toward Char Chine district, but the inhabitants were nervous and Taliban spies were everywhere. "No one would even give us food, let alone help," Mohammad Lal said. A nomadic herder, a Kuchi tribesman, fed them on the way, and the group slept in abandoned shepherds' huts. They could not raise supporters.

They retraced their footsteps. The Kuchi tribesman warned them that a Taliban search party had come through, and he advised them to go higher into the mountains. Mohammad Lal urged them to return to Durji where he could protect them. Hafizullah Khan urged Karzai to call his American contacts for help. The Taliban knew where they were and wanted to kill him, he told Karzai. They chose a rendezvous and lit fires in a clearing. Two nights later, helicopters swooped in in the dark. They ferried Karzai and seven of his commanders away to the safety of a Pakistani airbase at Jacobabad that the Americans were using for their operations.[4] The burly fighter, Rahim, and a few others stayed behind. They stashed the weapons and hid in the mountains, awaiting the call to regroup.

The future president was lucky to escape. Another resistance leader, Abdul Haq, had attempted a similar campaign, traveling into eastern Afghanistan on his own mission to rally followers. He found the Taliban hold over the population insurmountable. Haq was one of the most dynamic Pashtun personalities from the 1980s resistance and well known to American CIA officials. Like Karzai, he was a potential national leader. His family was prominent in eastern Afghanistan and had ruled Jalalabad during the mujahideen government. Haq had also seen the growing popular dissatisfaction with the Taliban and had been working to raise support to replace the Taliban with a more broadly acceptable form of government under the former king. He had organized several conferences to bring Afghan groups together, and his discussions had accelerated in the three months before 9/11 as terrorist threats escalated. The CIA had renewed its contacts with the main opposition figures and urged them to cooperate in tracking bin Laden and al Qaeda. Haq believed in the power of the Afghan tribal system and the old mujahideen networks from the resistance, and was convinced that many Afghans were ready to turn against the Taliban, his close friend Habib Ahmadzai told me.[5]

When the attacks of 9/11 occurred, Haq feared that a U.S. bombing campaign would anger the Afghan people and push them back into the arms of the Taliban. He also saw the danger of the Northern Alliance gaining power alone and alienating the entire Pashtun south and east. He and his brothers, who were also influential figures in the resistance, had always maintained close relations with the Northern Alliance and had joined the United Front for this reason. "He did not want American forces nor one side gaining power because this would be a cause of revenge and bloodshed," his brother Haji Din Mohammad told me.[6] "This country should be led through a big council," he said. "We wanted slowly to dissolve the Taliban administration and the Northern Alliance and bring them into one administration. That was Abdul Haq's plan to prevent bloodshed and revenge, and so there would not be an excuse to bring foreign soldiers into this country."

Abdul Haq sensed this was the moment to rally the Pashtun population. Pashtuns were the largest ethnic group in Afghanistan and for centuries had ruled the country. Haq knew that his fellow Pashtuns were tired of the mullahs but would not accept a victory by the northern tribes over the Taliban, a predominantly Pashtun force. There had to be a Pashtun opposition movement to provide a counterbalance for the Northern Alliance. Haq wanted to lead it. Above all, he insisted, it had to be a peaceful movement.

His plea for a nonviolent movement was ignored. Within a month of 9/11, the United States began its bombing campaign in Afghanistan. Twelve days after Karzai had slipped into Afghanistan, Abdul Haq did so too. He took a small group with him — including his close friend Ahmadzai and his handsome twenty-one-year-old nephew Izzatullah. They headed into a belt of territory southeast of the capital, Kabul. It was strategically important terrain, where the Taliban and their Arab allies ran training camps and military bases, and maintained control over the population through a network of intelligence informers. Like Karzai, Haq was greeted by old associates but warned that it was too dangerous for him to stay. The Taliban were close by and would not tolerate his presence. Haq and his companions stayed the first night in Azra, a remote and hilly district of Logar province, with a venerable tribal elder and longtime ally. Within hours, the elder received threats from the Taliban. He warned Ahmadzai that their mission was premature. The small party left for Alisher, on the border with Abdul Haq's home province of Nangarhar. There they stayed three days with elders of the Naser tribe. News came that the Taliban were preparing an advance against them. Although the elders of the tribe had agreed to protect Haq, the villagers were nervous. The Taliban would kill them and their families and burn their houses if he remained, they said. They could see Taliban vehicles ranged in the valley below. A Taliban commander sent a message asking them to leave the area or expect to fight. He was offering them an escape.

As darkness fell, the Taliban began advancing up the valley, and Abdul Haq's group left the village and climbed a rough track toward a pass into Pakistan. They were on foot, unarmed. At some point they found a horse for Haq, who wore a prosthesis after losing part of his foot on an antipersonnel mine in the 1980s. He had been struggling with the climb.

From the top of the pass, they saw the lights of dozens of Taliban cars snaking up the valley after them. They trekked through the dark until they approached a village called Tank, at around nine at night. They sent scouts ahead. One man returned running, saying the Taliban were in the village. Ahmadzai moved off the path to set up the satellite phone and call for help. Abdul Haq had refused to call earlier, saying it would be shameful to request American assistance. He especially did not want to be seen as relying on American firepower, but now they were in danger of being caught. Ahmadzai and Izzatullah decided to make the call, covering the phone with a shawl to hide the light.

They telephoned an American businessman friend and supporter in Peshawar, and gave him the coordinates of their position. They were closing down the telephone when suddenly the Taliban were upon them, ordering them to halt. The men split and ran as the Taliban opened fire. Ahmadzai leapt up the hillside as fast as he could, shouting to Izzatullah to follow, bullets ripping past him. He kept running until he realized he was alone. He found a hiding place by a rock and pulled his shawl over him. He could hear the Taliban shouting: "Sons of Americans, where are you? Where are you running to?" Taliban fighters climbed the hill, and he heard them pass within yards of his hiding place. "I thought it was the last moment of my life and they would capture me," he later recalled.

Then he heard shouting and recognized Abdul Haq's voice. The fact that he was shouting meant one thing: he must have been caught. The Taliban fired a rocket-propelled grenade, a signal that they had caught their prey. Ahmadzai crouched behind his rock without moving, long into the night. At first light he moved up to a narrow uninhabited valley where he hid for four days, eating dried mulberries, until a shepherd found him and took him to his house. Village elders had realized that one of the group was unaccounted for and sent the shepherd to him. He led Ahmadzai for six days through remote reaches of the mountains to safety.

That same night, the Taliban took their captives down the valley. Izzatullah had escaped to a village but was handed over to the Taliban. His body was found the next day, some distance away, shot and thrown down a well. Abdul Haq was beaten but survived the night. The next day, he was put in a jeep with several others from the group and driven toward Kabul. The Taliban interior minister, Mullah Abdul Razzaq, a man with an ugly reputation, stopped the jeep just south of the city, at Charasiyab.[7] He ordered the group out of the car. Haq knew what was coming and asked Razzaq not to harm his companions, among them his security advisor, his horseman, and a family retainer.

Haq was shot dead by a ditch just below the road. The date was October 25, 2001. It was an unworthy end for a brave and clever man in the dying days of the Taliban regime. His brothers blamed the CIA for pushing Haq to enter Afghanistan when conditions were still too dangerous. Those close to him claimed to see the hand of Pakistan in his assassination, too, since the interior minister was especially close to the ISI, and Haq was a strong, charismatic leader who opposed Pakistan's policies toward Afghanistan.

Abdul Haq was just one of scores of opposition leaders slain by the Taliban before and after 9/11, part of a ruthless strategy to remove potential leaders.[8] One of his brothers, Haji Abdul Qadeer, Karzai's vice president, was gunned down nine months later. At its time of greatest need, Afghanistan had lost its best military commander in Ahmed Shah Massoud and its strongest advocate for national peace and reconciliation in Abdul Haq. The United States had lost its two best potential allies. Afghanistan's future might have been brighter, and far fewer people might have died, had these men lived.

Within two weeks of Abdul Haq's death, Taliban rule collapsed. Their forces crumpled under the relentless bombardment, and the latent Afghan opposition, that Karzai and Abdul Haq both knew was there, began to emerge. By November 14, Kabul and Jalalabad, Abdul Haq's hometown, had fallen. American helicopters flew Karzai back into Uruzgan province with a U.S. special forces team to protect him. The next day tribesmen in Uruzgan rose up and seized Tarin Kot and called on Karzai to join them.

In Kandahar Mullah Omar and his lieutenants were in hiding as bombing raids hit the Taliban leader's home, along with barracks, police stations, and Osama bin Laden's farm near the airport. A group of Arabs went to camp in the desert outside the city for safety; they, too, were bombed. Mullah Omar made one last attempt to hold on to the south, dispatching a force to Uruzgan to retake Tarin Kot and capture Karzai. The Taliban streamed up in a long convoy of pickups and SUVs, forging into action in their signature mode of fighting, using reckless speed and large numbers that usually sent their opponents scattering.

But they had not counted on the American special forces, who coordinated airstrikes from positions on a ridge just south of Tarin Kot. The airstrikes demolished most of the vehicles heading toward the town, and more as they tried to flee back down a narrow pass. That was the last time the Taliban government mobilized troops into battle in southern Afghanistan, and it was a turning point in the war in the south. The demonstration of U.S. airpower broke the fear that had kept the population from supporting Haq and Karzai in those first weeks. The Taliban were in flight. Tribal elders, mujahideen commanders, and opposition groups rushed forward to join the winning side.

In many Pashtun areas, the Taliban handed over the keys of offices and vehicles to community elders or mujahideen groups and were allowed to leave unharmed. It was a typically Afghan change of power, where the possession of vehicles and weapons took precedence over anything else. In Kabul, the Taliban left under cover of darkness, abandoning homes and, in some cases, wives, as well as the nation's gold reserves — a last-minute attempt by some Taliban members to empty the government vaults was prevented by a quick-thinking bank official who broke a key in the main vault door. Despite their unruly image, neither the Taliban nor the mujahideen government before them had looted the country's treasury and the priceless museum collection stored there. Incoming officials found the treasure under the palace as they had left it in the early 1990s.

The leader of the Taliban, Mullah Omar, held on for another three weeks in his home province of Kandahar, but from then on his forces were scrambling for cover. The Taliban commander in the north, Mullah Fazel, trapped in Kunduz, was negotiating his surrender, and his forces began handing over their weapons. In the south, Mullah Omar faced a similar choice: a humiliating surrender or death under American bombs.

The one-eyed Mullah Omar was a hardheaded fighter who would never flinch from a challenge. He had grown up in a poor household, orphaned at a young age, and raised by his uncle who was a village mullah. A fighter since his teens, he had a reputation for toughness on the battlefield matched by an uncompromising adherence to Islam, in particular to a fundamentalist version of his religion taught by clerics of the Deobandi sect in madrassas in Pakistan and increasingly in Afghanistan.

While Afghans are famous for their tribal code of hospitality, Mullah Omar always explained his refusal to give up bin Laden to the United States in terms of his loyalty to his religion. He did not want to be known as someone who betrayed a fellow Muslim to infidels. In a speech he reportedly gave to his followers the day before the U.S. bombing began, he urged them to sacrifice themselves in the coming fight rather than become a friend of non-Muslims. "I know my power; my position; my wealth; and my family are in danger," he said. "However, I am ready to sacrifice myself and I do not want to become a friend of non-Muslims, for non-Muslims are against all my beliefs and my religion." He was prepared to give up everything, he said, and "to believe only in Islam and my Afghan bravery."[9]

Finally, toward the end of November, a large group of commanders came to see Mullah Omar where he was sheltering in Maiwand, thirty miles west of Kandahar city. The daily bombardment had become so heavy that there was a consensus among the leaders that it was time to pull out of Kandahar. No one wanted to say it to Mullah Omar. It took his longtime supporter and mentor, the powerful commander Haji Bashar Noorzai, who finally spoke.

"What is wrong with you?" Haji Bashar berated the Taliban leader. "You let Mazar-i-Sharif go, and you let Kabul go, and you surrendered all the other places, and now you cannot let Kandahar go and save it from destruction?"

Mullah Omar was studied in his reply. "I have known you a very long time and I know you very well," he said. "If it was not you saying this, I would have shot you right here."[10]

It was only then that Mullah Omar sent emissaries to negotiate his exit with Karzai, who was camped with his band of followers and a unit of American special forces an hour north of Kandahar, in the sawtoothed mountains of Shah Wali Kot. Karzai had just been named the interim leader of Afghanistan at a conference, organized by the United Nations, of anti-Taliban groups gathered in the German city of Bonn. Karzai was a compromise candidate, a moderate with no blood on his hands who had the backing of the United Nations and Western powers. Above all, he was a Pashtun who could continue the tradition of

Pashtun rule in Afghanistan, but was also known and acceptable to northern groups. For Mullah Omar, Karzai was at least a known quantity. He had promised that all Afghans had the right to live in their own homes, and all Taliban fighters would be offered amnesty if they gave up their weapons and went home in peace. The message appealed to many Afghans, even if the higher-ranking Taliban did not trust it.

It was not the first time that Mullah Omar had reached out to Karzai. Several weeks earlier, just after Mazar-i-Sharif had fallen, Omar had put a call through to Karzai. An assistant had spoken for the Taliban leader, asking Karzai about his intentions and how he saw the conflict ending. Karzai had told him what the United States was demanding: unconditional surrender of the Taliban regime. The assistant said Mullah Omar would call again.[11] Now, three weeks later, the balance of power had shifted. Tribesmen were rallying to Karzai's side, and the Taliban had fallen back to a few districts around Kandahar city with just three thousand men left under arms. The Taliban leader sent a delegation to Karzai to negotiate the surrender of Kandahar and the safe withdrawal of the Taliban leadership. To lead the negotiations, Mullah Omar chose Abdul Waheed Baghrani, a senior Taliban leader who was an important tribal figure and respected mujahideen leader.[12] Among those with him were Amir Mohammad Agha, a father-in-law of the Taliban leader, and Tayeb Agha, Mullah Omar's close assistant. They proposed that Mullah Naqibullah, a powerful opposition figure who was nevertheless acceptable to the Taliban, should take charge of Kandahar. They came to the negotiations with a signed letter of surrender from Mullah Omar agreeing to hand over the city in three days' time.

According to a member of the Taliban delegation, Karzai gave certain promises in return: to free the Taliban prisoners who had surrendered in northern Afghanistan and to allow each Taliban commander five armed guards for his personal security at home.[13] Yet Karzai refused to accept Mullah Omar's letter, perhaps in a gesture of conciliation. His close friend Hafizullah Khan was infuriated, judging that Karzai had passed up on an important historical document that could have been used to seal the peace. If Karzai had presented proof that

Mullah Omar had ceded power in an agreement, then the Taliban could not have justified their subsequent insurgency, Khan contended. "He did not understand," he said later of Karzai. "This was a very important document." Sure enough, a decade later, when Karzai sought to negotiate an end to the insurgency, the Taliban denied that Mullah Omar had ever offered a formal surrender.[14]

Mullah Omar did not wait for Karzai's answer anyway. When Baghrani returned to Kandahar from his second negotiating trip, he found the city abandoned, the Taliban forces and their leaders gone. It was December 6, 2001. There remained a few wounded Arab fighters, barricaded into a wing of the hospital, who fought a weeklong siege. Some reports said Mullah Omar had left in a beat-up station wagon, driving west toward his home area of Maiwand and narrowly escaping a U.S. missile attack. In the months afterward, American officials suspected he was sheltering in Baghrani's district in mountainous northern Helmand. The consensus of Afghan officials, who took over after the fall of the Taliban, is that he went to his father-in-law's house in the village of Sangesar. It had been home for Mullah Omar for most of his adult life. From there he probably headed south, across the Registan Desert and into Pakistan, a route he knew intimately from ten years of fighting against the Soviet Army.

For months U.S. forces conducted raids in parts of southern Afghanistan, pursuing smugglers and tribal figures with connections to the Taliban, including Baghrani, with little result. The word in Pakistan is that Mullah Omar left on the back of a motorbike, driving to the border town of Chaman, with the Pakistani militant Qari Saifullah Akhtar, a man who could ensure him protection in Pakistan. Gradually Afghan officials and ordinary residents reported sightings of Mullah Omar from the Afghan refugee community in and around Quetta, Pakistan. A number of sources, including a major in the Pakistani army, told me that he was living under Pakistani protection in a military camp near the border.

The fall of Kandahar and the end of the Taliban regime was, as so often in Afghanistan, a negotiated pullout. Even as he made plans to escape, Mullah Omar had tried to arrange for a transition that would allow many of his followers to remain in Afghanistan and for the leadership to withdraw in good order. His choice of Mullah Naqibullah, a leader who was acceptable to all sides, was one such attempt. His offer of a written agreement opened the door to reconciliation and showed him to be a more experienced statesman than Karzai.

Several years later, as the Taliban resurgence grew, critics began to question why there had not been a greater effort by the Western and Afghan forces fighting the Taliban to find a more inclusive settlement to the conflict and even a power-sharing agreement with the Taliban that could have prevented a return of hostilities. The veteran Algerian diplomat and peacemaker Lakhdar Brahimi, who headed the UN mission in Afghanistan and chaired the Bonn conference in 2001, concluded several years later that the Taliban should have been included in the Bonn settlement and not left out in the cold.

Baghrani said the strength of the opposition, American and Afghan, ranged against them left the Taliban with no option but to retreat. "At the time it was the right move considering the concentration of all the factions," he told me later. "That was a move for peace and stability. Things went wrong, turned out differently, but at the time it was in the interests of Afghanistan and the Afghan people." Mullah Omar was right to escape and not give himself up or try to negotiate a position in any future government, he added. "If you look at what happened in the north, the Taliban surrendered in a peaceful movement. Yet, even though it was a peaceful gesture, they were deceived, and they were killed and tortured."[15]

A week after Mullah Omar gave up Kandahar, Osama bin Laden made his escape too. For days, American B-52 bombers had pounded the caves and Taliban positions in Tora Bora in eastern Afghanistan in a terrifying but vain attempt to kill him. His forces took heavy casualties, but he managed to leave, probably on horseback, and made his way across the Pakistani border to North Waziristan. He knew the region, which had served as a training base for him in the 1980s and was controlled by a close ally from the jihad days, the Afghan mujahideen commander Jalaluddin Haqqani.[16] U.S. Delta Force members tracking him at Tora Bora caught a last intercept of a radio message from bin Laden to his men on December 13. "Our prayers have not been answered. Times are dire," he said, his voice apparently showing signs of stress and even despair. "We didn't receive support from the apostate nations who call themselves our Muslim brothers. Things might have been different." Apparently giving up on any vow to fight to the death, he ended, "I'm sorry for getting you involved in this battle, if you can no longer resist, you may surrender with my blessing."[17] The attacks of 9/11 cost him everything: his bases, his followers, and eventually his life, but he achieved one aim — dragging the United States into war on Muslim lands and creating a great conflagration between the Western and Muslim worlds.

By the spring, the Taliban were almost all gone from Afghanistan. In a last stand in April 2002, a group in southeastern Afghanistan, a mix of Taliban and some Arab and Central Asian fighters, fought a ferocious battle in the mountains of Shahikot in Paktia province. For American troops, it was their deadliest fight so far. Eight Americans dropped in by helicopter were trapped on the snow-covered mountain bowl and died fighting off an encirclement of insurgents. It was a sharp lesson in how the Taliban's well-trained foreign fighters could battle in the forbidding terrain of Afghanistan's mountains when they chose to make a stand.

The Taliban vanished after that. The survivors were seen trekking out along the well-worn mujahideen trail through the border village of Shkin, into Pakistan, by villagers living there.[18] In May 2002, British Marines made a painstaking sweep through the mountain range of Shahikot and found the insurgents were gone. The commander of the British task force, Brigadier Roger Lane, declared the fight against al Qaeda and the Taliban in Afghanistan "all but won." The Taliban were not showing signs of regrouping for offensive operations, he added. The British units packed up and left Afghanistan, and did not return in large numbers until 2006.

• • •

It was the end of Taliban rule in Afghanistan, a resounding defeat for
the radical Islamist movement and its leadership. It was also a defeat
for Pakistan's scheme to control Afghanistan by proxy. Several thousand Taliban fighters were killed in the six months after October
2001, and thousands more fled, badly mauled, hunted by vengeful opponents, and shell-shocked by the accuracy and power of American
bombs.[19] Those escaping from the north faced an arduous journey
overland through hostile regions where opposition groups were seizing power and arresting opponents. It took some of the Taliban fighters weeks to make their way out across the border. Even in Pakistan,
they were unsure of their welcome. The Pakistani leader, General Pervez Musharraf, had supposedly sided with the United States in the war.
The Taliban had no choice but to go to ground, seeking medical help
in private hospitals and shelter in the Afghan refugee community.

Yet they still had many friends in Pakistan, some of whom were
highly placed and influential. Their adopted homeland proved more
welcoming than threatening.

3

Pakistan's Protégés

"He was not even street smart. He was so stupid
it was easy for the ISI to use him."

— *Hafizullah Khan about Mullah Omar*

Mullah Omar never seemed marked for leadership. People who
knew him as a young man wonder to this day how he became
the driver of the great wave that swept the Taliban to power in
Afghanistan from 1994 to 2001. The main attribute that people recall
about him was that he was short on intelligence. That he was a brave
and dogged fighter was undisputed, but that was hardly unusual in
Afghanistan. Every family in the countryside gave heroes to the jihad.
But there was ambition beneath the stolid villager's exterior. He was
poor, landless, and an outsider from another province, and so was easily underestimated.

He came from a family of village mullahs. His father died when he
was young, and Omar was raised by his uncle Maulavi Muzafer. His
uncle took in the children and married Omar's mother. The custom
is common in parts of Afghanistan to ensure that the widow and off-
spring are provided for and kept within the family's embrace. The family belonged to the Hotak tribe, which made them Ghilzais, underdogs
in Afghanistan's tribal politics where the Durrani tribal confederacy
had long dominated.

Omar grew up in the village of Deh Wanawarkh in Deh Rawud,
the same mountainous area of Uruzgan where Karzai would raise a

force against the Taliban in 2001. He attended his uncle's mosque for a few years of basic religious education and later was sent to continue his studies at a madrassa in Kandahar. From there, soon after the Soviet Union invaded Afghanistan, he ran off to join the mujahideen. He never completed the religious training to become a mullah — but like all Taliban commanders and officials, he came to use the title as an honorific, although he always told acquaintances that he preferred the title of mujahid: holy warrior.

Omar joined a mujahideen group led by a commander, Faizullah, who commanded about 150 to 200 men in Maiwand west of Kandahar.[1] Their main base was in a village called Sangesar, which became Omar's adopted home. A mujahideen commander, Mohammad Nabi,[2] who came from a village near Sangesar, knew Omar well and often fought alongside him. He remembers him as a brave and good fighter but dull-witted. Omar was strict on moral issues and stubborn to a fault, once even refusing to leave the battlefield despite the fact that their ammunition had run out. "He would stick to his argument even when he was proved wrong," he told me.

It was that rigid stubbornness that brought Omar to lead the Taliban at the age of thirty-five. In the years after the Soviet withdrawal in 1989, after fourteen years of struggle in the mountains, the mujahideen took power. Many commanders began seizing land and businesses for themselves. Omar had an argument over land with his subcommander and was thrown out of his particular group of mujahideen. The commander complained that he was a troublemaker, like a "virus."[3]

The whole country was going through similar upheavals. The seven main mujahideen parties established the Islamic Republic of Afghanistan and formed a coalition government, but within months the alliance had fallen apart. Afghanistan slid into civil war as the different factions vied for power in Kabul, and armed militias across the country turned to brigandry. In the countryside and provincial towns, already decimated by war with the Soviets, mujahideen established their own mini-fiefdoms. In Kandahar, militias fought each other for control of the highways and set up checkpoints where they hung chains across the roads to stop vehicles and extort money and goods. By the spring of 1994, the criminality was annoying even the most powerful commanders of Kandahar whose own businesses and smuggling rackets were being disrupted. The militias had splintered into a plethora of criminal gangs. Every man with a gun was stepping onto the roads to steal cars or demand money from the local population.

A group of the most powerful commanders west of Kandahar gathered in the spring of 1994 and decided to organize a force to clear the worst offenders. They agreed to support a stern judge, Maulavi Pasanai, who presided over an Islamic court in the village of Zangabad to move against the checkpoints and help bring order to the chaos. Three commanders drove the plan: Haji Bashar, who wanted to clear impediments to his lucrative transport and drugs network; Haji Berget, a tribal leader who controlled smuggling routes; and Hafizullah Khan, a major landowner alarmed at the lawlessness. He would later accompany Hamid Karzai into Uruzgan in 2001. They gave Judge Pasanai half a dozen guards each for his protection so he could crack down on the worst criminals as both judge and enforcer.[4] The aim was to clear fifteen checkpoints between Maiwand and Kandahar, and fifteen on the other, east side of Kandahar up to the Pakistani border.

Mullah Omar was one of the men sent to work with Pasanai. At that point Omar was just an ordinary fighter living in Sangesar with ten followers. The commanders saw him as a religious man and a fighter with a clean reputation. As an outsider from Uruzgan province, he could act freely, unhampered by tribal loyalties. Hafizullah Khan, who lived near Pasanai's court, dealt with Omar regularly in 1994. "He was studying with a mullah in my village. He would work, building a wall, and then he would study," he recalled. "He was a *very* stupid man" but "he was a good man, and very humble."

Soon Omar became Judge Pasanai's trusted emissary, carrying letters back and forth and coming to Hafizullah Khan for money, food, and support for their work. With vehicles donated by the big commanders and court orders from Pasanai, the group began moving against militias and criminals west of Kandahar. Justice was harsh. A particularly notorious checkpoint commander, Nadir Jan, resisted arrest, so Mullah Omar killed him on the spot with a pistol shot to his head.[5]

The Taliban had begun with barely a penny among them. Pasanai would send Mullah Omar out with requests for money, and Hafizullah Khan would gather people together to drum up resources for the group. Khan remembers giving Omar vegetables and yogurt from his farm. Yet within months, Pasanai's men had seized enough weapons and gained such stature that people were volunteering money and assistance. At some point, Pasanai replaced his commander of operations, Abdul Samad, because he had executed a former Communist without authority. Pasanai gave the top job to Mullah Omar. From that moment, his power began to grow. He talked of clearing checkpoints and subduing militias all the way to Kabul.[6]

In September 1994, in a lightning strike, Mullah Omar cleared the main highway and swept up to Kandahar city in just twelve days. Some of the most fearsome commanders had supported his appointment since they knew him as a good mujahid and a religious man, and they let him advance without opposition. The most powerful commander in Kandahar, Mullah Naqibullah, pledged not to resist Omar's advance and even handed over the military barracks in the city. Over the next six weeks, Omar steadily neutralized the different militia groups in and around Kandahar city. It was a masterful action, ruthlessly removing petty criminals; amassing popular support, weapons, and men; and gaining overwhelming moral momentum before turning on the most powerful commanders.

So the Taliban movement was formed. Mullah Omar was now the one calling meetings of mujahideen commanders back at his old base in Sangesar. Mullah Abdul Salam Zaeef, who served with him from the beginning and later became the Taliban ambassador to Pakistan, recalled forty to fifty mujahideen commanders gathering at the white mosque in Sangesar in the autumn, each taking an oath of allegiance to fight against corruption and criminality.[7] The group came to be known collectively as the Taliban, which means "religious students" or "seekers of knowledge" (Taliban is the plural of "Talib"), since most of them had religious training.

Although Pakistan did not create the Taliban, it acted swiftly to co-opt the movement. Before the summer of 1994 was over, Mullah Omar had acquired Pakistani advisors. People in Kandahar remember a Major Gul, along with Colonel Imam, the Pakistani special forces trainer. Imam was a distinctive figure. He sported a 1942 British paratroopers jacket, a long beard, and a flat white turban shaped like a car tire, as one Pakistani journalist joked. He was from a military family in the Punjab. He would come to epitomize the Pakistani officers who adopted the mujahideen cause as their own. He was familiar to thousands of Afghan mujahideen who had taken his training courses. He later told me that he had no memory of training Mullah Omar, though the Taliban leader told him that Omar had been his student on an extended three-month course in 1985. Omar always addressed the colonel by the honorific title of "Ustad" or "teacher." The respect was mutual. Colonel Imam described the madrassa students as the most "formidable" of all the fighters he had trained because of their religious zeal. Omar, he said, was the only honest leader for Afghanistan.[8]

Soon after Omar secured a base in Kandahar city, he attacked the border town of Spin Boldak. This time the Taliban showed clear signs of Pakistani support, including cross-border artillery fire. Local journalists reported that among the attackers were hundreds of Afghan students from Pakistani madrassas run by the Pakistani religious party politician Maulana Fazlur Rehman. They left a trail of wrapping paper as they unpacked brand-new weapons.[9]

Two weeks later, Colonel Imam tried an odd Pakistani stunt, purportedly opening up a trade route linking Pakistan to Central Asia via Afghanistan. It was labeled a "peace convoy" but it was not cleared with the Kabul government and seemed to be an attempt to promote the Taliban as a new highway police force. Trucks bearing Pakistani medicines and goods for export drove out from the Pakistani town of Quetta, passing through southern and western Afghanistan en route

to the Turkmen border. The Pakistani Interior Minister Naseerullah
Babar and the government of Benazir Bhutto claimed credit for the
plan. It was stage-managed by the ISI.[10]

Colonel Imam, along with another ISI man, Major Gul, were de-
puted to lead the convoy comprising some thirty-five trucks. They
took two Taliban commanders with him, Mullah Borjan and another.
Not far inside Afghanistan, the convoy was stopped and the trucks im-
pounded by Afghan militia. The mujahideen commander of the border region, Mansour Achakzai, famously pulled Colonel Imam's beard
and told him to get out of Afghanistan. "Why did you come to our soil
without our permission?" he demanded.[11]

Colonel Imam and Major Gul were released to the Pakistani consulate, but Mansour kept custody of the trucks and their seventy men,
drivers and helpers. In Kandahar, Colonel Imam appealed to Mullah Omar to help release the vehicles and personnel, and the Taliban
leader mobilized a force against the militias.

They battled each other for two days at Takht-e-Pul, east of Kandahar,
until finally the Taliban routed the militias. They pursued Mansour
south to Dand, where they killed him. They hung his body from a tank
barrel in front of Kandahar airport in a grisly lesson to all. Opposition
dropped away after that. One of the most feared commanders, Ustad
Aleem, told his men to surrender their weapons to the Taliban while
he slipped away across the desert with a single companion. The Taliban
moved on to Kandahar and took charge. Units of bearded Pakistani
commandos in civilian clothes appeared and took up positions at the
prison and several other strategic sites. "They were advising the Taliban
and beating anyone who was a member of the mujahideen," Mohammad Nabi recalled. If the mujahideen had understood their real intentions, they would have slaughtered the Pakistanis right then, he added.

Through murderous methods and with Pakistani help, the Taliban
took power in the south. They enforced a strict, fundamentalist code
of behavior that harked back to the time of the Prophet Mohammad.
They banned music, television, and almost all recreation. They ordered the male population to attend prayers in the mosque five times a

day and to grow their beards long. They dealt out punishments such as whippings, amputations, and executions of criminals. They had little knowledge of how to run an administration or handle international relations, but they did deliver law and order, gaining a monopoly of force and disarming the population.

The Afghan people, and the majority of the mujahideen, were so weary of the lawlessness and desperate for some strong moral leadership that they embraced the Taliban and accepted such harsh justice.

The most powerful commanders were steadily disarmed or forced to flee, and the Taliban established themselves as the dominant force throughout Kandahar province and the adjoining districts. Even Mullah Omar's early protectors were not spared. Haji Bashar was detained and had his head shaved. Hafizullah Khan was beaten so badly by the Taliban that he needed skin grafts. Others, however, accepted the new rulers because of the Taliban's religious standing. Omar's old comrade in arms, Mohammad Nabi, was disarmed and detained for a few weeks before being sent home. "We were happy to be done with this whole jihad thing," he recalled.

With control of Kandahar, Mullah Omar was on his way to dominating the southern and eastern Pashtun belt of Afghanistan. Within a few months, he had tanks, armored vehicles, artillery systems, and an army thousands strong.

Borne along by a sense of righteousness and by substantial military and logistical assistance from Pakistan, the Taliban rolled across half the country in the next six months. They took control of some Pashtun regions without a fight, but as they advanced further north, resistance intensified. They lost hundreds of men in a bloody encounter with the Northern Alliance as they advanced on the western city of Herat, only succeeding in seizing the city in September 1995 after Pakistani commandos arrived to boost the Taliban assault, Mohammad Nabi said. He spotted Major Gul counting out ammunition for the offensive at one point.

Colonel Imam was appointed Pakistani consul in Herat and was open about his involvement in the military campaign. The American reporter Steve LeVine visited the consulate there in June 1996 and found Imam directing the Taliban assault on the Shomali Plain north of Kabul from his desk, barking orders down the telephone. Colonel Imam remained close to Mullah Omar for the next seven years, serving as a Pakistani diplomatic envoy in Afghanistan for most of that time. Journalists and Western diplomats who met him in those years described him as wielding a remarkable level of influence. One Pakistani journalist saw him speak to a roomful of Taliban in a government building in Kandahar. His listeners all sat before him with their heads bowed in obedience, in the manner of students before a revered teacher.

Wrenching Herat from the control of its leader, the independent-minded Tajik warrior Ismail Khan, was a milestone for the Taliban and their Pakistani mentors, and they next turned their sights on the capital, Kabul.

For the previous two decades, Pakistan had fostered Afghan protégés in order to have a friendly ally in power in Kabul that would protect its western flank. Pakistan was a young nation and paranoically insecure about defending its territory. Since its formation and partition from India in 1947, Pakistan had fought three wars with its larger neighbor, India, and lost half its territory when Bangladesh broke away in 1971. Rulers in Islamabad were constantly concerned that regional rivals, whether India, Iran, or Russia, would use Afghanistan as a springboard to attack Pakistan. Pakistan's generals wanted Afghanistan firmly in their own camp to provide "strategic depth." Some even advocated annexing Afghanistan as Pakistan's fifth province, as an ISI official once told me. For allies Pakistan had favored Islamists, who could be counted on to resist non-Muslim foes such as the Soviet Union and India, and ethnic Pashtuns in Afghanistan, who were affiliated to Pakistan's own large Pashtun population. Besides external threats, Pakistan was concerned about controlling Pashtun nationalism. Some Pashtuns supported the creation of Pashtunistan, a separate state for themselves. Such a notion was unthinkable to the Pakistani military, and so it had long supported Islamist Pashtun groups to counter the nationalists. The Taliban, a primarily Pashtun band of radical mullahs, fitted the bill and by 1995, became Pakistan's new instrument of policy in Afghanistan.

Mullah Omar's vision was to overthrow the Kabul government and establish an Islamic Emirate of Afghanistan across the whole land. Yet few of his old acquaintances believed Mullah Omar was doing the thinking by himself. There were brighter minds within the Taliban leadership, such as his deputy, Mullah Mohammad Rabbani, but the strategic plan and the tactical and logistical organization of the military campaign were on a scale much too advanced for Omar and his band of fighters.[12] "He was not even street smart," said Hafizullah Khan. "It was easy for the ISI to use him."

Yet the Pakistanis who came into contact with Omar often described him as an able leader with an unmatched ability to manipulate and command. Robert L. Grenier, who served as the station chief for the CIA in Islamabad, recalls a Pakistani associate who knew Omar well and described him as head and shoulders above the rest of the Taliban. A friend told me that Mullah Omar possessed three elements that appealed to Afghans: He came from Deh Rawud, known for the exceptional bravery of its fighters. He was a mullah (even if only half-qualified), and Afghans will follow their religious leaders whatever they say. And he was a mujahid, which was essential for any leader in the post-Soviet era in Afghanistan. Meanwhile his supporters spun myths of his holiness and uncompromising attitude toward right and wrong. His ruthless punishments earned him a fearful esteem.

In fact, Mullah Omar was not so pure. He behaved like the typical mujahideen commander made good. After taking power in Kandahar, he flew one of the captured Russian Mi17 helicopters up to his uncle's house in Deh Rawud to fetch all his furniture and household belongings to bring them down to Kandahar. He took four wives, which is permitted under Islam but frowned upon among Afghanistan's middle classes. He also broke a taboo in Pashtun culture when he forced a family to give him their daughter even though she was engaged to someone else.[13]

In April 1996, he took a step to augment his religious authority and head off any challenges to his leadership. He gathered hundreds of mullahs and supporters at a grand assembly in Kandahar, entertaining them for days. He called them to a ceremony at the city's holiest shrine, the turquoise-domed Shrine of the Blessed Cloak, where a robe belonging to the Prophet Mohammad is kept alongside the grave of the great Afghan conqueror Ahmed Shah Durrani. Mullah Omar took out the cloak, a venerated relic that is rarely ever removed from its multiple caskets. Before the crowd, he raised the cloak and wrapped it around himself as followers proclaimed him Amir-ul-Momineen, Commander of the Faithful, one of the most elevated titles in Islam.[14]

Omar may have been gathering support for his next campaign. His next target was Kabul. Pakistan piled support and money onto the Taliban offensive on the capital. The Taliban itself poured volunteer fighters into the assault, sending them racing across minefields in fleets of pickups east of the city. Even when a pickup blew up, more rushed into the gap, a Northern Alliance officer told me. The rapid advance surprised the Northern Alliance, and Ahmed Shah Massoud beat a retreat rather than fight in the city. His troops regrouped in the Panjshir Valley where they had survived repeated Soviet offensives, and Taliban forces swept into Kabul. In one of their first actions, the Taliban murdered the former Communist president Najibullah and his brother, who were living in the city in a United Nations guesthouse.

Just days before the assault, the top operational commander of the Taliban, Mullah Borjan, had told a Pakistani journalist that ISI officers had given him orders to execute Najibullah as one of his first acts upon taking Kabul. Borjan had come from the frontline to Quetta, ostensibly to undergo treatment for his kidneys — but in fact to meet with his handlers in the ISI. The journalist met him in the house of a mutual acquaintance and asked what the Taliban planned to do about the Afghan Communist leader. Hated by the mujahideen and the Taliban for his brutal regime, Najibullah was nevertheless an influential Pashtun figure, and the journalist suggested to Borjan that the Taliban would lose the sympathy of many Pashtuns if they executed him. Borjan said he agreed. He wanted to arrest the former president and send him to Kandahar to be put on trial.

"But are you aware of the black gates?" Mullah Borjan added. "I have just come from there. The gates are in your cantonment area," he said.

"Do you mean the ISI?" the journalist asked.

"Yes. They are insisting that the first thing we do is kill Najibullah. If I don't, I am not sure what will happen to me," he said.[15]

Mullah Borjan never made it to Kabul. He was assassinated on his way back to the frontline, reportedly by his bodyguard, a Pakistani from Kashmir. The journalist summed it up: "The Taliban do not have minds of their own."

When the Taliban took Kabul days later, the first thing they did was drag Najibullah through the streets and string him and his brother up on Ariana Square, where the CIA now has its offices, just yards from the presidential palace. The first ring of Taliban fighters controlling the gawping crowds were Urdu-speaking Pakistanis. Some of them were dark-skinned and wearing sunglasses, Abdul Waheed Wafa, a colleague who was there, told me.[16] The ISI's demand had been met.

The Taliban were entering difficult territory from then on. Herat and Kabul were majority Persian-speaking cities inhabited by sophisticated, educated populations who mostly hated the mujahideen and welcomed their departure, but were equally revolted by the Taliban's coarse justice and draconian rules, as enforced by the dreaded Department of Vice and Virtue. In one of the first protests against the Taliban, women in Herat demonstrated against the banning of women from the public baths. In the countryside, the Taliban's campaigns were marked by mass killings and plunder. In one of the worst acts of the war, the Taliban laid waste to the fertile Shomali Plain north of Kabul, burning houses, orchards, and vineyards, killing villagers and abducting women. A UN special rapporteur described it as nothing less than a scorched-earth policy.

The mujahideen groups in central and northern Afghanistan saw the Taliban as an instrument of Pakistan's colonial ambitions and vowed to resist their advance. Undaunted, the Taliban continued their march north. They brought in thousands of foreign fighters, including Arabs, Uzbeks, and Pakistanis, to strengthen their extended frontlines. By 2001, the Northern Alliance had been pushed back to the far northeastern corner of the country.

Mullah Omar was sure of victory. He thought the last resistance would wither away eventually, according to the Pakistani former interior secretary Rustam Shah Mohmand, who shuttled between the Taliban and the Northern Alliance leaders in the late 1990s in an effort to bring peace.[17] Yet Omar also recognized that he needed non-Pashtun partners in his government if he was to sustain his power. In a three-hour meeting in the late 1990s — the longest meeting Omar had ever held, according to aides — Rustam Shah won Omar's agreement for his foreign minister to meet the Northern Alliance leader Ahmed Shah Massoud on neutral territory in Central Asia and work out a power-sharing agreement.

"He was a very simple fellow, a man of few words, but very straight-forward and very clearheaded," Shah later said of Omar.[18] But then General Pervez Musharraf seized power in Pakistan and promptly ended the peace efforts for Afghanistan. When Shah sought instructions to continue the peace effort, Musharraf's chief civilian aide, Tariq Aziz, relayed a message from the general: "Please tell this fellow that I have better things to do." Musharraf's view was that "the Taliban are in power, and they are our people, why fiddle with this arrangement," Shah told me.

Pakistani officials, including senior military officers, often say that they could not control the Taliban. And it is true that, as the movement grew stronger, it fell under the influence of Osama bin Laden and increasingly began to resist requests from Pakistan and Saudi Arabia. The realization came as a shock to Pakistan according to retired general Jehangir Karamat, who served as chief of army staff in the 1990s.[19]

When, in 2001, there was a world outcry against the Taliban's plan to blow up the colossal Buddhas carved into the rockface in Bamiyan, the Pakistani government tried to intervene. Mullah Omar rebuffed its intervention. "We reached out to them and they told us to get lost," Karamat said. Earlier, when the Saudis had gone to Omar to ask him to give up bin Laden, they were also rebuffed. "That was again a shock," Karamat told me.

There is evidence showing that bin Laden became an increasingly powerful influence over Mullah Omar in the last few years before 2001. Omar's actions revealed a growing radicalism, and moderates in the Taliban leadership were sidelined. Pakistani diplomatic cables found in Kabul in 2001 warned that the Arab militants in Afghanistan were growing "too big to handle."[20] Retired Brigadier General Ziauddin Butt, who served as ISI chief under Nawaz Sharif before being removed by Musharraf, visited Kandahar three or four times to see Omar after al Qaeda bombed the American embassies in Kenya and Tanzania in 1998. It was a sign of the importance of the relationship that the head of Pakistani intelligence himself traveled to see the Afghan leader. "Mullah Omar told me bin Laden was 'like a bone in my throat,'" Butt said.[21] Yet when he advised Omar to get rid of bin Laden, the Taliban leader asked, "How do we send him out?" The man who was ruthless with his own warlords and criminals apparently could not move against his Arab guest.

Bin Laden's son, Omar bin Laden, relates a revealing episode in the book *Growing up Bin Laden*. After the embassy bombings, Mullah Omar told bin Laden that he and his men should leave Afghanistan. Yet bin Laden used religion to persuade Omar to allow him to stay longer, saying that if Omar gave in to the demands of infidel governments, his decision would be against the tenets of Islam.[22] American journalist Gretchen Peters, in her book *Seeds of Terror*, describes how bin Laden's terrorists were part of the narcotics mafia making millions of dollars out of Kandahar and bankrolling the Taliban along the way.[23] Certainly the money helped buy influence. But it was bin Laden's Islamist dreams and commitment to help create an Islamic Emirate of Afghanistan that wielded the strongest influence over Mullah Omar.

The CIA chief in Islamabad, Robert Grenier, concluded that Omar was convinced of his own religious mission. "He really thought he was Amir-ul-Momineen and saw himself as the leader of a global jihad. He saw himself as more important than bin Laden," Grenier told me.[24]

Pakistani military and intelligence support for the Taliban remained extensive and committed right up to 2001. The Taliban's most dogged opponent, Ahmed Shah Massoud, wrote in an open letter to the American people in 1998 that, according to his intelligence, more than 28,000 Pakistanis, including paramilitary personnel and military advisors, were part of the Taliban forces arrayed against him. He said he was holding more than five hundred Pakistani citizens as prisoners of war in his jails. "Afghanistan, for the second time in one decade, is once again an occupied country," he wrote.[25] Western diplomats agreed that Pakistan was helping the Taliban's military campaigns with specialized troops. "You would see a sudden qualitative improvement in the Taliban, such as in coordinating artillery fire," Grenier said.

Pakistan even encouraged the Taliban's waywardness. The government and the ISI conducted a deliberate policy of keeping the Taliban cut off from the wider world in order to control them, Rustam Shah Mohmand told me. "This was the basic tragedy. They thought to keep them solitary and ostracized, then they would be dependent on us." Mullah Omar was a reticent man, unversed in worldly affairs, and over time he became a virtual recluse. Even after the Taliban took Kabul, he only ever ventured there once, preferring to rule from his base in Kandahar. He generally refused to meet with non-Muslims. Western officials had difficulty obtaining meetings with him, and no Western journalist ever gained an interview with him. When Spozhmai Maiwandi, director of Voice of America's Pashtu service, first interviewed him by telephone in 1999, she said Omar was nervous speaking to a woman.

Nevertheless, Mullah Omar was not so cut off that he did not know what was happening inside Afghanistan. Although the Taliban deny it, the Taliban leadership certainly knew something of bin Laden's impending attack against the United States in 2001. Taliban fighters knew about it. Arab fighters bragged about a huge forthcoming attack on America to a driver at a gas station in Kandahar, a Kandahari tribal leader told me. The Taliban foreign minister, Wakil Ahmed Mutt-awakil, learned of the planned attacks from Uzbek foreign fighters and attempted to warn a U.S. consulate official in Pakistan, according to British reporter Kate Clark.[26] Mullah Omar also certainly knew about the plot that assassinated Ahmed Shah Massoud two days before 9/11. The two al Qaeda assassins arrived in Kandahar from Pakistan and stayed in the southern city for two weeks. An official from the Ministry of Foreign Affairs was sent from Kabul to meet their plane in Kanda-har. There was such importance attached to the visit that the official spent several days traveling back and forth to the airport in anticipa-tion of their arrival.

The ISI also undoubtedly knew of their trip. The Pakistani embassy in London had granted one-year, multi-entry journalists' visas to the men, Tunisians traveling on forged Belgian passports. Such lengthy vi-sas to Pakistan, as every reporter in the region knows, are notoriously difficult to obtain and always vetted by the ISI.

After 9/11, when the United States threatened war and demanded again that the Taliban hand over bin Laden, Mullah Omar was at a loss as to what to do. He telephoned a variety of contacts, including journal-ists, in the days and weeks that followed. When Spozhmai Maiwandi called to interview the foreign minister about five Christian mission-aries in a Taliban jail, she was unexpectedly offered an interview with Omar. The Taliban leader did not care that he was endangering the lives of his people, Maiwandi remembers. He railed against U.S. policy toward Muslims and its support of secular dictators in Muslim lands. To give up bin Laden would be cowardly and bring shame upon the Taliban, he told her. "Giving him to the U.S. would in fact be smashing Islam's prestige on the ground," he said.[27]

Some in the Taliban urged him to hand over bin Laden. The council of clerics, the highest religious body in the land, ruled that bin Laden should be asked to leave. The Taliban foreign minister Muttawakil even traveled to meet with American officials in Islamabad to discuss the mechanics. But it came to nothing.

Omar was listening to his Pakistani intelligence advisors, who wielded the greatest influence. Colonel Imam joined him in Kandahar in the days after 9/11. He urged Omar to ignore demands to hand over bin Laden and to resist the American attacks.[28] Colonel Imam believed that the Americans would not bomb the country for long, and assumed they would not be able to sustain a ground war so far from home. He advised Omar to pull back into the mountains and wage a guerrilla war, as they had done against the Soviet Army.

The head of Pakistani intelligence, Lieutenant General Mahmud Ahmed, traveled twice to Kandahar to talk personally with Mullah Omar in the weeks after the 9/11 attacks. General Mahmud did not do as his American counterparts and his president, Musharraf, had requested. "Musharraf wanted that they should come to some sort of compromise and allow bin Laden to be sent away or handed over to the Americans," Talat Masood, a retired lieutenant general and well-known political analyst, told me. Instead, Mahmud, who was deeply caught up in the Taliban cause and a committed Islamist, told Omar to hold on to bin Laden and resist the attack. "He gave just the opposite signal. There is no doubt about it. I think Musharraf did not have full control over what was happening," Masood said.[29] General Mahmud even told the Taliban leader what he knew of American attack plans and how best to withstand them.

General Mahmud's support for the Taliban became so obstructive that the Bush administration demanded his removal from the top intelligence post. Musharraf replaced him on October 7, 2001, the day the bombing campaign began. Colonel Imam remained at Mullah Omar's side even after the bombing began, until an exasperated Musharraf sent orders: "What are you doing there?"[30]

For years American officials failed to recognize the huge investment in time, money, and military effort that Pakistan had put into the Taliban from 1994 to 2001. It was much more than the infiltration of a single intelligence operative. It was a seven-year bloody campaign waged by the Pakistani military. It was the continuation of a policy to dominate

Afghanistan pursued by Pakistan since the early 1970s when it first began supporting Afghan Islamists. It meant that when Musharraf agreed to cooperate with America after 9/11 and abandon the Taliban, he was going against nearly thirty years of Pakistani strategic thinking. American officials should have realized that it was inconceivable for Pakistan to give up on so much time and investment, or that the military and security establishment could change its institutional thinking so easily.

· **4** ·

The Taliban in Exile

"America should have selected to crush al Qaeda and the
Taliban in Pakistan, rather than go to war in Iraq."

— *Habib Jalib Baloch, Quetta politician*

May 2003. As the heat left the afternoon and the time for evening
prayers approached, dozens of men began to fill up the square
at Mizan Chowk, one of the main intersections in the center of
Quetta, Pakistan. The crowd was mostly Afghan: bearded men wearing the heavy black turbans of southwestern Afghanistan and younger
men in the tightly wound white turbans worn by students. They
greeted each other in the Afghan way, placing a hand on the chest of
their friend and leaning into an embrace, bringing their heads close.
Pulling back, they would stand chatting, holding each other's hands
in a prolonged handshake, intoning the traditional Pashtun greetings,
blessings, and inquiries about health and family. They wore shalwar
kamize, the loose-fitting shirt and pants that is common attire in much
of Pakistan and Afghanistan. Most had embroidered cotton shawls
thrown over one shoulder. The shawl serves as a sheet, blanket, prayer
mat, and cushion, depending on the need. Some displayed a short pant
length that stops above the ankle, a sartorial affectation of the most
fundamentalist among them.

They were all Taliban, some of them former fighters, officials, and
supporters of the rump movement, and some of them were *taliban* in

the original sense of the word, religious students studying in Quetta's numerous seminaries. Often part-time volunteer fighters, these students were foot soldiers of the movement.

Eighteen months after their defeat and flight from Afghanistan, the Taliban were gathering openly in the center of this Pakistani town. Every Thursday evening they could be seen mingling at Mizan Chowk, where newsstands sold Taliban newspapers and CDs of Taliban sermons, catching up on news before attending evening prayers together at nearby mosques.[1]

A longtime base for the mujahideen during the 1980s, Quetta had become since 2001 the Taliban's home in exile. It was a quiet, provincial center of low-rise buildings and orderly streets. Once an outpost of the British empire that guarded the southern gateway from India through the Bolan Pass to Afghanistan, Quetta now served as an important military garrison town for Pakistan. It is the provincial capital of Baluchistan, home of the Baluch tribes as well as a large population of native Pashtuns. For decades the city and surrounding region provided a refuge to Afghans fleeing war and poverty. It has hosted hundreds of thousands of refugees ever since the Soviet invasion of Afghanistan in 1979. After thirty years in Pakistan, many of these Afghans have become so well settled and integrated that they do not want to return to Afghanistan. The air is thin and cool in Quetta, even in the height of Pakistan's torrid summer. Orchards bearing apples, pears, apricots, and plums thrive in the green valley beneath the barren brown of the surrounding mountains. Many of the Taliban spent their youth in refugee camps in and around Quetta and knew the area well. Some had homes, relatives, and small businesses in Pakistan from that time. Many had studied in madrassas in the region. Almost all carried refugee papers, or forged Pakistani identification cards, allowing them the right to reside in Pakistan. They blended in easily.

The Taliban were easy to find, though they were on their guard. I went to Mizan Chowk with two Afghan colleagues and a driver in a small hired minibus. It had curtains on the windows, and I sat in the back, hidden from view. The sight of a foreigner would generally attract the attention of police or crowds of passersby, who would then warn people off and break up any street interview. My Afghan colleagues — an interpreter and a friend who knew some of the Taliban — went off to find people willing to be interviewed. Several young Talibs came over to the window of the car and chatted easily. They were confident and defiant. They talked in slogans, boasting that they would fight the Americans and return the Taliban to power. They criticized the presence of foreign troops in Afghanistan and called the government of Hamid Karzai illegitimate.

"We don't like the Americans, and Karzai is a puppet of George W. Bush," said Abdul Karim, twenty-six, a soldier in the Taliban until he left Afghanistan in 2001. He was now studying at a madrassa in Quetta. "We want an Islamic government in Afghanistan," he said. Several in the group told me they had left Afghanistan because of fear of arrest by the Afghan authorities. "It is too difficult to study in Afghanistan, because all the time people demand: 'Who are you?' and 'What are you doing?'" said Mullah Shahzada, a religious teacher and former fighter from Helmand province.

A student called Nasrullah said he had left his home in Kandahar two weeks earlier, after the governor of the province ordered Taliban supporters to leave unless the elders of their village could vouch for their good behavior. "If the situation continues and the Americans do not behave well, I am ready to fight, because jihad is the duty of every Muslim," he said.

Within minutes of starting the interviews, my Afghan colleagues were warned to stop. The students did not have permission to talk to journalists, only the Taliban spokesmen could, a young Talib said. He told us to leave. The Taliban security apparatus was still strong. Orders had come from somewhere in the crowd. The Taliban did not want their presence in Quetta publicized, and they did not want foreign journalists writing about them. The young Talibs moved away obediently. We closed the car window and curtains, and pulled out into the traffic. That warning more than anything indicated to me that the Taliban movement was intact and functioning. Unseen officials had political control over this group of refugees and students, and their orders were obeyed.

We went to pay a visit on a former Taliban commander. He was staying in a small house down a back street in Khoratabad, a sprawling refugee settlement on the west side of Quetta where many Afghans lived and the Taliban had found shelter. We approached down a narrow, twisting alley, like a "camel's neck," our host joked. The driver inched the minivan between high walls and through a gateway into a small courtyard. We ducked under a piece of canvas hung across to prevent visitors catching sight of the women of the household.

Along a concrete path beside the one-story, whitewashed house, we entered a side door into the guest room. Most Afghan and Pakistani houses have separate rooms for entertaining guests and holding meetings. The guest room often has its own entrance and is designed to allow visitors to be entertained without disturbing the sanctity of the women's quarters. Many Afghan and Pakistani families, especially the conservative tribal and religious ones, still continue the practice of purdah. Women only mix with their extended family and do not meet unrelated men.

As a foreigner I was exempt from such rules. I had little difficulty working as a woman in Afghanistan and Pakistan where hospitality is a much-honored custom, and I often had the bonus of being invited into the inner sanctum to visit the women of the family. Only occasionally did conservative clerics refuse to meet with me or ban me from entry to their mosques and madrassas because I was a woman or a non-Muslim.

It is a strictly honored custom that no one enters an Afghan's home without being invited, and no man unrelated to the family enters the women's quarters. This becomes second nature to anyone living in Pakistan and Afghanistan, yet the readiness of foreign soldiers to violate this cherished custom in their search for militants, kicking down doors in house-to-house raids and searching women's quarters, became one of the most upsetting issues for Afghans across the country. The American and NATO forces violated a code that could have worked in their favor: when you are invited into someone's home, you are under the protection of your host. I felt no fear going to interview a Taliban commander in the warren of Quetta's back streets. I knew and trusted my host, who had organized the meeting. He would make sure I came to no harm.

The room, like any simple Afghan home, had no furniture. Mattresses and cushions were placed on the floor around the walls, and white cotton fabric was hung over the window, softening the bright sunlight. The commander was half-lying on a mattress, propped up on a bolster with a cup of green tea on the floor beside him. We sat down on the floor. Someone brought more tea. The commander said his name was Mullah Habibullah Akhund (not his real name, I later learned). He was in his thirties and had served as a logistics commander in the Taliban's Defense Ministry, supporting the frontline on the Shomali Plain north of Kabul. He had moved south to Kandahar with the rest of the Taliban army as their positions were smashed in the bombardment. When Kandahar fell, he escaped across the border to Pakistan.

Commanders like Habibullah, who had served in the Taliban from the beginning, did not trust Hamid Karzai's promise that they could return to their homes and live in peace. They had lost the support of the people, and they fully expected retribution from opponents and arrest or even worse from American forces. They came to Pakistan even though here, too, they did not trust the authorities. Allies in the ISI were on their side, but President Musharraf was cooperating with the United States.

Those years — 2002 and 2003 — when the people rejected the Taliban and embraced the new vision for Afghanistan, were their lowest moment, a Taliban commander told me years later. Habibullah came to Quetta and went into hiding, living in a friend's house, barely going out, worried he would be arrested and handed over to the Americans. "They were scared of the Pakistanis," the Afghan refugee who hosted

Habibullah told me later. "There were rumors that the Americans would arrest a lot of them in Pakistan like they did in Afghanistan."

In the meeting, Habibullah told me he was unsure what to do. Remnants of the Taliban movement were already conducting an insurgency inside Afghanistan, he knew, but he was waiting to see which way things would go. "There are different groups of Taliban," he said. "Some are fighting, and some, like me, are waiting to see what the government will do. If they make an Islamic government in Afghanistan, then it will be all right."

Officially, Pakistan had turned against the Taliban. When pressed by U.S. Secretary of State Colin Powell in a phone call in the days after 9/11, General Musharraf had declared his full support for the United States and promised cooperation in the fight against the Taliban and al Qaeda in Afghanistan. Musharraf was not in a strong position. Since seizing power in a military coup in 1999, he had been largely ostracized internationally. Although he had a liberal reputation—of a whiskey-drinking, bridge-playing officer—he was a military hardliner in his support for the Taliban in Afghanistan and Kashmiri militants. He had nearly sparked a nuclear war with India after seizing Kargil in Indian-held Kashmir in May 1999 and had stonewalled U.S. requests to help get bin Laden. Perversely, 9/11 offered Musharraf a chance to improve his relations with the United States and his own standing internationally. He gave a national television address on September 19, 2001, and told his people that Pakistan would help America with military intelligence, over-flights, and logistics. He sent eighty thousand troops to guard Pakistan's frontier with Afghanistan.

By his own account, Musharraf was ready to cut off support for the Taliban after 9/11, and for the next two years, Taliban members went into hiding to escape the official crackdown. Pakistani forces rounded up and deported a large number of al Qaeda members and foreign fighters during this time. But Musharraf was not ready to dismantle the thousands of homegrown guerrilla fighters — Afghans, Pakistanis, and Kashmiris — who had been trained as proxy insurgent forces as part of Pakistan's thirty-year-old defense strategy. Musharraf planned to keep the thousands of fighters who returned from Afghanistan in reserve, hidden somewhere.

He told the then-U.S. ambassador to Pakistan, Wendy Chamberlain, that Pakistani militants and the Kashmiri groups would be off limits in any action against terrorism.[2] Senior leaders of the Afghan Taliban were secretly taken into the protective custody of safe houses. The rest were left to fend for themselves.

A few days after 9/11, Musharraf invited several political analysts to a meeting, among them the retired lieutenant general Talat Masood, who was an influential liberal voice well known in diplomatic circles, on talk shows, and at conferences. Musharraf asked them for advice on what the government should do. Masood told the general that he should cease support for the Taliban and all militant groups, including the Pakistani ones that operated in Kashmir.[3]

"My advice to him was you should completely stop supporting the Taliban and the jihadi forces in Pakistan, in the sense that the government, the state, must follow the policy, completely stopping support," Masood told me. Musharraf agreed that support for the Taliban should end but insisted that the government would continue its support for the Pakistani groups in Kashmir. The two could be "compartmentalized," he said. Masood, the senior in age, says he warned Musharraf that, from experience, it would not be possible to close one operation down and not the other. Still, Musharraf insisted he could do it.

"Yes, I think we should stop supporting the Taliban but we will continue supporting the jihadis in Kashmir," Musharraf told him.

"That's very difficult for you to do that," Masood said.

"Sir, you are becoming an apologist," the general retorted.

"I am telling you from my experience it is not possible to compartmentalize the way you are talking," Masood protested.

"As a matter of policy, he did want the Taliban to be controlled," Masood told me. "But when this invasion took place, the Taliban were pushed into Pakistan, along with al Qaeda. And as there was no anvil, and there was only a hammer, and the border was porous, there were large, large numbers in Pakistan, and they filtered all over the place in Pakistan, wherever they found it more convenient to carry on their activities and to feel safe. And Pakistan did not really understand the implications of having the Taliban based in Pakistan, and that in turn gave rise to their own Talibanization." Masood was not the only person to warn Musharraf in the months after 9/11, but the general was set on keeping at least some militant groups alive. His decision was to have dangerous repercussions for Pakistan and the wider region.

Only a single prominent Taliban official was arrested and handed over to the United States in the first years after 9/11: the Taliban ambassador to Pakistan, Mullah Abdul Salam Zaeef, who was living openly at his residence in Islamabad. Mullah Zaeef had irritated the Bush administration by holding strident news conferences in the garden of the Afghan embassy in Islamabad in the months after 9/11. A founding member of the Taliban, Zaeef doubted bin Laden was behind the 9/11 attacks, and he denounced the American intervention. On American insistence, Pakistan detained Zaeef in January 2002 and allowed his rendition to the CIA. He was taken to the USS *Bataan* and spent four years in Guantánamo Bay. Afterward, he reserved his greatest vitriol not for his American captors but for his betrayal by Pakistan.

The main Taliban leaders disappeared from sight into safe houses or the homes of sympathizers. Those who were detained were put on notice to cooperate with the ISI. Lower-level commanders and fighters like Habibullah were warned by their leaders to lie low — until the pressure gradually eased in 2003.

The American bombing of Afghanistan in 2001 had meanwhile lit a fuse in Pakistan's border regions, and they erupted in a volatile mix of militancy, religious fervor, and tribal solidarity. The border regions were populated by Pashtuns and Afghan refugees who held close ties to their fellow tribesmen in Afghanistan, and they were angered at the intervention.

One of the first to act was a militant cleric named Sufi Mohammad who raised a force of hundreds to join the Taliban in their fight against the United States. Sufi Mohammad was a Pakistani Pashtun from the Swat Valley. He had been a member of Jamaat-e-Islami, Pakistan's foremost religious party, formed along the lines of Egypt's Muslim Brotherhood, but he had split away after he came under the influence of Arab Wahhabists, including bin Laden. He formed his own movement, Teherik-e-Nefaz-e-Shariat-e-Mohammedi, the Movement for the Enforcement of Islamic Law (usually known by its Urdu acronym TNSM), calling for the establishment of Sharia law in Swat and the surrounding region.

As the American bombing of Afghanistan began, he urged every able-bodied man to help the Taliban and go and fight jihad in Afghanistan. Hundreds of villagers, old and young, most of them subsistence farmers, heard the call in mosques and on the radio and dutifully climbed into the buses provided for them. They were ferried into Afghanistan, though they were of little use to the Taliban. Hundreds of them arrived in the north just days before the Taliban began their retreat. With few weapons or organization, they were quickly captured by United Front forces as the northern towns fell. Scores of them were killed, and hundreds taken prisoner. I interviewed some of the prisoners in Mazar-i-Sharif. They were illiterate laborers who had little idea what they were doing in Afghanistan. As survivors straggled home with news of the debacle, families turned on Sufi Mohammad in fury.

The Pakistani government took him into custody—apparently for his own safety. He was detained by the ISI for seven years until 2008. He was neither charged nor put on trial for inciting his countrymen or endangering their lives. It was typical of the way the ISI dealt with militant leaders who went too far. They were removed from circulation but never formally punished. Some were even allowed to continue to run their organizations from behind a smoke screen of detention. In Sufi Mohammad's absence, his son-in-law, Mullah Fazlullah, a radical firebrand with close-set eyes and a bushy black beard who had fought alongside the Taliban in Afghanistan, took on the leadership of his father-in-law's movement with disastrous consequences. Less dependent on the ISI, intoxicated with power and al Qaeda's grand ideas, the new generation of militants represented by Fazlullah would prove uncontrollable.

In the month after 9/11, the mainstream religious parties in Pakistan began holding rallies to protest the war in Afghanistan and denounce Musharraf's alliance with the United States. As they gained momentum, Musharraf detained their leaders, including Qazi Hussain Ahmad, the leader of Jamaat-e-Islami, and Maulana Fazlur Rehman, head of Jamiat Ulema-e-Islam, a close supporter of the Taliban who had supplied thousands of madrassa students to fight in Afghanistan over the years. Qazi Hussain was placed under house arrest in a government guesthouse at Tanda Dam in Kohat, a remote spot in Pakistan's tribal regions, a three hours' drive from the city of Peshawar. Guarded by forty or fifty soldiers, he was the only "guest." He was detained for four months and then allowed to move to Lahore for health reasons. Although his party is known for cooperating with successive military governments, Qazi Hussain clearly resented his detention. He complained that the ISI had always sought to control the religious parties through a policy of divide and rule. It was during his detention that he formed the idea for a coalition of religious parties to campaign in provincial elections in 2002. He wrote to the other leaders of religious parties and urged them to come together in an alliance coalition. "I wrote that people are disheartened and in depression and if we do not come together they will be disappointed."[4]

Musharraf not only agreed to the idea of the religious parties' coalition but released their leaders from detention and gave them help. Six religious parties came together and formed the Muttahida Majlis-e-Amal, the United Council of Action, or MMA. Cynics later dubbed it the "Mullah-Military Alliance," for certainly the Musharraf government assisted its formation and rise to prominence. He was intent on keeping his rivals, the mainstream democratic parties, out of power. He needed democratically elected allies. The religious parties had never been hugely popular but had always been a useful and cooperative ally for the military, supporting the proxy wars in Kashmir and Afghanistan and channeling social dissatisfaction into religious causes.

Now in 2002, even as they campaigned vociferously against the U.S. intervention in Afghanistan and Musharraf's betrayal of the Taliban, they were again useful to the general because they siphoned support from his political rivals. Musharraf wanted to sideline the main threats to his power: the Pakistan Muslim League — led by Nawaz Sharif, the former prime minister whom Musharraf had ousted in 1999 — and the Pakistan People's Party led by Benazir Bhutto, a longtime opponent of military rule. Both leaders were in exile outside the country. Sharif had been imprisoned and then exiled to Saudi Arabia by Musharraf after the coup. Bhutto, whose father Zulfiqar Ali Bhutto, the founder of the People's Party, had been executed by a former military dictator, General Zia-ul-Haq, had gone into self-imposed exile in 1998 after her husband was jailed and she faced a slew of corruption charges.

Ahead of the October election, the ISI went into action, imprisoning some candidates, persuading others to defect, and impeding supporters from canvassing and voting. The tactics were standard practice by the intelligence service. The man who led the political campaign for the ISI, Major General Ehtisham Zamir, the head of the spy agency's domestic wing, later regretted helping Musharraf crush his opponents and went public about his manipulation of the elections.

The 2002 election changed the makeup of the Pakistani assembly, sweeping the religious parties to power in two border provinces and winning them sixty-eight seats in the national assembly, where previously they had only ever held a handful. Many saw it as an ISI plan to control the border areas through the MMA. But even the ISI was surprised by the strong wave of anti-American feeling that caused the swing. On the day after the election, as they sat in an outer room at the grand colonial Governor's House in Peshawar, a leading politician accused a senior ISI official of masterminding a landslide victory for the religious parties. The ISI man defended himself. "We did not expect them to be so successful," he said.[5]

• • •

The election of the MMA into the provincial governments of the North West Frontier province and Baluchistan was a great boon for the Taliban and Islamists inside Pakistan. The alliance was openly sympathetic. One new member of parliament in the North West Frontier province, Tajul Amin Jabul, twenty-six, admitted to having fought as a member of the Taliban in Afghanistan. Wearing a white shalwar kamize and white silk turban, his beard worn long and untrimmed, he looked as if he had stepped straight out of a Taliban madrassa as he greeted supporters on the lawn of the provincial parliament. He spoke with a soft voice and the gentle, even shy manner that students and mullahs often adopt, yet his eyes showed a wariness, and a proud insolence, when he replied to my questions. Along with a dozen female parliamentarians who were dressed all in black, veils covering their faces but for narrow slits for the eyes, Tajul Amin represented the new radical face of Pakistani provincial politics. During a break in the proceedings, I was chatting with a senior female parliamentarian in the women's common room when the call for prayer sounded. A younger woman from an Islamist party asked the legislator accusingly why she was not joining them to pray. The question forced her to state to the whole room that she was menstruating, and thus, according to custom, should not partake in communal prayers. The tyranny of the Taliban had entered Peshawar's parliament.

With friends and supporters in power in Pakistan's border provinces, the Afghan Taliban began to move around more freely and reorganize. Mullah Omar emerged from a long silence in February 2003, sending a letter from hiding calling on all Afghans to wage a holy war against American forces. He also made an audio recording with a similar message, distributed on cassette tapes that were duplicated and passed among his followers. It was the first sign that he was reassuming leadership in over a year. In the letter, sent by fax to a Peshawar newspaper, Omar accused American forces of committing atrocities against Muslims. He urged all Muslims to join the struggle against the United States and warned that anyone who collaborated with U.S. forces or the Afghan government would be killed.

Infidels have encroached on Islam and today America is committing atrocities against Muslims, so Jihad is absolutely compulsory for all Muslims.

Wage Jihad against America and its allies, and if someone cannot fight, he should quit his job and separate himself from them.

Vacate all offices, ministries, provinces so that the distinction between a Muslim and a crusader is made.

Anyone of you who helps infidels, or serves them in any manner, deserves to die.[6]

Up until then, there had been only intermittent attacks against U.S. and government forces in Afghanistan. A gunman who had joined the police tried to assassinate Hamid Karzai in Kandahar in September 2002. A teenager threw a grenade into a U.S. Army jeep in Kabul in December. The following day, a suicide bomber — the first to strike in the capital — blew himself up at the entrance to a German peacekeepers' base. They were one-off attacks, and mostly unsuccessful. The grenade-throwing teenager was caught and told police that he and a dozen others had spent a week in weapons training in a camp in Pakistan, just across the border from his home province of Khost. They were then sent into Afghanistan and told to attack Americans.

Earlier in 2002, Afghan police had caught a twenty-nine-year-old member of a Taliban gang operating in a mountainous part of Kandahar province, and I was able to interview him. They had locked him up in a windowless room on their base in Kandahar city and brought him out in chains. He was thin and dirty, with long tousled black hair. He squinted in the sun. He wore a surly expression but was not hostile, and he answered questions as his guards looked on. His name was Juma Khan. He was from a village in the mountains. He had been a member of the Taliban and had fought under a commander from the same village. He said he was part of a group that had killed four Afghan officials who were helping to organize elections for the loya jirga, the grand assembly being convened in Kabul to decide on a new government. The gang had stopped them on the road as the officials were returning home from a canvassing trip. When the gang found sheaves

of papers about the loya jirga in the car, they shot the officials and
threw their bodies off a mountainside. Then they set fire to their car
and left. Juma Khan seemed to be a casual Talib who rejoined his old
unit without much thought and for lack of anything else to do. He said
his former commander had pressed him to join and start guerrilla attacks against the government and American forces in March. "He told
me: 'This is jihad and we will fight the Americans,'" Juma Khan said.
"My mind was not working but he is our leader and he told me to join
him." Juma Khan's account was typical of the Taliban at the time: small
gangs, a village commander with a few men, yet already following instructions from somebody.

Mullah Omar's call to arms in February 2003 brought a change in pace
to the Taliban's activities. Police posts in the districts came under frequent attack. Fliers, announcing jihad and warning the Afghan public
against collaborating with American forces and the Karzai government, started turning up in towns across southern and southeastern
Afghanistan. They became known as "night letters," left at shop doors
and scattered in the street at night by unknown couriers. In the southern border town of Spin Boldak, the town's police chief, Lieutenant
Colonel Mohammad Arif, pulled one from a drawer of his desk and
showed it to me. It was entitled "The Taliban's Emirate" and announced
a "last warning" to Afghans to keep away from Americans and not
work for them, "because our target is the Americans." The language
was virulent. "Those who do not stop helping the Americans, we will
slit their throats, target them with bombs and shoot them, especially
those who work as spies," it said. "If they do not stop, their punishment
will be very, very harsh, and we will blow up their houses."

"They have lost power and so they are trying to change people's
minds against the government," Colonel Arif told me. "They want to
seize power again."

On March 27, 2003, the Taliban struck a blow that they knew would
reverberate far beyond Afghanistan's outlying provinces. A group of
gunmen came down from the mountains and set up an impromptu

checkpoint on the main road running from Uruzgan province to Kandahar. It was the same road where U.S. special forces had called in airstrikes and smashed the Taliban advance in December 2001. The road
was a single-file dirt track through the mountains, ideal for an ambush
site. The group began stopping cars at gunpoint, ordering passengers
out of the vehicles. Soon they had two dozen people lined up. A convoy
of vehicles belonging to the International Committee of the Red Cross
came along, three white Land Cruisers with the red cross insignia on
the doors. The personnel were Afghan but for one foreigner, Ricardo
Munguia, a water engineer from El Salvador who had been working
on projects in Uruzgan and was returning to base in Kandahar. The
Taliban stopped these cars too and ordered everyone out.

The Red Cross was widely known and respected by most Afghans.
The organization had been providing free medical care and humanitarian assistance across the nation and in refugee camps throughout
the last two decades of war. When the Afghan employees explained to
the Taliban who they were, the leader of the group answered that he
knew the Red Cross very well and had been to their clinic. He pulled
up his pant leg to show that he was an amputee wearing an artificial
leg, which he said was from the Red Cross. But then he took out his
satellite telephone and called someone for instructions.

"What shall we do with the foreigner?" he asked.

"Kill him," came back the reply.

The gunmen did not hesitate. They walked Munguia off away from
the cars, behind some rocks. A burst of automatic gunfire shattered the
air. Twenty bullets ripped into Munguia, killing him instantly.[7]

The Taliban warned Munguia's colleagues and the other Afghans
standing at the roadside that if they found them working for foreigners
again, or for the Karzai government, they would also be killed. Then
they set one vehicle alight and headed off in two stolen cars into the
mountains.

The murder of a civilian was shocking. Most chilling, however, was
the order over the satellite telephone. The Taliban government, despite its collaboration with al Qaeda and brutal treatment of its own
people, had always allowed international assistance groups to work in

Afghanistan. While it had imposed restrictions on the organizations, the Taliban leadership had recognized the services of humanitarian groups and the needs of the Afghan population. The murder of Munguia appeared to end that. The Red Cross suspended its work in southern Afghanistan, and other aid groups pulled out or cut back their operations.

The commander on the other end of the satellite telephone was Mullah Dadullah, often called Mullah Dadullah Lang, Dadullah the Lame. He too was an amputee. Dadullah gave an interview to BBC radio the following day, bragging that his men had detained sixty-five Afghans and killed two Americans on the road at Dar-e-Noor. It became common for the Taliban to announce the damage they had inflicted on others, and they rarely missed a chance to claim responsibility for attacks. They knew how to play the media to increase their notoriety and often inflated the numbers of their victims. Dadullah said the Taliban were starting to wage jihad against the "Jews and Crusaders" who had invaded Afghanistan. "You know that the Russians were also saying that they would stay for a long time. The ground became hot for them, and so maybe the ground will also become hot for the Americans," he taunted.[8]

Dadullah was emerging as one of the most energetic organizers of the Taliban resurgence in those early days in Quetta. A native of Uruzgan province in southern Afghanistan, he was one of the younger batch of Taliban commanders who had joined up to fight the jihad against the Soviet occupation as teenagers. He was about thirty-six in 2003, with all the drive and religious fervor of a young madrassa student. He also had the brashness of someone who had cheated death — he had evaded capture at Kunduz and transfer to Guantánamo in 2001 — and the ruthlessness of one who had killed with his own hands. People in northern Afghanistan talked of him as the most brutal of all commanders, known by the way he killed people. "He used to thrust his fingers up a man's nostrils, jerk his head back, and then slit his throat," one villager told me in 2001.

• • •

The governor of Kandahar reacted to the killing of Munguia with fury. Gul Agha Shirzai was a bear of a man in both physique and temperament. The son of a famous mujahideen leader, he was better known for his love of music and parties, some of them notoriously debauched. He had grabbed power in Kandahar as the Taliban fell and claimed the governorship against the wishes of Hamid Karzai, who had negotiated with the Taliban for the city of Kandahar to be handed over to Mullah Naqibullah, a man of greater military and tribal standing. But Shirzai wanted power and seized it; Karzai the conciliator let it go. Now, after Munguia's death, Shirzai led a force up the road into Shah Wali Kot, raiding houses and arresting some former members of the Taliban. On his return to Kandahar, he announced that Taliban members had ten days to leave the southern provinces unless they could provide endorsements from their village elders. All Taliban working in the government or army had to leave their posts, he added. "I have ordered my commanders not to allow any Taliban in the villages; if they are caught they are to be punished severely. I will fill the prisons with them."[9] Shirzai was rising to Dadullah's bait. Many former Taliban members, even ordinary fighters, left for Pakistan.

Dadullah the Lame did not let up. He deployed assassins to hit prominent figures in Kandahar, attacking senior clerics who supported the government and Afghan aid workers who worked in rural communities. Dadullah himself was following orders. In June 2003, Mullah Omar announced the appointment of a ten-man leadership shura, or council, to organize the resistance.[10] The council came to be known as the Quetta Shura, as intelligence reports filtered out that the Taliban council meetings were held in and around that city. The Taliban appointed a spokesman who over the next few years maintained a steady barrage of phone calls and press statements that made us think he was sitting in an Internet café rather than on the top of a mountain. Mullah Dadullah even gave an interview to a Pakistani television station in 2005, prompting Zalmai Khalilzad, the U.S. ambassador to Afghanistan, to question why the Pakistani authorities could not detain Taliban members. "If a TV station can get in touch with them, how can the intelligence service of a country, which has nuclear bombs, and a lot of security and military forces, not find them?"[11]

In July 2003, representatives of the Taliban leadership came together with the longtime Pakistani asset, mujahideen leader Gulbuddin Hekmatyar, and members of al Qaeda. It was another critical council of war, and a level up from that of December 2001. Former deadly foes, Hekmatyar and Mullah Omar, agreed to cooperate in the fight against American forces in Afghanistan. Al Qaeda, which had always pursued its own aims, was with them. They divided the country into areas of responsibility. Their calculation was that American forces were not going to increase their presence in the Pashtun areas, and since the United States was now heavily engaged in Iraq, it was an opportune moment to reassert control.[12] The ISI was aware of the meeting. It had ties to all three parties. While some Pakistani officials warned of the danger of the new nexus, the agency as usual thought to co-opt the Afghan insurgency for its own interests rather than fight it.

Dadullah did not have widespread support among Afghans. Most Afghans I met at the time were still hoping for peace and opposed the violence. Haji Emal Zhrak was a former employee of Afghanistan's agriculture ministry during the Taliban regime, and was one of the elders among the refugee population in Quetta. His tribe had always been aligned to Hekmatyar and later to the Taliban, but when I met him, the elders of the tribe had just decided to withdraw their support for the insurgency since they were concerned it would drive away reconstruction projects from their districts. "People support the Taliban but they do not support the attacks they are conducting," he told me.

I was not the only one encountering this reaction. Talatbek Masadykov, a UN political officer in Kandahar at the time, received repeated warnings about the campaign that was building. Masadykov had worked in Afghanistan since the late 1980s when he was a young Soviet diplomat. He came from the Muslim Central Asian state of Kyrgyzstan and spoke fluent Pashtu, and so had an immediate rapport with the Afghans. He passed through Quetta regularly in the years after 2001. On one such trip, a group of Taliban came to see him. They were former commanders and elders who said they did not agree with the new insurgency. "We were fighting on the side of the Taliban but we do not want to be part of the new campaign," they told him. They said they wanted to return home to Afghanistan peacefully, and were looking for guarantees they would not be arrested. In the months that followed, Masadykov met with dozens of former fighters, low-level commanders, and pro-Taliban tribal elders. They warned him that the ISI was reorganizing the Taliban and pushing people to go and fight. ISI officials were threatening former fighters and commanders and their families with arrest, telling them that they would be handed over to the Americans and sent to Guantánamo Bay if they did not start an insurgency in Afghanistan. The ISI was offering satellite telephones and motorbikes, and telling former Taliban members they had to go and fight. "This we heard many many times," Masadykov told me.[13]

For many Taliban members in exile, there were few options. The ISI was threatening to use force against them if they tried to avoid taking part in the insurgency. Meanwhile, in Afghanistan, none of the main parties were interested in making peace. Karzai, despite many promises and public statements, never offered the Taliban a serious peace plan or safety for defectors. Karzai's cabinet was also strongly anti-Taliban. Some members had been imprisoned by the Taliban or forced to flee their homes in the 1990s, and felt threatened by them still. They often warned that the Taliban had only one goal: to overthrow the government and return to power. The Bush administration showed it too was not interested in wooing the Taliban. In January 2002, the Taliban foreign minister Wakil Ahmed Muttawakil had offered to cooperate with American forces. But instead of treating him like a valued ally, the Americans detained him in Bagram prison for two years. Such treatment deterred other Taliban members from coming forward and strengthened the ISI's leverage over the rump movement. The Americans considered the Taliban irrelevant once they were defeated, according to Bruce Riedel, a former CIA official who wrote a strategic review on Afghanistan for the incoming Obama administration in 2009. The Bush administration never gave instructions to its intelligence officials in Pakistan to follow the Taliban in exile, he said. "The Taliban were defeated much more quickly than we expected. I was looking at them as a spent force," the CIA station chief in Pakistan, Robert Grenier, recalled.[14]

It was a lost opportunity. In the first months and years after their defeat, many Taliban members could have been persuaded to rejoin Afghan society if they had not been pursued and arrested. If handled skillfully, some of their leaders could have been used to bring the bulk of the Taliban movement to a negotiated peace. Instead, influential leaders were imprisoned and removed from the scene, leaving a vacuum for men like Mullah Dadullah to fill. Midlevel figures, men like Mullah Habibullah, the commander I met in Quetta in May 2003, who had served in the Taliban army and government, were at loose ends in those first years. They knew little other than their lives of fighting and religious instruction, were unable to support their families, and worried about survival. Habibullah lodged with friends for months and then moved into a madrassa where he met up with some old acquaintances. Some of the mullahs at the madrassa were from the Taliban and were reorganizing and recruiting for the insurgency in Afghanistan. They pushed Habibullah to go with them, his former host told me. Finally, Habibullah rejoined the Taliban because, with his madrassa training, he had no talent for business and no job, whereas the Taliban offered him money and status. Around 2005, he went back to southern Afghanistan and found as a commander that he enjoyed considerable respect in the community. By 2012, he had become one of the most powerful commanders in all of southern Afghanistan.

In June 2003, coalition forces fought pitched battles with two groups of insurgents in southern Afghanistan. The guerrillas were easily defeated and fled across the border into Pakistan. "I never had any doubts that we had an insurgency on our hands, the breadth of which I was unable to measure. Most of that had to do with [the fact] we had so few people," General Dan K. McNeill, who commanded the coalition force in Afghanistan from 2002 to 2003, told me. McNeill had 11,500 men in his force when he left in mid-2003, a tiny contingent compared to the 140,000 NATO-led forces and 300,000 Afghan security forces that would be deployed at the height of the war seven years later. He did not have the special operations forces under his command, nor did he have the concentration of intelligence and surveillance units he needed.

Beyond weekly radio addresses, Karzai did little to galvanize popular sentiment. He relied on his personal appointees in the provinces to maintain support, the traditional Afghan way. Yet his governors and security officials were often inadequate, and in some cases grossly corrupt and predatory. They soon lost the support of large sections of the population. Governors who tried to manage more honestly were hamstrung by lack of money, infrastructure, and security. District officials had neither vehicles nor fuel to run them nor police to staff their offices. For years Kabul ignored their difficulties.

For the next five years, the Taliban was quietly allowed to regenerate in Pakistan. Pakistan's religious parties ruled in the border provinces after their 2002 election victories. Provincial ministers supported madrassas, spoke at funerals, and became a conduit for covert support for the Taliban. Residents of Quetta noticed that the rules guiding Friday mosque sermons were changed. In the first years after 9/11, sermons always emphasized Musharraf's policy of "Pakistan First." There were men from Pakistani intelligence present, and some mullahs were even arrested for talking out of line. But once the religious parties came to power, speakers began openly urging the faithful to go and wage jihad in Afghanistan. All throughout this period, the ISI steadily increased its ties and assistance to the insurgency.

"America should have selected to crush al Qaeda and the Taliban in Pakistan, rather than go to war in Iraq," the former senator and leader of the Baloch National Party in Quetta, Habib Jalib Baloch, told me in

May 2003. He warned that the Taliban were being reorganized with funding from Arab countries, and that Mullah Omar and the top Taliban commanders were all in Pakistan, protected by their links to the Pakistani establishment. "You need to cut the funding," he said. "You will not kill them with a hammer. You must cut the funding and the connection."[15]

· 5 ·

Al Qaeda Regroups

"This regime has handed over the entire
tribal belt to al Qaeda."

— *Mahmood Khan Achakzai, Pashtun nationalist leader*

I n January 2003, I set off with a driver and translator for Shkin, a village far down in southeastern Afghanistan on the border with Pakistan. An American soldier had been killed there while on patrol the previous month, the first U.S. casualty in Afghanistan in four months, and Afghans were telling me that al Qaeda fighters, based across the border in Pakistan, were behind the attack.

It was a two-day journey to the border, over a snowy pass to the town of Gardez, through frozen, muddy villages of one province, across a desert into Paktika province, and then ten hours of bumping through riverbeds and along stony tracks to the border. It was the route that the last known group of foreign Islamist fighters had taken when they pulled out of Afghanistan in March 2002. They had put up a fierce fight. Seven Americans had died in Operation Anaconda, the heaviest toll of any battle in Afghanistan to that point. It was four months after bin Laden had fled Tora Bora, and the foreign fighters and Afghan Taliban had sheltered in hamlets in the Shahikot mountains through the winter. During the battle, they hugged the mountain ridges, pinning down U.S. forces for hours and bringing down two helicopters.

A famous Afghan mujahideen commander, Mansour, led that fight. Yet the foreigners under him, thought to be Arabs, Uzbeks, Chechens, and other Central Asians, fought better than the usual standard of the Taliban.[1] After the battle they retreated in good order to the border crossing and passed into Pakistan, villagers told us.

Ten months later, there was no sign of Taliban on the road down. We passed groups of tribesmen in silk turbans sharing taxis to go to market or visit government offices. We did as they did, setting out before dawn to get an early start and never driving after dark when gunmen and thieves come out. We lodged in government offices and police stations on the way. Often the district offices were bullet-ridden ruins, with leaking roofs and sheets of plastic covering the windows and only a single warm room. We would fetch bread and kebabs from the bazaar for everyone and bunk down on the floor in our sleeping bags around the embers of a wood stove for warmth. The government was barely functioning in the provinces, and district officials frequently had no communication with the provincial capital, much less with Kabul.

The province did have telephone communications with Pakistan, however. From a public telephone office in the bazaar in some towns, you could call anywhere in the world. Paktika was still hooked into the Pakistani phone system, a leftover of the Taliban era when the Pakistani government extended telecommunications services into the main provinces of Afghanistan. It represented strategic assistance to the Taliban regime, but it seemed like annexation.

By 2003 district police chiefs and administrators had been appointed by Karzai but had no budget and were managing largely on their own. Local police chiefs tended to use family members as bodyguards and drove their own cars. The most effective ones were former mujahideen commanders who had loyal networks of fighters and informants who knew the area and the population. In the years after 2001, these men were often criticized as predatory thugs. While there certainly were some who abused their power and preyed on the population, I met many in small communities who were natural and energetic leaders, with deep ties to their communities forged in times of war. They spent a lot of their time trying to make money to run their operations and keep their enemies at bay. Yet they also resolved many local issues, working with influential elders, and they were an important part of their communities.

In Shkin, on the border, we discovered a village grappling with insurgency. The settlement was a miserably poor collection of mud-brick shops along a single dusty street, with adobe houses scattered beyond. Villagers were living under rocket fire, and officials were living under death threats. I realized this was the frontline. The Taliban and al Qaeda were just across the border, and still saw themselves at war. Their enemy, American special forces and CIA officers, had taken over the only substantial house in the village, a mud-walled *qala,* a fortress house on the edge of the village. On the road in front, we met Engineer Amin. That was how he was known to everyone. The title "Engineer" is often conferred on those with higher education. Amin was a tall, big-chested Waziri tribesman with a black bushy beard. He wore a jacket and waistcoat over traditional shalwar kamize and a pakul, the roll-brimmed wool hat worn by many mountain men in Afghanistan and Pakistan. He was President Karzai's representative in the area, and he was worried.

Hundreds of al Qaeda and Taliban supporters across the border were starting a campaign of attacks against the Shkin area, he said. Their aim was to attack the American base — the compound had come under repeated rocket attacks in recent weeks, he said — but insurgents were also threatening any Afghans working with U.S. forces or the Karzai government. The death of the American soldier, killed when his night patrol surprised insurgents smuggling rockets across the border, was just one sign of the growing threat.

Engineer Amin's concern was visible; shadows from sleeplessness ringed his eyes. He moved only with well-armed bodyguards. He did not want to meet us in his home, arranging instead for me to interview him in a house some distance from Shkin, out of sight. His home had come under rocket attack twice in previous weeks.

Fliers scattered in the bazaar had warned townspeople not to collaborate with the Americans. One letter named Engineer Amin as a key collaborator and offered a bounty of ten thousand dollars to anyone who killed him. The engineer's father and brother, who opposed his work with Karzai's government, had left for Pakistan after the first rocket attack, but his wife, children, and cousins remained at home, he said.

Over the next few days in Shkin, I met a number of people from Pakistan's tribal regions of North and South Waziristan just over the border. The Wazir tribe, which gives its name to the two regions, lives on both sides of the border, and people move freely across the unmarked frontier. These men told me of their fears that war was brewing in their region. Hundreds of foreign fighters and al Qaeda members who had fled Afghanistan in 2001 and 2002 had settled on the Pakistani side, guests of tribesmen who had fought in Afghanistan with the Taliban. No one questioned their presence at first. They were fellow Muslims, mujahideen, and esteemed as such.

But in recent months, they had started mobilizing for war and threatening those who got in their way, the tribesmen told me. I spoke to one tribal elder from South Waziristan who gave his name as Reghduanullah. He described Arabs, Africans, and Central Asians, men from Sudan, Uzbekistan, Yemen, and Muslim regions of Russia and China. They would visit the central bazaar in his town, Wana. They were equipped with walkie-talkies, carried assault rifles and grenades, and were always accompanied by the armed Pashtuns who were hosting them, he said. To anyone who asked, they vowed to continue the fight against U.S. forces: "We swore we would fight against the Americans until they leave Afghanistan or we die. We will not give up our holy war against America." The fighters were planning operations in Afghanistan, and more volunteers were arriving to join them to fight Americans, Reghduanullah said. The leaders were Taliban mullahs and were telling people if they killed an American, they would go to paradise, but if they so much as met with an American, they would be branded an infidel.

The tribesmen I interviewed told me of six men who had been recently murdered in South Waziristan because they were suspected American informants. One of them had been killed on the road from the border. His killers had daubed a message on a nearby bridge: "We have killed a spy of America, he had dollars, an expensive watch and a GPS reader." No one dared bury the body. That alone was shocking in a culture that placed high importance on respect for the dead and performing a Muslim burial.

The men said that tribal elders and Pakistani government and intelligence officials were sympathetic to the foreign fighters. They were tipping them off ahead of government raids so they could avoid capture, and allowing them to cross the border on frequent incursions into Afghanistan. "Until all these refugees leave the place we will not have peace," an elder from Shakai warned.

In the months that followed, the attacks around Shkin increased. Small groups of guerrillas, among them foreign fighters, would stage hit-and-run ambushes and then escape back across the border into Pakistan. Two U.S. soldiers were killed in an ambush on August 31, 2003. Two months later, at the end of October, two CIA agents were killed in another attack in the same border area. Coalition forces clashed with militants around Shkin that same day and said they killed eighteen, among them foreign fighters. It prompted the U.S. military spokesman in Afghanistan to describe Shkin as the "most evil place in Afghanistan."[2]

It was no secret to anyone in the border region that Taliban and al Qaeda fighters had escaped into Pakistan after the fall of the Taliban in 2001. By the end of 2003, Pakistan claimed to have captured no fewer than 450 al Qaeda members — almost half of whom were Yemenis and Saudis. By 2006, the official count would grow to 709, although the numbers were impossible to verify since the government never showed the detainees to journalists or independent observers.[3] Rarely mentioned was the huge number still at large in the tribal areas who were settling down to stay. Officials denied their existence. Few people dared talk about them. One former legislator and Pashtun nationalist leader, Mahmood Khan Achakzai, a longtime opponent of Islamists in the Pakistan military establishment, did speak out. "This regime has handed over the entire tribal belt to al Qaeda," he told me in 2003.[4]

By the beginning of that year, reports started to trickle out that militant training camps were forming along the Afghan-Pakistan border. Afghan security forces were capturing poorly trained insurgents who talked of receiving only a week or so of preparation. An Iraqi with a suicide vest, caught trying to blow up the vice president's motorcade, said he had been in a training camp in Pakistan-administered Kashmir for four months. The United Nations reported that al Qaeda was operating mobile training camps in eastern Afghanistan. In February 2003, I traveled east to the province of Khost, which borders Pakistan and serves as one of the main crossing points from Pakistan's tribal regions into Afghanistan. Police on the border told me that they were hearing from informants that there was a camp for insurgents called Dewabi, just across the border in Pakistan's tribal areas, and another called Ettebad, near the capital, Islamabad. According to their informants, anyone who went there for training to fight in Afghanistan was promised Pakistani citizenship. It reminded me of ethnic Uighurs from China whom I had once met on a bus to Kashgar in 1990. They were Muslims from China's western province of Xinjiang sent by their parents to obtain a religious education in Pakistan since such study was restricted in China. This group was returning home after months in various madrassas in Pakistan, topped off with a month's "jihad" training in Afghanistan. They had been issued brand-new Pakistani passports, which they proudly showed me. They were part of a covert Pakistani government-sanctioned program that was creating an army of mujahideen and spreading Islamist ideology to Central Asia and beyond. Figures in Saudi Arabia had long encouraged and funded the spread of their brand of Sunni Islamist teaching; this was proof Pakistan was doing the same.

In the police station in Zazi-Maidan, a nineteenth-century mud-brick fort with thick, white-washed walls, the district commander told me that militant leader Gulbuddin Hekmatyar had been moving covertly through the district to garner support for an insurgency.

Hekmatyar told his recruits that al Qaeda was with him. The official showed me the fliers he had left behind.

Publicly Pakistani officials denied that foreign militants were sheltering in the tribal areas in the same way that they denied Taliban members were hiding in Quetta. Foreign journalists were soon banned from traveling to Pakistan's tribal areas — ostensibly for our safety but almost certainly to prevent us from reporting. We had to rely on secondhand accounts. Pakistani journalists were able to report from the region but had to tread carefully. A growing number of journalists lost their lives over the years covering the tribal areas, as both the military and militants sought to control the flow of information. Pakistani officials undoubtedly knew about the foreign fighters. A former senior ISI official who served in the North West Frontier province and the tribal areas told me years later that his agency had estimated there was a minimum of a thousand foreign fighters in the Waziristan area in the spring of 2002.[5] Yet in internal discussions, officials had often played down the threat, whether out of sympathy for the Islamist fighters or from a reluctance to confront the problem.

By 2004, Musharraf had a personal incentive to go after foreign militants in the tribal areas. In December 2003, he narrowly escaped two assassination attempts. Both attacks tried to blow up his motorcade near his military headquarters in the garrison town of Rawalpindi, first with a bomb under a bridge and eleven days later with two suicide attackers driving truck bombs. Musharraf survived only thanks to electronic jammers and his armor-plated car.

The investigation into the attacks revealed that the instigator was a Libyan member of al Qaeda operating from Pakistan's tribal areas. Al Qaeda was opposed to Musharraf for cooperating with the United States against it. Two important findings should have set alarm bells ringing for Pakistan's generals. One was that al Qaeda had spread its tentacles into the Pakistani armed forces, even recruiting conspirators from army special forces as well as the air force. The second was that al Qaeda had maintained its operational expertise. The two assassination attempts were run by separate cells, unknown to each other, and planning was decentralized.

In early 2004, Musharraf ordered a large military operation to root out militants in a fifty-square-mile area of South Waziristan. What happened next astounded the Pakistani public and broke wide open the scale and ambition of the foreign militants in the tribal areas.

Two thousand troops moved into an area west of Wana in South Waziristan to conduct a sweep for foreign fighters reported to be sheltering there. The particular target was a twenty-six-year-old tribesman, Nek Mohammad, and his uncles, who had gained renown fighting in Afghanistan against the Soviets. The family were the main hosts of al Qaeda in the tribal areas after 2001. The Frontier Corps, the tribal paramilitary force that polices the border areas, spearheaded the operation with support from the army. On March 16, 2004, a group of three hundred men from the South Waziristan Scouts regiment went to Kaloosha, a village in Asam Warsak near the Afghan border. Nek Mohammad was thought to be housing up to twenty-five foreign militants in a large, mud-walled farmstead. Villages in the green Wana Valley are spread out, and farmhouses stand alone, or in small clusters, among fields and apple orchards against a backdrop of bare, craggy mountains. As in Afghanistan, the houses consist of a series of rooms and outbuildings around courtyards, surrounded by strong outer walls creating large, protected compounds.

The scouts moved toward the compound at 6:30 in the morning. Their plan was to set up a cordon, then call on the tribesmen and ask their cooperation in handing over any foreigners. As they were approaching, a motorcyclist came out of the compound, spotted them, and zipped back inside. A few minutes later, a pickup truck of armed fighters roared out of the compound and barreled through the government cordon, shooting as they went. At the same moment, gunmen opened fire from positions behind the scouts' lines. The pickup truck crashed into a nearby building, but its riders escaped as gunfire erupted from all sides. Tribesmen rallied from all around when they heard government troops were attacking a family of their own community. The fighting grew so ferocious that the scouts were nearly overwhelmed and had to call for reinforcements. They took refuge in the village mosque, and the commander of the unit, a Pakistani colonel, had to be protected by village elders.

Fighting erupted in three different places that day in reaction to the military operation. The militants had prepared fortifications. They ran through trenches and tunnels between compounds — one tunnel was a mile long — and used radios to coordinate. At one point, some of them were heard calling for help in a foreign language to evacuate their wounded leader, whom they called the Sheikh. The Pakistani army struggled to gain the upper hand over the next few days, and resorted to artillery and airstrikes. One airborne assault unit, dropped in by helicopter, was surrounded and cut down as soon as it landed. A supply convoy was attacked and burned east of Wana as it traveled toward the battle area.

The scouts had stumbled upon one of the most experienced and motivated groups of foreign fighters: the Islamic Movement of Uzbekistan. They were members of the same organization that had precipitated the prisoner uprising at Qala-i-Janghi in 2001, and that had shot down U.S. helicopters in the mountains of Shahikot during Operation Anaconda. Fearful of capture and deportation home, where they faced torture or death, they were fighting for survival.

Their leader, Tahir Yuldashev, was a charismatic Muslim preacher who had cofounded the movement. (His cofounder, Juma Namangani, had been killed in northern Afghanistan in November 2001 as were hundreds of followers.) The remnants of the group made their way to Pakistan and regrouped in South Waziristan in 2002. Yuldashev soon became a well-known figure among the tribesmen of Waziristan. He gave fiery speeches in local mosques and was respected for his religious learning. When news spread that day in 2004 that Yuldashev was wounded, many local tribesmen rushed to his defense.

The government forces could barely manage the ferocity of the resistance. Although the militants lost more men — thirty-two, twenty-seven of whom were foreigners, compared to sixteen for the government — Pakistani forces took an unexpected mauling over the next ten days, losing fifty-four more men by the operation's end. Another twenty soldiers and two government officials were taken hostage. The militants threatened to execute them if the army did not withdraw from the area. Soon, militants left eight of those soldiers in a ditch, shot in the head with their hands tied. To compound the army's humiliation, the deputy head of al Qaeda, Ayman al Zawahiri, released an audio message to the Arabic television station Al Jazeera calling on members of the Pakistani army to turn against Musharraf and refuse orders to fight.

After two weeks, the military claimed it had captured seventy-three foreigners and killed over fifty militants across an area of fifty square miles. Yet in the end it decided to sue for peace and withdraw its forces, in return for the twelve soldiers still being held hostage. A month later, on April 24, 2004, Lieutenant General Safdar Hussain, the overall commander for the tribal areas, embraced the militant leader Nek Mohammad at a peace ceremony before hundreds of tribesmen from the Shakai area, the untamed mountains stretching toward Afghanistan. The agreement was a capitulation by the government: Nek Mohammad and his group agreed to curb attacks in their area, and the army agreed not to pursue them. The foreign fighters, still estimated to number three to four hundred, would be allowed to remain in South Waziristan with only a fig-leaf concession: they were supposed to register with the authorities within a week.

Even that weak agreement failed to hold. It was the first of half a dozen peace agreements over the next three years between the Pakistani government and the armed fighters and their respective tribes. Each time, the military seemed to be wooing the militants, and the fighters only became bolder. They soon clashed again with the Pakistani army and the Frontier Corps.

It was clear already then that the influx of foreign fighters was radicalizing the Pashtun tribesmen among whom they lived, and was drawing them into confrontation with the Pakistani state. The foreign fighters and al Qaeda wanted the tribal areas for themselves as a free zone where they could train fighters and plan operations. Yet instead of removing the foreigners or containing their extremist influence, Pakistan's generals sought to use them and direct their zeal across the border against the American and NATO presence in Afghanistan. General Hussain, the man who had entered the first agreement with the militants, had told the Pakistani journalist Zahid Hussain a year before the Kaloosha operation that he expected, and wanted, to see American forces bogged down in a guerrilla war in Afghanistan.[6]

By 2004, General Musharraf was walking an increasingly difficult tightrope between the demands of Washington and Western countries for action against terrorism and the generals and religious groups at home who were pushing back against his pro-American agenda. Musharraf had demanded economic and political concessions from the United States in return for his cooperation after 9/11. On the economic side, Musharraf got what he wanted. He received large amounts of financial assistance including a lifting of sanctions, debt relief, and reimbursements for the cost of military operations along the Afghan border. From 2001 to 2013, Pakistan received nearly $26 billion in assistance from the United States, a large portion of it defense-related, which helped to provide handsome assistance and equipment for the army.

Yet on Afghanistan, Musharraf's demands were not heeded. He had wanted to keep the Northern Alliance from gaining any power, since they were no friend of Pakistan's, but with the Taliban gone, they were the strongest force in the country and took power in Kabul. The Bush administration and British troops in Kabul accepted them as a reality. Karzai understood where local power lay and worked with the main Northern Alliance leaders since they possessed military muscle and political networks, which meant in due course they could deliver votes in elections. For Pakistan, it was the worst possible scenario. Islamabad had supported the Taliban regime in order to maintain influence in Afghanistan. Overnight, Islamabad lost what it had worked for over two decades to build.

• • •

By 2004, with the United States embroiled in the war in Iraq, Musharraf's generals began to think that the Americans would soon leave Afghanistan. The prospect gave them reason to strengthen links with Pakistan's main asset and former ally in Afghanistan, the Taliban. In October 2004, Musharraf appointed Lieutenant General Ashfaq Parvez Kayani as the head of the ISI. Kayani was an advocate of formal strategic assistance for the Afghan Taliban. He couched it in terms of the need to maintain intelligence contacts with them. A taciturn, chain-smoking infantryman from the Punjab, Kayani had attended the U.S. Army Staff College at Fort Leavenworth and so was known and acceptable to the United States. Western diplomats and military officials described him as the brightest and deepest thinker of the top Pakistani generals. Yet it was under Kayani, first for three years as ISI chief and then as chief of army staff, that the Taliban received consistent protection and assistance from Pakistan, and came to threaten the entire U.S.-led mission in Afghanistan.

Musharraf began to tell interlocutors that the Taliban were a reality and that Pakistan had no other option than to deal with them. The retired general Talat Masood noticed the shift in Musharraf's stance around 2003 or 2004. "It was not that he wholeheartedly supported the Taliban, but because of his [strained] relationship with Karzai, he became indifferent. He would say of the Taliban: 'At least they are our friends.'" A few years more and Musharraf would justify ties with the Taliban as a necessity. "He came to say the Taliban are here to stay, we have no option," Masood said.[7]

Musharraf's double dealing may have gone as far as helping al Qaeda's top leaders escape capture. In 2005, a senior Pashtun tribal elder told Afghan officials that al Qaeda's deputy leader, Ayman al Zawahiri, was staying as a guest at the house of a senior Pakistani government official in Kohat. The official was none other than the governor of the North West Frontier province, a retired general and Musharraf appointee.

The tribal elder who went to the Afghans with the information was sent by none other than an uncle of Nek Mohammad, the Pakistani tribesman who was the main facilitator for al Qaeda in Pakistan. Nek Mohammad's family had themselves hosted Zawahiri until a rocket attack caused him to move. He left the house and went to stay in Kohat, a sizable town in an adjoining tribal agency. He traveled in a bulletproof car. In Kohat, he negotiated to stay for one month in the governor's home. The al Qaeda leader paid forty thousand dollars for that protection. Nek Mohammad's uncle, a man named Sadiq, accompanied Zawahiri on the trip, and it was he who sent a senior tribal elder to relay the information to Afghan national security officials. They regarded both the source and the man selected to carry the message so highly that they passed the information on to President Karzai.

I also learned of the information at that time but found it impossible to corroborate. I never published it. Several years later, Sadiq died, as did the elder who had relayed the message. One of his Afghan friends told me that they had not dared reveal the identity of the messenger at the time lest they endanger him, but he was an honorable man so they did not doubt the veracity of his account.

In those days, it was hard to believe that senior Pakistani officials would protect top al Qaeda members, yet we journalists occasionally heard such reports. Afghans and Pakistanis who were opposed to the Taliban and their supporters in the Pakistani establishment often warned us as much, and sometimes helped us to investigate reports. For years these reports were discounted as conspiracies by Pakistani officials and Western diplomats. Only after bin Laden was discovered living in Abbottabad, a few hundred yards from Pakistan's foremost military academy, did many of these earlier stories make sense. I never doubted Sadiq's account, but it was only after bin Laden's death that two American counterterrorism officials told me that the account of Zawahiri's hiding place was entirely possible and that they had seen similar such reports.

As for the man at the pinnacle of al Qaeda, Osama bin Laden, he spent three years in Pakistan's tribal areas before disappearing from view in 2004. A video passed to the Arab news channel Al Jazeera in October

2003 showed bin Laden and Zawahiri picking their way down a rocky, tree-covered mountain trail amid scenery that resembles the terrain of the northern border areas.

One militant commander in Pakistan told me that he saw bin Laden in North Waziristan in 2003. The commander had spent many years fighting, and training fighters, in Kashmir and Afghanistan with the Taliban. He said he had met bin Laden twice, once before 9/11 in Afghanistan and the second time in the spring of 2003 in a village in the Shawal mountain range of North Waziristan. The commander said bin Laden was accompanied by a personal guard of Arab and Chechen fighters, and arrived unexpectedly at a large gathering of eighty to ninety fighters in the village. The commander was in a house meeting other fighters when bin Laden arrived. They greeted each other before the commander departed with his group.

The commander said that bin Laden was moving from place to place in the border areas for about three years after 9/11. "Everyone was aware in the region where he was." It was a time when the Taliban and foreign militants were living relatively unmolested in the tribal territories. Pakistan's forces were making occasional raids, but it was before the United States started its campaign of drone strikes and before the Pakistani military began its large-scale operations in 2004. People were aware there was a price on bin Laden's head and that the United States was spending money to look for him, but the tribespeople stuck together and did not give up his whereabouts.

Then, when Pakistani military operations increased in North and South Waziristan, and Nek Mohammad was killed in a drone strike in June 2004, bin Laden dropped out of sight. Two former commanders I talked to assumed that he had been moved by the military to a safe house in a city. In December 2004 in Washington, D.C., General Musharraf announced that the trail had gone cold.[8]

Journalists in the region never saw the glimmer of a lead on bin Laden's whereabouts after 2004. In fact, bin Laden had moved outside the tribal areas and then gone to live in Haripur, a small provincial town northwest of Islamabad, sometime in 2004. Bin Laden's youngest wife, questioned by Pakistani intelligence officials after the 2011 raid that killed her husband, told investigators that they had lived in the Swat Valley for six months, then two years in Haripur before moving to their last home in Abbottabad in 2006. Each move happened under Musharraf's watch, just as he was proclaiming to the world that the trail had gone cold.

6

The Wrong Enemy in the Wrong Country

"Our people were victims of al Qaeda, and it is not fair that
they should be victims of the American campaign."

— *Abdullah Abdullah, foreign minister of Afghanistan*

July 2002. Southern Afghanistan turns into an oven in the summer
months. The heat is so dry it cracks your skin, and the light so
blinding that it drives everyone inside by mid-morning. In the villages there is no electricity, and Afghans live in dark rooms, often underground, which offer cool relief from the heat as soon as you duck
in through the low doorway. Farmers sleep in the day and work their
fields after sundown. A fierce heat still bounces off the hard-packed
earth at night, and people sleep on the flat roofs of their houses or sit
up late to catch the cooler air.

So it was that Mohammad Sharif and his family entertained a large
party of guests late into the night, celebrating the engagement of his
sixteen-year-old son, Abdul Malik. They lived in the farming village of
Kakrak in Uruzgan province. The villagers had been early supporters
of Hamid Karzai in his stand against the Taliban. The brother of the
groom, twenty-five-year-old Mohammad Shah, had joined Karzai, as
had their uncle, who had since been appointed a senior army commander in Kandahar.

Over two hundred people from their extended family were gathered
at their home for the party. Women and children were together in the
inner courtyard while, as is the tradition at Afghan weddings, the men

congregated separately in the outer courtyard. They had eaten a meal of soup, and mutton and rice *palau*. By one o'clock in the morning, the women were seated on cushions on the long flat roof of the house, playing drums and singing the traditional wedding songs long banned under the Taliban regime. Young children were asleep in the rooms downstairs. Older ones were watching the dancing, eating sweets and dashing about. The men were relaxing after cooking cauldrons of food for the guests, sitting on rugs and chatting. "People were singing, we were drinking tea, small boys were going round pouring tea for people," Mohammad Shah recalled.

Without warning, a fighter plane descended out of the black sky and slammed a missile into the roof where the women were sitting. A second later another explosion burst above the men's courtyard, shredding guests with shards of metal. The women and children fled in panic through a garden door into the orchard as more rockets exploded around them. Cannon fire raked the compound walls. Eleven-year-old Saboor Gul was sitting up on the roof with her mother when the first bomb struck. They threw themselves down the stairs into the courtyard. A second explosion struck them, knocking Saboor Gul unconscious. She woke up in the hospital in Kandahar, a day's drive away, her back and legs lacerated with shrapnel. She did not know that her mother had died in the attack. "The airplane was very big," she told me. She was frightened to see a foreigner at her bedside.

"The children were running, they were scared," said Chenara, a twenty-year-old sister of the groom who was watching the dancing in the courtyard when the planes struck. She was wounded but fled outside with everyone else.

The planes circled and attacked again, cutting down a group of women and children in the orchard. The grandmother of the family, Nazaka, had snatched up her grandson and pulled a wounded woman along by her shirt. They ran into the orchard and reached the far corner when another explosion showered them with shrapnel.

Sadiqa, a slim fifteen-year-old girl, unhurt by the first strikes, sprinted out behind the house through the fields. She hid in a dry river gully some distance away. Women were standing on the bank of the gully when the planes came round again and strafed their group. A bomb raised an enormous dust cloud in the field. Most of the women were killed. Sadiqa survived, wounded in both legs.

In the men's courtyard, Laik, a thirty-five-year-old farmer, was drinking tea with two other guests when the first bomb hit. One of his friends was killed instantly. The other two men rushed up out of the compound but came under fire as they sought cover. Laik's second friend was cut down as they ran. Laik reached the field in front of the house and dove into a small ditch. "The Americans were bombing the house and we could not believe it, we were running everywhere to hide," he recounted. Unknown to him, his wife and three children had been killed. Laik lay in the ditch until dawn as the planes circled again and again, pouring fire onto the fields and the neighboring farmhouses.

Mohammad Shah, the brother of the bridegroom, was knocked off his feet by the first bombing but escaped into the fields. There he came under fire again and was badly wounded in the arm. He wandered back to the house and collapsed in a relative's arms.

Abdul Khaliq, twenty-four, was not even at the engagement party but lived nearby. He was sleeping on his rooftop when the bombing began. He rushed downstairs and fled into the fields, thinking to get away from the houses that were the target. But planes were shooting into the fields, and he was struck in the hip and the arm. "I was frightened I was going to die and I was desperate for water," he said. As the bombardment receded, he limped back home. Villagers were collecting the dead and carrying the wounded to the village mosque, and he made his way there too.

As the planes receded, Pir Jan stepped in to check a relative's house across the street from the engagement party. He found seven children dead and wounded in the courtyard. Two boys — Ahmad, seven, and Shirin, thirteen — lay dead where they had been sleeping on the rooftop. Five more were wounded as they tried to hide.

Sahib Jan, a twenty-five-year-old neighbor, was one of the first to reach the groom's house after the bombardment. Bodies were lying all over the two courtyards and in the adjoining orchard, some of them in pieces. Human flesh hung in the trees. A woman's torso was lodged in an almond sapling. Cannon fire had gouged long scars into the mud walls of the compound. Missiles had blown wide holes in the flat rooftops of the buildings, and bodies lay in the dust and rubble of the rooms below. A mother and her five children were dead in one room. The groom's parents were killed, as were thirteen children of the house. Seven children lay dead by the gate in the orchard. Sahib Jan knew every one of the dead. He named them at each spot as he walked us through the compound several days after the attack. He found a twelve-year-old boy lying under an archway in the men's courtyard, slain by a piece of metal shrapnel in his head.

"His name was Shirin, he was the son of Zaher Jan," he said, staring at the bloodstained ground. He had carried the dead boy to the mosque. The villagers collected dozens of bodies and carried scores of wounded to the mosque. They found body parts strewn about, human ears, teeth, a woman's skull in one corner, a hand tossed aside. Fifty-four people died and more than one hundred were wounded that night. According to custom, the engaged couple were not present at the party and so they had survived, but their union was forever benighted.

As dawn broke, American and Afghan soldiers surrounded the village and advanced on foot, searching houses and detaining people. "When they came right into the village and saw the dead women and children they were very sad and their attitude changed towards us," said Pir Jan, who was helping gather up the dead. "They told me through a translator that they had made a mistake. They said: 'We are sorry but what's done, we cannot undo.'" At the mosque, the American soldiers found the wounded men Abdul Khaliq and Mohammad Shah. "They came and asked: 'Who was shooting?' I said, 'No one was shooting,'" Abdul Khaliq said.

Later, Afghan officials, including provincial governor Jan Mohammad Khan, arrived to investigate. "They were collecting body parts in a bucket," the governor told us. I had driven from Kabul with a translator and driver for three days over dusty and rutted roads. A team from the *Los Angeles Times* had come with us. Four days after the bombardment, the place was still a scene of unspeakable gore. Blood stained the ground and putrefying flesh was still entangled amid the bright scarlet blossoms of a pomegranate tree.

Five miles away, a village called Siya Sang had also come under bombardment that night. Villagers told us six people had been killed. It was a poor settlement of small mud houses. A woman named Jamala wept as she showed us a pile of bloody clothes in her courtyard. She pointed to the blood on the wall where her teenage son had fallen dead, and a corner where she had found her daughter and grandson dead. A female neighbor had also died. "My grandson and daughter's mouths were full of dust," she said, pulling her veil across her face. "Write about this so it will stop, so they leave us in peace to pray and fast."

These villagers lived simple lives. Their houses were unfurnished. Everyone ate and slept on the floor. The women tended cows and chickens in the yard and cooked on outdoor stoves fired by animal dung. The children ran around barefoot and played games in the dust. These people were not al Qaeda. They were not remotely connected to international terrorism. They were not even Taliban. They were not hostile to us foreign journalists even after such unspeakable killings. They answered our questions and patiently walked us through the ruins. I would leave, my heart full to bursting.

The men were angry. They warned that the U.S. military had made a grave mistake. The sixteen-year-old groom, Abdul Malik, veered wildly between declaring undying enmity to the Americans and intoning an acceptance of God's will.

In the hospital in Kandahar city, we found four wounded men, including his sole surviving brother. "This is the third time the Americans have made a mistake in our district of Deh Rawud. And they did not kill any Taliban, or arrest anyone," Mohammad Shah said. Twenty-five members of his extended family had been killed in the bombing. "We were the first to help Hamid Karzai, so we did not think they would bomb our village." The family was already receiving threats of revenge attacks from the Taliban who remained at large, he said.

"Why are they killing women and children? They are not al Qaeda or Taliban. If they want to arrest us men, they can, but not kill the women," his neighbor Abdul Khaliq said. "And did they find any weapons caches in the village? No," he added bitterly.

Laik, the farmer who lost his wife and three children, said they had been firing a Kalashnikov in celebration. "We were shooting from happiness," he explained.

The villagers told us they did not want American forces to leave Afghanistan; they wanted them to continue to pursue al Qaeda and the Taliban. Yet there were already signs that they would not forgive the killing of family members. "Those people who bombed our women and children, they are our enemies now," warned Khudai Nazar, forty-five, who lost several members of his family.

The attack on Kakrak was part of a large nighttime operation by U.S. forces involving several hundred troops in convoys of trucks and jeeps, and airborne assault teams. The target was a suspected Taliban position north of the village. When a U.S. unit heading toward the target spotted gunfire, they called in airstrikes on Kakrak even though it was not the intended target. Pilots had reported antiaircraft fire from heavy machine guns at several positions along the valley during reconnaissance flights. Ground forces moving up the valley also reported gunfire at several other places that night. Villagers used to fire their guns at night when they heard the American planes overhead, sending arcs of red tracer rounds into the blackness, residents told me later. Some were pro-Taliban and hated the Americans, some would do it for fun. In Kakrak, however, they had no antiaircraft gun. They had simply celebrated an engagement by firing a Kalashnikov into the sky, a favorite custom at weddings and parties.

The planes worked the skies for two hours. The AC-130 airplanes attacked four villages in the area, and a B-52 bomber dropped a two-thousand-pound bomb on a hillside in a show of force. Troops then entered the village on foot. Yet they found no Taliban positions in Kakrak. No heavy machine gun was found there, a U.S. military spokesman said afterward. Kakrak was indeed loyal to Karzai.

The two targets of the operation were Mullah Omar and his operational commander, Mullah Baradar, who had been reported to be sheltering further north, American officials said. Local Afghan officials were incredulous. "If Mullah Omar and Mullah Baradar were sitting up the road with a whole load of soldiers, would we be sitting here?" Abdul Rahim, the district chief of Deh Rawud and a longtime opponent of the Taliban, asked.[1]

There were sporadic reports of senior Taliban figures moving around the remoter parts of southern Afghanistan. They always proved elusive. One of the villagers in Kakrak, a taxi driver, said he had seen Taliban vehicles on the road to Kandahar a couple of months earlier. Afghan workers from an aid group saw a convoy of Taliban vehicles passing through a nearby area just three days before the Kakrak bombing. The convoy was traveling through the northern Helmand district of Baghran, across the Helmand River Valley from Deh Rawud. Taliban guards ordered drivers off the road at gunpoint as the thirty-two-car convoy, with black windows and armed guards, swept past.[2] The convoy may have belonged to Abdul Waheed Baghrani, the man who negotiated the surrender of Kandahar with Hamid Karzai in 2001. The Baghran Valley was his home region. Yet the size of the convoy suggests that he was escorting senior leaders and as many as two hundred men.

The failure to catch any significant Taliban figures at Kakrak and its neighboring villages, combined with the devastating death toll, revealed the ineffectiveness of heavy-handed military forays when a police or intelligence operation would have been more appropriate. Afghan villagers and officials asked the question that would dog the NATO coalition for the rest of the decade, and to which Afghans have never received a satisfactory response: were the airstrikes proportional to the threat? Abdul Rahim said he asked that question of an American commander who visited the scene. "Mullah Omar and Mullah Baradar are just two people and you bombed four villages. Why?"

The wedding party bombing, as it became known, was not the first deadly mistake U.S. forces had made in Afghanistan. Hamid Karzai narrowly missed being killed in a misguided airstrike in Uruzgan in December 2001. Sixty-five tribal elders traveling to Karzai's inauguration were killed when their convoy was mistakenly bombed that same month. Twenty-one commanders and fighters loyal to Karzai were killed in raids in Khas Uruzgan just one month later. The latter two mistakes were both cases of faulty intelligence fed by local enemies.

Yet Kakrak was particularly shocking for its level of violence and the high death toll of women and children. Afghan leaders reacted angrily. President Karzai remonstrated with the American commander of coalition forces, Lieutenant General Dan K. McNeill, who promised an investigation. Abdullah Abdullah, the Afghan foreign minister, warned that it would turn the people against the government and play into the hands of al Qaeda. Provincial leaders demanded an end to air raids. Afghans had been subjected to relentless bombing for ten years by Soviet forces, and the experience had left deep scars in the population: a permanent hatred of the Russians as well as devastating destruction and impoverishment to the country. Whole valleys were turned into dust bowls in the 1980s. Centuries-old irrigation systems were destroyed forever. Villages were smashed and abandoned, and orchards and vineyards blasted in that merciless war.

A third of the population, five million people, had been forced to flee the country. An estimated one million died, the vast majority of them civilians. Men abandoned their livelihoods and education and took up weapons. Women wove pictures of enemy jets and helicopters into their carpets. Karzai and Abdullah had lived through the Soviet occupation and knew that their people would not tolerate being bombed again. "The enemies of peace and stability could utilize this situation," Abdullah warned. "Our people were victims of al Qaeda, and it is not fair that they should be victims of the American campaign."

He cautioned that U.S. forces had to check their intelligence more carefully before conducting airstrikes. "We have no doubts for a single second of the coalition's objectives to eradicate al Qaeda, which poses a threat to our country. But what is needed is for strong measures to be taken to avoid civilian casualties," he said. "Mistakes can take place, human errors are possible, but our people should be assured that every measure was taken to avoid incidents," he added. "It must come to an end. It will not be acceptable for the people of Afghanistan if that becomes a pattern."

Yet the U.S.-led military force struggled to change the way it fought. Military officials promised better coordination with Afghan officials, but they continued to operate alone and circumvent Afghan officials they considered unreliable. Commanders often tightened the rules of engagement, or paused operations after a particular calamity, yet they never contemplated operating without air support or rethinking their counterterrorism operations. The Americans started conducting joint investigations, but Afghan officials came to view them as an attempt to control the message.

The U.S. and NATO forces on the ground displayed too great a readiness in their use of devastating firepower. Whenever forces were ambushed or pinned down by enemy fire, they called in airstrikes. Special forces troops especially went looking to provoke insurgents into fights and then requested air support. Sometimes troops pulled back from the firefight and called in airstrikes on the Taliban firing positions, even though they were no longer in danger. Villagers often complained that planes struck after the Taliban had left the area, or they destroyed a whole house in pursuit of a single gunman. On the occasions when we were able to reach bomb sites, we frequently found that they had hit the wrong targets.

In 2004, nine children and a teenager were killed in front of a house in Ghazni. Seven small boys were playing marbles in the dirt, and two little girls were fetching water from the stream. The teenager was walking beside the house. By the time we arrived at the village, hours after the attack, they had been buried but their rubber galoshes and embroidered caps, shredded with shrapnel, lay in the dust beside caked pools of blood. The owner of the house, a suspected Taliban facilitator, was not even at home, American soldiers at the scene told me. American officials told President Karzai they had not noticed the children when they fired the missiles.

From the beginning of the war, coalition operations all over the

Pashtun lands of southern and eastern Afghanistan killed one to two thousand Afghans every year. The number climbed relentlessly as fighting intensified, and we started hearing of young men running off to join the Taliban to take revenge for the deaths of relatives.

A frustrated Afghan official once asked me if the British Army would be allowed to bomb a house in Northern Ireland because it suspected an IRA gunman was inside. So why did it think it could do so in Afghanistan, he asked. The level of the insurgency in 2002 was so low that security operations should have shifted to a more careful intelligence and police operation. "If you are looking for one man you should not use a B-52. You should use spies, not bombs," Abdul Manan, the owner of a teahouse in Ghazni, told me when we stopped for lunch on one of our many trips across the country.

Yet it was many years before the American military changed its approach. After he retired, General McNeill told me in an interview that the human loss at Kakrak was one of the things that lived on in his thoughts from his two tours in Afghanistan. The mistake, he said, had been to keep pursuing the people fleeing into the fields.

It took the military most of the decade to adopt a counterinsurgency strategy that would scale back its use of airpower and put massive levels of troops on the ground to protect the population. McNeill did not stop using big military sweeps to disrupt the increasingly active insurgents, or airstrikes to take out Taliban firing positions. He had no mandate to act across the border in Pakistan to get at the source of the militancy, so he did what he could in Afghanistan, he said.

Karzai early on protested the high number of civilian casualties and warned American officials to be wary of false intelligence. He pleaded with Afghan villagers not to harbor Taliban or fire weapons, and asked American and NATO forces to be more careful, to work with Afghan officials, and to stop raiding homes. Over time, his repeated protests sounded hollow to his countrymen and only emphasized his powerlessness to prevent the airstrikes and casualties. As the violence spread and the casualties escalated, Karzai became more strident in his criticism. The frustration among the population was growing. Karzai began to complain that the U.S. Army and NATO-led International Security Assistance Force (ISAF) were targeting the Afghan public as a whole, while the source of the insurgency was in the training camps, madrassas, and even the headquarters of the ISI in Pakistan. Diplomats explained away his criticisms as nationalist grandstanding. Yet Karzai was right, and official American accounts were often short on the truth. The U.S. military routinely denied casualties or confirmed much lower figures than Afghans reported — often because they did not have access on the ground. As the dispute grew, the United Nations began gathering information about casualties and produced reports that showed much higher casualty rates than the military was acknowledging.

Six years after the Kakrak wedding party bombing, I was walking through another bombed village in western Afghanistan, inspecting the destroyed houses and counting the freshly laid graves on the edge of the settlement. In the dust and rubble of a small house, the smell of decaying bodies was overpowering. The villagers began to dig into the rubble. They uncovered the body of a tiny baby, tucked tightly into the corner of the ruins of a room, its skull crushed and its body caked in pale golden dust. Missed by the first rescuers, the baby was the ninety-second victim of a raid ten days earlier by a U.S. Marine Special Operations Company.[3]

The U.S. military command had been insisting that only five to seven civilians and thirty to thirty-five militants were killed in what it called a successful operation against the Taliban: a special operations ground mission backed up by American air support. But gradually the weight of evidence, wounded survivors, eyewitness accounts, cell phone footage of bodies laid out in the mosque, and freshly dug graves, many of them belonging to women and children, forced the military to open an investigation.

We were in western Afghanistan, in the district of Shindand, south of the cultured and largely peaceful city of Herat. I had been reporting in the same area just over a year earlier. When a similar raid by U.S. forces had killed fifty-seven people, U.S. and NATO commanders tight-

ened rules on calling in airstrikes on village houses. This time the damage was done by a team from the Marine special operations command.
They were following a tip that a Taliban commander, Mullah Sadiq,
was in the village of Azizabad. They had been misled by a business rival
of the main family in the village, officials and villagers said. There was
a particularly troubling detail. A female survivor had described how
American troops and armed Afghans had entered the village on foot
and executed her male relatives, the villagers told me. Karzai's officials
also interviewed the woman and sent her to India for medical treatment. When I later asked a presidential aide if he believed the woman's
story, he told me he did. "We have heard worse things than that," he said.

As we toured the bombed-out ruins, we heard the same complaint
that I had heard so many times before. "This is not fair to kill ninety
people for one Mullah Sadiq," said Lal Mohammad Umarzai, the district chief. "If they continue like this, they will lose the people's confidence in the government and the coalition forces." Another member
of the presidential staff told me, "People are sick of hearing there is
another case of civilian casualties."

Karzai by this time was sounding like a broken record. "It seriously
undermines our efforts to have an effective campaign against terrorism," he told me in an interview earlier that year. "I am not happy with
civilian casualties coming down; I want an end to civilian casualties,"
he said. "As much as one may argue it's difficult, I don't accept that
argument." He said that American officials had been trying to reduce
casualties, and he commended them for it. But his main complaint
was always the same: the United States was bombing Afghan villages
when the source of the insurgency was in Pakistan. "Because the war
against terrorism is not in Afghan villages, the war against terrorism is
elsewhere, and that's where the war should go."[4]

The casualties did not stop, however. In 2009 in another western
district, U.S. planes bombed the village of Granai, killing 147 men,
women, and children in the worst single incident of civilian casualties of the war. A group of Taliban had been fighting from the village but they withdrew before the bombers pulverized the place with

thousands of pounds of explosives. One family of refugees had called a relative in panic during the bombing, but when he reached Granai, he never found their bodies. All trace of them had been erased.

"Why do they target the Taliban inside the village? Why don't they bomb them when they are outside the village?" a villager, Sayed Malham, asked wearily as he sat beside his wounded daughter in a hospital. Seven members of his family had been killed and four wounded. "The foreigners are guilty," he continued. "Why don't they bomb their targets? Instead they come and bomb our houses."

It was not until General Stanley A. McChrystal took over command in Afghanistan in 2009, with General David Petraeus at the helm of U.S. Central Command, that U.S. forces switched to a counterinsurgency campaign centered around protecting the civilian population. McChrystal, more than anyone, ended the litany of mistakes, enforcing very strict rules of engagement that demanded that soldiers take much more risk on the battlefield before calling in airstrikes. Petraeus described it to me as a completely different approach. But by then the damage was done. The Taliban were so deeply entrenched in the southern provinces that to clear them was going to demand intense firepower and destruction. The people of southern Afghanistan were close to the breaking point and no longer trusted their president or the Americans.

McChrystal's arrival also brought a new development: a dramatic increase in night raids in the form of airborne assaults by special operations forces teams who dropped into villages and compounds to capture or kill Taliban commanders and affiliates. Special operations forces made scores of raids a week, with teams going out sometimes several times a night to roll up cells and whole networks of Taliban across the country. Afghan officials in the regions often praised the campaign for its accuracy and the devastating effect it had on the Taliban leaders. But reports filtered out that the teams were on kill missions, executing people as they slept, shooting unarmed villagers without warning. The military insisted that they were more interested in taking people alive, since they could glean intelligence from them on the wider circle of operatives. Yet the reports kept coming: a provincial police chief in Ghazni, troubled by the slaying of a woman alongside her husband, leaving four orphaned children and no relatives; three women, two of them pregnant mothers, killed along with their husbands, who were government officials, in a raid on a house in Paktia; several cases of angry villagers bringing the corpses of the latest massacre on tractors to the doors of provincial authorities.

The military often questioned the veracity of the Afghan accounts. Yet whenever I or other reporters managed to reach the scene and interview eyewitnesses, we found their accounts were straightforward and checked out. Soldiers, we found, were not always truthful in their reports.[5]

One day an Afghan I knew and trusted told me a story he had never dared tell anyone, even his closest family. He had worked as an interpreter for the U.S. military for several years. One night he had accompanied U.S. special operations commandos on a raid. Helicopters dropped off the team a mile or so from their target village, and they hiked in silence to its edge. The unit split up, and the interpreter went with a group of four men to a house in the center of the village. Two men were in front of him and two behind, armed with American assault weapons with silencers attached. They moved without noise, communicating with hand signals. They kicked in the door of the house and entered a room. A gas lamp was burning very low but enough for the interpreter to see the astonished faces of a young couple in their twenties as they leapt up from their bed on the floor. "Why? Why are you shooting?" the man asked. The Americans did not answer. They crouched and shot them both. They fired four or five rounds, the silencers making a dull "tick, tick" sound. As the woman fell, she let out a dying gasp. A child sleeping beside them began to cry. The Americans moved straight on to the next room. The translator began to shake. This time he did not enter the room but stopped at the door. He saw four people by the lamplight. A grandmother stood, her head uncovered, and asked, "What's happening? Why?" Three teenagers, a boy and two girls, were cowering on the floor, wordless, trying to hide among their bedclothes. The Americans did not speak. They fired two or three rounds. The translator did not see who was shot. He was never asked to translate anything. "You have to wait until they ask. If you say anything, or translate anything, they say 'Shut up, mother-fucker, or I'll shoot you.'"

December 2002. A year after the fall of the Taliban, Afghanistan seemed to be regaining a measure of peace. Karzai had been in office a year. His position had been confirmed by a loya jirga, a grand assembly of 1,500 elders and tribal representatives gathered in Kabul from all over the country. A commission was working on a new constitution. Elections were set for 2004. The country was setting itself to rights and breathing with relief. A seven-year-long drought had broken, and the harvest had been good. In eastern Afghanistan, the Taliban had been gone for months, and a power struggle led by a maverick royalist tribal commander, Bacha Khan Zadran, was over. The nation dared to hope that a durable peace was attainable. The Muslim festival of Eid al-Fitr, celebrating the end of Ramadan, was approaching. Shoppers were cramming the towns and bazaars to buy sugar and sweets for the traditional three days of entertaining and feasting. The roads were full with families on their way to visit relatives and workers traveling home.

A young man named Dilawar set off from his home in his new taxi to find fares in a nearby town. His mother had asked him to fetch his married sisters and bring them home for the festival, but he said first he would go and earn some money since they needed to buy more fuel. They lived in a farming village called Yakubi, not far from Khost, in eastern Afghanistan. His father and brothers grew wheat, peanuts, and corn. Dilawar was a shy man who had never been to school. He was twenty-two, married, and had a two-year-old daughter, Rashida. He spent his free time sitting out in the fields chatting with his best friend and neighbor, Bacha Khel. He worked on the farm, driving the tractor, and earned money fetching stone from a nearby quarry and bringing it down in the tractor to market. Quarrying was heavy work, though, and so a few weeks earlier, the family had borrowed money to buy a taxi, a secondhand Toyota station wagon, for Dilawar to start a new job as a taxi driver.

He drove the forty-five minutes to Khost, passing the American military base, Camp Salerno, on the edge of the city. At the taxi stand in town, he found two passengers who lived in a village near his home, and at noon the three set off on the road back to Yakubi. As they passed the American base for the second time, the Afghans guarding the road pulled them over to search the car. When the guards found one of the passengers carrying a broken walkie-talkie, and then found a stabilizer, used to regulate electricity, in the trunk of the car, they detained the three. At nine o'clock that morning, Camp Salerno had come under rocket attack. The guards accused the three of involvement in the attack. They handed them over to American soldiers on the base and pulled the car into the base. Dilawar, who had never spent a night away from home, was about to spend the most terrifying days of his life.

On December 4, he was flown to Bagram Airbase and interned in the detention camp there. It was a makeshift jail set up inside a dilapidated two-story hangar, once used by the Soviet military as a machine repair workshop. The outer walls were clad in rusty metal sheets that covered the windows on both floors. No light or sound emanated from the building. Inside, eighty to one hundred people were held in pens divided up by chain-link fences the length of the ground floor. Prisoners were allowed to read the Koran but were forbidden to talk. Electric lights shone day and night. Interrogation rooms were on the second floor, along with a line of isolation cells. Dilawar was taken to one of the cells upstairs where new prisoners were held. A hood was placed over his head. His hands were cuffed and then chained to the wire mesh above his head, forcing him to stand with his hands stretched out and up. It was standard treatment, used to deprive new prisoners of sleep between interrogations. Several prisoners remember seeing Dilawar over the next few days. They did not know his name, but the interpreters told them he was from Yakubi. Abdul Jabar, a thirty-five-year-old taxi driver, was also from Yakubi and tried to whisper encouragement. He saw Dilawar struggling as guards were leading him down the stairs on the way to the bathroom. "He was very young and when they put on that hood, maybe he could not breathe," Jabar suggested.

When the guard released his chains, Dilawar lay down on the ground. "I was sure he was uncomfortable. I told him, 'Don't struggle because you make it worse for yourself. Don't worry, you'll be there a few days, and then you will be moved downstairs where it's better.' He was scared because he could not get enough oxygen."[6]

All the detainees knew what happened upstairs in the isolation cells. A farmer and former mujahid, Hakim Shah, was held upstairs for sixteen days. For the first ten days, he was kept standing, stripped naked, with a hood over his head and his arms chained to the ceiling. "I had no clothes on at all. It was very cold. They did not let you sleep, day or night," he said.[7] He was let down to pray and go to the bathroom, and for interrogations, but then chained back up, day and night. The rooms were divided into cells by chain-link fencing covered with cloth. Military police guards would kick a soccer ball against the wire mesh or kick the door whenever a prisoner nodded off to sleep. By the tenth day, Shah's legs had swelled so much that his shackles became tight and he lost all feeling in his legs and feet. A doctor came, and the guards released the shackles and let him sit down. Yet they still dragged him off for interrogations, naked and hooded.

One day a soldier held him in a kneeling position, his arms behind him as a female interrogator kicked him hard in the thigh. "She kicked me with her boot. She was just asking me a question," he said. The pain was excruciating, and he could not use his leg for about a week, he said. The blow, a peroneal strike, a disabling blow to the side of the leg above the knee, was a favorite punishment that the military police guards and some interrogators used to subdue prisoners or to stop them falling asleep.

Dilawar spent five days in isolation and received repeated blows to his legs. Hakim Shah said he saw him one day being made to sweep the big room downstairs. "He did not look healthy," Shah said. "His face was a dark color. His feet were chained so he could not move well. He was looking very worried." Parkhuddin, one of Dilawar's passengers, who was detained at the same time, heard a man in a neighboring cell calling for his mother and father, and believed it was Dilawar.[8] On December 10, Dilawar was found dead in his cell.

A week later, the U.S. military announced that a man had died of a heart attack in U.S. custody. It was the second death of a detainee in Bagram within a week. Another man had died on December 3 of a pulmonary embolism, we were told. The Army Criminal Investigation Command completed an inquiry into the deaths without seeking charges against any of the soldiers involved. I was nevertheless curious to find out more about these detainees and why they were still fighting American forces. It took us weeks to track down their families. When I visited his family in Yakubi in February, Dilawar's brother, Shahpoor, showed me a death certificate they had been given along with the body. The certificate was in English, and the family did not understand fully what it said. It was dated December 13, 2002, and was signed at the bottom by Major Elizabeth A. Rouse, a pathologist with the Armed Forces Institute of Pathology based in Washington, D.C., and medical examiner Lieutenant Colonel Kathleen M. Ingwersen from the Army Medical Corps based in Landstuhl, Germany. It gave the circumstances of death: "Decedent was found unresponsive in his cell while in custody." Under "Cause of death" was typed, "Blunt force injuries to lower extremities complicating coronary artery disease." Mode of death, it stated, was "homicide."[9]

I gasped as I read it. I had been looking to learn more about the Afghans being detained. I had not expected to find a homicide committed by American soldiers.

We traced the other man who died in Bagram. He was from Uruzgan. His name was Habibullah, and he was the brother of a prominent Taliban commander. Reportedly related by marriage to the Taliban leader Mullah Omar, Habibullah was not a combatant. He was about thirty-five years old. He had worked in an office in Kandahar during the Taliban government and, trusting Karzai's call for the Taliban to go home in peace, had returned to his father's house in the provincial capital of Tarin Kot after the Taliban fell. He was arrested from his house by the Afghan governor of Uruzgan, Jan Mohammad, and handed over to American forces. Although he may well have possessed information of interest to interrogators, his treatment seems to have been entirely one of beatings and kicking. He died within three days of arriving at Bagram. The U.S. military said at first that he had died from natural causes but later stated that he had died from a pulmonary embolism, a blood clot that stops the blood flow to the lungs. The clot, we later learned, was caused by heavy blows to his legs. His death certificate also gave mode of death as "homicide."[10]

The alleged homicides of two Afghans in American custody passed almost unnoticed when I first reported it in March 2003.[11] The attitude from U.S. officials toward detainees had been aggressive and accusatory from the start. President George Bush had said in January 2003 that "all told, 3,000 suspected terrorists have been arrested in many countries." Many others had met a different fate, he added. "Let's put it this way, they are no longer a problem to the United States and our friends and allies."[12] The American general public seemed to be just fine with that state of affairs. By March, the United States was absorbed in preparations to invade Iraq.

A criminal investigation into the deaths was reopened but took two years to reach a conclusion. No one was ever charged with homicide.[13] Meanwhile, the military intelligence team in charge at Bagram was redeployed to another prison, Abu Ghraib in Iraq, where they continued the same practices that were eventually exposed in the Abu Ghraib scandal of 2004.

More than anything else, detention at Bagram Airbase signaled to Afghans that they were an occupied country. A decade later, Karzai insisted on taking over jurisdiction of all Afghan detainees — years after he should have. Following the deaths of Dilawar and Habibullah, the U.S. military did improve conditions in Bagram, and there were no further deaths in custody there. Yet Bagram remained a black hole for inmates. Some were detained for years without trial and without contact with family or lawyers. It was not until 2008 that families were finally able to talk to detainees through a secure video link organized by the Red Cross. Many inmates were unjustly held, fingered by malicious or misguided informers with flimsy evidence and hearsay that would never have held up in a court of law. But there were no courts. There was no way for families to appeal or protest detention. "We don't know who to complain to," Gul Shah Khan, told me in 2008. His son, Ahmad Murid, twenty-four, had been held in Bagram for two and a half years without trial or investigation. "There is no place to make an appeal, to say what is true and what is false."

For nearly the entire duration of the war, Afghanistan had no Status of Forces Agreement with the United States, which would formalize the right of American forces to detain and imprison Afghans. The Obama administration did eventually introduce military tribunals at Bagram, but the Afghans still felt many of those held were unjustly detained. It was not until 2012 that the two presidents signed an agreement for all detention facilities to be handed over to Afghan authorities.

American forces were fighting a war and capturing insurgents. They had a right to expect them to be detained and kept off the battlefield. Yet they cast their net too broadly. Thousands of Afghans passed through the humiliation and pain of Bagram and other detention centers around the country. Of them, 220 Afghans were sent to Guantánamo Bay. Only a dozen of those were important Taliban figures. The rest were minor figures or ordinary Afghans who were wrongly arrested, accused by rivals, or simply in the wrong place at the wrong time.[14]

Some of those detained and killed were influential tribal figures, and their mistreatment did great harm to America's image in Afghanistan. Whole tribes were angered by the harsh treatment meted out to respected elders. As their elders were locked up or killed, Afghans withdrew from cooperating with U.S. forces and the Karzai government. A Pashtun nobleman in Khost warned me of the problem early on in 2003. Haji Spin Bacha Zadran was an upright figure in a black turban, sixty years old and a former mujahideen commander. He lived in a mud-walled fortress on the edge of the town and was the first commander in his community to surrender his weapons to U.S. forces in a gesture of support for the new government. Yet soon after, led by a local rival, American forces arrested Haji Zadran. He was transferred to Bagram with a black hood over his head and spent the night standing chained to a pillar. He was held and interrogated for a month in Bagram and Kandahar. He did not show anger afterward, but he told me he had warned his interrogators that they were alienating the population. "I told them they should not arrest innocent people. They should try to be close to the people and should not make the people angry. Now the people do not like them because they are arresting people who are not guilty."

When American forces detained a tribal elder from Kunar and former peace envoy, Haji Rohullah Wakil, 1,500 tribesmen descended on Kabul to ask Karzai to intercede for his release. "He has great fame, his father, grandfather, and ancestors were tribal leaders. They mediated and solved problems between tribes. That is why they are so important and why they have support," one of the elders, Ghulam Nabi, told me. "We need him urgently in our region. That is why we came to say he is innocent." Karzai knew such men personally and risked losing the support of their tribal followers with such blunders. Yet even the president struggled to win their release from the Pentagon, which oversaw Guantánamo Bay detentions. Kunar was one of the most troublesome provinces, where U.S. forces fought a grueling insurgency. Men like Rohullah Wakil, who knew people on both sides, could have prevented much of the conflict. Despite repeated requests for his release, he was detained in Guantánamo for nearly six years.

One of the gravest missteps alienated an entire tribe in southern Afghanistan. One night in May 2002, American troops made an airborne assault on a village on the edge of the blistering hot red desert of Registan. Bandi Temur was a smuggling crossroads, where opium and heroin passed down from the poppy fields of Helmand and Uruzgan and across the desert to Pakistan and Iran. It was the home of Haji Berget, one of the first sponsors of Mullah Omar. He was a mujahideen leader and prominent smuggler, and his tribe, the Ishaqzai, dominated the opium business. Yet by 2002, Haji Berget was old and frail. Villagers said he was a hundred years old. That night he had wandered from his home to the village mosque and lay down on the cool stone floor. American soldiers shot him where he lay, with a bullet to the head. They took his body away along with fifty-five men detained in the village. They left behind a bullet mark and shards of his skull in a pool of blood on the mosque floor.

Incensed, Ishaqzai tribesmen marched on Kandahar and threatened to storm the governor's office. "They are thinking of when the Russians came and killed a lot of people, and they are thinking that the Americans and British are going to repeat that," General Akram Khakrezwal, the police chief in Kandahar, warned. Hundreds of tribesmen from three provinces turned out for Berget's funeral, lining the hillside by his village. The tribe had threatened to withdraw its support for the Karzai government unless his body was returned and the villagers released, elders told me. The Ishaqzai thus became deadly opponents of the foreign forces across a swath of territory. Haji Berget's sons took up arms and joined the Taliban. By targeting their leader, American forces had incurred the enmity of an entire tribe.

There was one American officer who seemed to understand Afghans better than most. Colonel John W. "Mick" Nicholson Jr., a lanky, energetic ranger and paratrooper, was commander of 3rd Brigade, 10th Mountain Division, in eastern Afghanistan in 2007 when I first met him. In his sixteen-month tour, he oversaw a threefold increase of U.S. forces in eastern Afghanistan in a serious push to combat the growing insurgency and cross-border infiltration. The extra troops came with a new orientation toward counterinsurgency and tactics designed to win over the Afghan population. Nicholson deployed troops to remote outposts in the mountainous province of Kunar where they tried to befriend the local populace, a policy that he defended as strategically, tactically, and operationally necessary. At the time, bin Laden and other high-level targets were thought to be hiding in the northeastern border region, and insurgents were using the region to filter in from Pakistan to target central regions around Kabul.

Nicholson's tenure in eastern Afghanistan was one of the first and most impressive efforts to switch U.S. forces away from the broad sweeps and house raids of counterterrorism operations. By placing his troops way out in the regions among the community, he wanted to build a positive government presence. "Always seek to do no harm to the Afghan people because ultimately it is the people and their connection with the government that we are trying to nurture and grow," Nicholson told troops at a change of command ceremony on June 1, 2007, at a small mountain outpost at Naray, in Kunar province. "Central government has never meant anything good or brought anything good to them," he told me. "So we have to overcome the skepticism and we do that mainly through actions, not words," he said. "You have to show them that you mean it."

He would run with practiced rapidity through the three stages of counterinsurgency strategy, what he jokingly referred to as the Nicholson Doctrine: separate the people from the enemy; connect the people to the government by providing security and basic assistance; and then turn that connection into an enduring relationship so the people see their future with the government, not with the insurgents.

Nicholson's affinity for the Afghans may have had something to do with a family connection — a distant relative, Brigadier General John Nicholson, had served in the same tribal areas in the British imperial army. Or it was his own strong sense of right and wrong. That stood out with his public reaction to a calamity on March 4, 2007, when a U.S. Marine Special Operations Company ran amok along a busy main highway that runs from the town of Jalalabad toward the Pakistani border. The thirty-man platoon was hit by a suicide car bomb in the midst of heavy traffic at a village called Spinpul. One marine was wounded in the arm by shrapnel, but otherwise the unit was unharmed. Yet in the panic and confusion after the bomb, the Marines reacted ferociously, blasting through the supposed ambush, firing indiscriminately at passing cars, pedestrians, and even people working in the fields. Along a ten-mile stretch of road, they killed as many as nineteen people and wounded fifty others. One of those killed was a young bride, Yadwaro, only sixteen, who had been cutting grass for the family's animals in the field outside their home. She hoisted the bundle onto her head and was walking back to the house when she was struck down by a Marines' long-range machine gun. She fell dead across her own threshold. "They committed a great cruelty," her father-in-law, Ghor Ghashta, said. Another victim was a neighbor, seventy-year-old Shin Gul, who was waiting beside the road to catch a ride to town to do some shopping. He was cut down on the spot. His body was so torn apart that his son, Mohammad Ayub, thirty-five, said he could not recognize him. "I saw a notebook in his pocket and then I knew it was him," he said.

A former mujahideen commander called Lewanai was driving along a side road toward the village when he heard the explosion and halted his car a few yards short of the main highway. He had three passengers with him: his eighty-year-old father, Haji Zarpadshah; his uncle, Haji Shin Makhe; and a sixteen-year-old nephew, Farid Gul. The Marines came into sight, and the gunner opened fire on his car, shredding it with dozens of rounds. Lewanai ducked and rolled out of his side door and took cover behind a mound of earth. His three passengers did not have time. They died in their seats, their bodies ripped apart by the barrage of fire. "They opened fire and were shooting for ten minutes," Lewanai told us afterward. The car was struck by 250 bullets, Afghan investigators counted. Further along the road, the Marines shot at cars stopped at a gas station, killing four people in a minibus including a one-year-old baby.

The Marines claimed that they had come under a complex ambush from several directions after the blast, but Afghan and U.S. military investigators disputed that assertion. When the same unit shot up two civilian cars five days later, commanders ordered them out of Afghanistan. "It is a matter of training, leadership, and discipline; there were lapses in all three," Nicholson told me later.[15] The training is to shoot your way out of an ambush, but the leader of a unit has to understand the situation, work out if the troops are receiving fire and where from, he said. To the Afghan survivors and relatives, he made the most heartfelt apology of any American commander in Afghanistan at a ceremony with relatives of the victims in Jalalabad. He repeated his apology in full to a news teleconference with Pentagon reporters:

> So I stand before you today, deeply, deeply ashamed and terribly sorry that Americans have killed and wounded innocent Afghan people. We are filled with grief and sadness at the death of any Afghan, but the death and wounding of innocent Afghans at the hand of Americans is a stain on our honor and on the memory of the

many Americans who have died defending Afghanistan and the Afghan people. This was a terrible, terrible mistake, and my nation grieves with you for your loss and suffering. We humbly and respectfully ask for your forgiveness.

His statement that he was ashamed of American Marines created anger back home, particularly among the Marines command. It nearly cost him a promotion. When I asked him later why he reacted to the shooting so strongly, his answer showed a deep sympathy and affinity for the Afghans. "These people, they have lives of such hardship and endure such deprivation that if you take away their respect, if you show disrespect to them, you have offended them much more deeply than, say, a Westerner can be offended by a similar action," he said. "It is inconceivable how damaging it is to show disrespect to these people."

Nicholson got his promotion and went on to command American forces in southern Afghanistan at the beginning of the 2009 surge. He returned for a third tour in December 2010 as a major general, promoted to deputy chief of staff, operations, at the ISAF command headquarters in Kabul. By now the coalition was deep in the surge and preparing for the transition to Afghan-led security and the drawdown of U.S. forces. Nicholson was assigned to conduct an inquiry into civilian casualties and the U.S. conduct of night raids, which had become by then the source of the Afghan president's greatest complaints against American forces. I went to interview him on the subject of night raids — and found he was a supporter of them, even though they were killing so many Afghans. By then the Taliban insurgency had become so prevalent that a full surge, and a pitiless campaign of dozens of raids a night, had become necessary. Nicholson reminded me of Lieutenant Colonel John Paul Vann, the fearless and upright American officer who fills the pages of *A Bright Shining Lie,* Neil Sheehan's epic chronicle of the Vietnam War.[16] Vann gave more than a decade of service in Vietnam, exposed much of the brutality and ineffectiveness of U.S. strategy there, but also refused to give up on the idea of winning. Nicholson seemed to be the same: one of a growing number of American officers who have invested much of their careers in Afghanistan,

who believe wholeheartedly in the mission, and who remain unswerv-
ingly optimistic.

Yet despite the best intentions of men like Nicholson, the American-
led campaign has destroyed much in the process of trying to build, and
has left many Afghans vowing revenge and Afghanistan to an uncertain future.

7

The Taliban Return

"We told the government for months the situation was bad,
that the Taliban were coming and killing people, and that it
would get difficult if they became too numerous."

— *resident of Kandahar*

2005. The mujahideen had been part of life in Afghanistan for over
two decades. Recruited from the villages and refugee camps to
fight the Soviet occupation, they were mostly rural men — virtually every family in the countryside had sons among them. They
fought a guerrilla war in the mountains for over a decade, and then
in 1992 they seized power and invaded the cities. They occupied compounds and bases in every town. Their guards lolled on chairs outside
the gates, and gunmen careered in and out in pickup trucks, rockets
and machine guns strapped to the back. The Taliban carried on in
much the same way when they took power. They used the same bases
and showed the same love for weapons and cars. When the Taliban
left, the mujahideen reappeared and took back their old compounds.
They were mostly a rough lot, and were often loathed by city dwellers,
but I learned early on that the mujahideen were always friendly to a
foreign journalist, offering cups of tea and the latest news. They knew
what was going on and were open with information.

By the spring of 2005, though, the mujahideen were taken out of
business. All over the country, the familiar compounds where we had
often stopped by to ask about security or recent events stood aban-

doned. The mujahideen were being disarmed and demobilized under a UN-sponsored program. In the northern town of Balkh, a compound that had served as a barracks for mujahideen and Taliban for twenty years was returned to the adjacent hospital. In Herat in western Afghanistan, two sprawling bases that took up an entire hillside of the city were emptied. A few guards were left at the main gate, watching over a pile of rusting ammunition awaiting disposal. In Gereshk, in the southern province of Helmand, a base we had often visited was deserted, the gate left ajar.

The commander of Gereshk was a man called Haji Mir Wali, a tall, barrel-chested fighter with a gray beard and a silk turban. His forearms were so big they made the Kalashnikov he carried look like a toy. His guards wore caps embroidered with glittering rhinestones, typical of Helmand and Kandahar. I had first met him back in January 2002, on a lonely stretch of road in Helmand when armed mujahideen had stopped our jeep. They were insisting that we proceed with an armed escort, and were offering us their services. It felt like a scam. We were standing in the middle of the road, arguing, when a large convoy of SUVs approached and I waved it down. Mir Wali emerged, Kalashnikov in hand. He listened in silence and then sent the mujahideen packing with a few short words. He gave us an escort of his own guards. As we drove off, they told us who he was: a leader of Hesbe-Islami, the largest Afghan mujahideen faction, now appointed the corps commander of Helmand, and the most powerful man in the southwest.

Like many mujahideen, Mir Wali came from humble beginnings. A twenty-five-year-old secondary school teacher at the time of the Russian invasion in 1979, he formed a thirty-man-strong defense group with fellow teachers and students in their village. Their band grew as others joined them, some of whom had had guerrilla training, and they began attacking Soviet forces. Gradually their following stretched along a swath of the Helmand River Valley, which gave them a supply route from Pakistan and positions from which they could ambush Russian military convoys along the main ring road. By the early 1990s, Mir Wali commanded over a thousand men and had pushed out rivals to control half of Helmand province. His followers were students, engineers, and teachers like himself, and illiterate farmhands, shepherds, and laborers. They were hardy, canny fighters who knew the terrain, and he managed them with an iron fist. He and his men caused their share of strife in the 1990s as they battled other groups for local supremacy. Mir Wali was eventually forced out by the Taliban, but seven years later, when the Taliban fell, he and his fighters returned. All over Afghanistan people accused U.S. forces of bringing back the warlords and unruly militias, which had plagued their lives in the 1990s, but many people in the villages had long ties with the mujahideen, and soon tribal figures and village elders swamped Mir Wali's compound at Gereshk bearing greetings or petitions for jobs or assistance, or offering information. He was someone they all knew. He became the face of the new government in their district.

For the next few years after 2001, Mir Wali served as the army corps commander in Helmand province, controlling 1,200 men including 225 officers from all over the province. Many of them were old comrades in arms or their sons and younger relatives from the villages. His role, he said, was to watch for any regrouping or buildup of Taliban, but the provincial governor, Sher Mohammad Akhundzada, and his security chiefs saw Mir Wali as a rival for power in the province. The corps commander and his men were among the first to be slated for disarmament and demobilization under a UN program in 2004.

The United Nations and the U.S.-led coalition were intent on a nationwide disarmament program to reduce the power of the militia commanders and prevent any repeat of the factional violence of the 1990s. There was a strong sense in Kabul that peace was finally within reach after twenty-five years of war, and that, with a UN peacekeeping force in place — in the capital, if nowhere else — the warlords and their militias should be disarmed and prevented from destabilizing the fragile government. The mujahideen's big guns and old Soviet tanks, booty from the Russian occupation, were put under wraps in government bases. A national army arose, built from scratch. Mir Wali was told by the president's national security advisor that he could go into the highway police or run for parliament. He chose to run for parliament.

He complied with the disarmament program, handed in his weapons, and tried to find jobs for his men, keeping just four bodyguards for his personal protection. In April 2005, he was one of eight former mujahideen commanders who made an all-expenses-paid trip to Japan. The Japanese government was the main donor financing the disarmament program, and the commanders were given a tour of Japan's achievements of postwar reconstruction, including the peace memorial at Nagasaki and a Toyota factory, a highlight for the Afghans. For years they had fought their battles with Toyota pickup trucks.

Yet back in Afghanistan, U.S. forces raided Mir Wali's home twice to search for illegal weapons, apparently on the urging of his rival, the governor. He was humiliated. His men saw that he no longer had the power to protect them or provide them with jobs and drifted away. The Afghans understood that the Americans were siding with the governor, Sher Mohammad. Some of Mir Wali's men transferred into a new highway police force intended to secure the main ring road from Taliban attacks, but soon that force too was disbanded under criticism that its men were extorting money from travelers.

Western officials viewed this entire process as a success story. It was the first time that the UN had managed a disarmament program without a neutral peacekeeping force in place around the country to enforce it. The armed militias, estimated to number 100,000 men, so often criticized for their lawless behavior, were disbanded. The warlords, defanged, were encouraged to turn into responsible citizens in parliament and government. Karzai, who had little clout in the regions, would be strengthened.

The Karzai government pushed for the disbanding of the mujahideen in order to weaken those it saw as rivals or troublemakers, in particular the Northern Alliance that dominated Kabul. Some around Karzai wanted to crush the mujahideen because they saw them as Islamist fundamentalists, similar to, if not as extreme as, the Taliban. Such was the reputation of the worst offenders of the 1990s violence that there was little support for the mujahideen among policymakers. Since 9/11 it had become popular to blame the problem of Islamist terrorism on the U.S. policy of the 1980s of supporting the mujahideen against the Soviet occupation. I had always rejected that theory since the vast majority of Afghan mujahideen who fought the Soviets did not support terrorism.

The mujahideen saw it differently too of course. They had sacrificed blood and livelihoods through twenty-five years of war and deprivation defending their communities from the Russians, the Communists, and then the Taliban. Now they were being excluded from power and any formal role in the new state that they had helped to bring into being. They were being sent home with a pack of farming tools or a two-week vocational training course.

What was missed in the hurry to disarm the mujahideen was the fact that — however self-serving these men were — they were natural leaders, resilient, resourceful, and brave, men who had organized and held together the resistance in their communities under very tough circumstances. At one disarmament ceremony, I met a distinguished-looking commander in a silk turban from Ghor province in northwestern Afghanistan, Ahmad Khan Murghabi. He had risen to the post of general in the mujahideen army. "The war is over and peace has come, and I don't want to continue in the military," he told me. But he added that he had not volunteered to disarm. "We accepted to take this package, but it was the government that fired us in fact."

A few people did warn that the mass demobilization, and the denigration of the mujahideen across the board as war criminals, was an error. Haji Nasrullah Baryalai, a brother of the war hero Abdul Haq and a presidential candidate against Karzai in 2009, cautioned that the Karzai government was losing touch with the people because it was pushing away so many local mujahideen who were the bedrock of the rural communities. "We have to integrate a wide spectrum of mujahideen who are a threat to the government," he told me during the election campaign that year. "They are threatening that they have sacrificed a lot and they have no share in this government." Every rural family had had men in the mujahideen, and the Taliban were benefiting from the growing disaffection, he warned.

Karzai also wanted to do away with the mujahideen political parties, which he blamed for causing so much of the factional fighting in the 1990s, and he prevented them from canvassing in elections. Yet the mujahideen parties, which were generally conservative and Islamist in outlook but supported cooperation with the West and the democratic process, were best placed to offer a political alternative to the Taliban.

Only later would the Disarmament, Demobilization, and Reintegration program, known as DDR, be recognized as an ill-timed mistake. To me, it was as grave an error as the policy of de-Baathification and the demobilization of the Iraqi Army in 2003. The Afghan program disabled rivals to Karzai, but in a single action it removed the strongest anti-Taliban forces from service to their country. It created a vacuum of power and left tens of thousands of former fighters across the country sidelined and resentful. The Karzai government had just lost another large constituency of support.

The disbanding of the mujahideen had a drastic effect on stability in the south of the country. There was no Afghan Army contingent in Helmand at the time. The police consisted of just a few hundred men, with units dispersed in a dozen district towns. U.S. special forces had a small presence in Gereshk, conducting counterterrorism raids, but they were not concerned with improving general security. Driving in southern Afghanistan became increasingly dangerous. Taliban attacks were on the rise, and the only serious deterrent had been removed.

It was Mir Wali's men who first alerted me to the scale and ambition of the Taliban resurgence. A group of them accompanied us as a security escort to the village of Shurakai, an hour's drive north of Gereshk, for an interview in June 2004. They warned me the village was pro-Taliban. While we were there children threw stones at the men, even though they were armed. But we completed the interview, with a pro-Taliban mullah who had been tortured by Afghans working with American special forces, without mishap. We took a different route home, across the desert, in case of a Taliban ambush. There were no roads in this part of the country, and we relied entirely on the mujahideen who knew every track and ambush spot. They led us along dry river beds and desert tracks across a moonscape of fine white sand. Our four-wheel-drive vehicles stirred up choking clouds of dust visible for miles. We encountered only one person out in the desert, an old hunter with his slender Afghan hounds, out chasing hare since dawn.

Eighteen months later I ran into the same guards in Kabul at the opening of parliament in December 2005. Mir Wali had won a seat in the lower house. The guards told us that the Gereshk region was now infested with Taliban. "You know that village we went to?" Yaar Mohammad, the chief bodyguard, told me. "Now even if we had two hundred men we could not go there."

To many in Kabul, including the UN, the Western diplomats, the human rights organizations, and the Karzai government, Mir Wali was another warlord successfully removed from his home base, cut off from sources of illegal racketeering, and given a generous consolation prize as a member of parliament. Yet within a year, Mir Wali was no longer able to visit his constituency. The Taliban had moved into the vacuum he left behind. They now held sway in the countryside. When the highway police force was disbanded, the rest of Mir Wali's men were made jobless. Some of them checked in with him with a question: Was it all right if they joined the Taliban?

2006. Afghanistan's largest reservoir lies like a bright blue jewel amid the brown mountains of Kajaki, a district in the far north of Helmand province. The area is remote and sparsely populated. The villages and district center, a sleepy, one-street town, lie in a green ribbon of irrigated orchards and wheat fields along the river valley. Beyond is rocky desert. The district had been largely peaceful since the fall of the Taliban. A few aid projects had reached this faraway corner, including a small health clinic beside the dam. Despite years of neglect, the American-built dam was still operating and generating electricity. An American security company was guarding the dam turbine and the camp beside it with a handful of Afghan guards. The district chief, Abdul Razziq, hoped more aid was heading their way. There was a U.S. government plan to install a third turbine and increase the electricity generated by the dam. NATO peacekeepers were expanding into southern Afghanistan in 2006, and British troops would soon be deployed to Helmand.

Razziq was a local landowner. He had grown up in a village near the district center where he went to school. Like most farmers, he had joined the mujahideen when the Soviet Union invaded. He opposed the Taliban and fled his home when the mullahs took power, returning home only after their fall in 2001. He knew the people of Kajaki did not support the mullahs. The farmers had suffered economically under the Taliban, from the seven-year drought and the effects of constant war, and they hoped international aid would bring some relief. The district had turned out in big numbers, including sixteen thousand women, to vote for Karzai in presidential elections in 2004, he said.

By the spring of 2006, however, Razziq was starting to feel squeezed. Helmand had been growing increasingly dangerous for men like him. Four district chiefs had been murdered in Helmand in the previous six months. The Taliban had the run of nearly half of the province — six of Helmand's thirteen districts — and were ambushing government convoys and outlying police posts. In February 2006, they mounted coordinated attacks in three districts adjoining Kajaki. Taliban fighters stormed the town of Musa Qala, pinning down the police and firing rockets into government buildings, killing the district chief, Haji Abdul Qudous, inside his office. Fighting raged for two days and left twenty-eight people dead. Twenty of them were police. British troops, caught in an ambush in Sangin district at the same time, were forced to call in airstrikes. Police fought off a third attack on their station in Nawzad. Taliban fighters had repeatedly cut the road through Sangin to Kajaki, searching cars, threatening people, and ambushing government and NATO forces. In March, the district chief of Sangin was killed while visiting his home in Musa Qala.

In Kajaki, Razziq had fifty policemen and a small Afghan National Army unit with French advisors. The police were a rough group. They had been badly mauled in Musa Qala in February and had pulled back to Kajaki with their commander. They had asked for relief, but they knew reinforcements would be ambushed if they tried to come. Razziq kept holding out for assistance.

The first newcomers that spring were not peacekeepers or aid workers. They were the Taliban. Two powerful commanders, Mullah Maruf and Mullah Janan, arrived. Razziq knew them both. They were from his own tribe, the Alizai. Like him, they had fought with the mujahideen against the Russians. But unlike him, they had joined the Taliban and held senior positions in that government. Mullah Maruf was the brother of Mullah Abdul Rauf, a former corps commander of the Taliban army, and one of the top Taliban members detained in Guantánamo Bay detention camp in Cuba.[1] The two commanders brought followers with them. They settled back in their homes, billeting their men with supporters in the villages. They began traveling around and preaching at village mosques. The Taliban regime had always forced the men of the community to attend prayers at the mosque five times a day under threat of punishment. This time, the commanders encouraged villagers with a friendly invitation. People obeyed and went to hear them preach. They began warning the villagers of the forthcoming expansion of the foreign military into Helmand and urged them to resist. "We are Muslims, we should not cooperate with the government. We should wage jihad."[2]

The Taliban were skilled at preaching, and they knew instinctively how to influence the Pashtun tribesmen. They had prepared the way for months across southern Afghanistan, posting official notices from the "Islamic Emirate of Afghanistan" in mosques and dropping fliers in the bazaars. The notices warned that jihad was every Muslim's duty, that the foreigners were coming with evil intent and would trick them with promises of assistance. They countered the government in every way they could: instructing people not to send their children to school, ordering them to grow opium poppies, and warning that government workers and collaborators would be beheaded.[3]

In Kajaki, the Taliban commanders pressed the same message. They urged villagers to grow poppy and make some money, but warned them that the foreigners would come and try to destroy their crops.

They told the villagers that the United States was not coming to help them, that the infidels had darker aims in occupying the country. It was an argument designed to tap into the Afghans' deep historic distrust of foreign invaders. The Soviet invasion was still a living memory that had affected every single Afghan family, and the three wars British imperial armies fought in Afghanistan are alive in Afghan folklore. Most families in the south have an ancestor who fought against the British.[4]

Razziq knew this was a direct challenge to the government, but his police force was too small to confront these men, and there was little chance of a stronger force reaching Kajaki. Instead he worked to counter their propaganda by congregating 450 clerics and tribal elders from around the district to push back against the Taliban call for jihad. Jihad is a struggle in the name of Islam, and is the duty of all Muslims. Yet in the Afghan tradition, jihad has to be declared by a prominent religious leader and can only be called against the government if that government is deemed to be un-Islamic. Razziq's gathering of religious leaders selected ten spokesmen who announced that the Karzai government was legitimate and indeed Muslim, and that jihad was not warranted. Razziq called on the governor and the central government to reinforce the message but never heard back. The Taliban meanwhile continued their aggressive campaigning. They were assiduous in touring every mosque and village. They began to behave as if they were the rightful rulers, and they carried weapons with them wherever they went, right into the mosque.

Abdul Razziq went out as much as he could among the people with his own message. "I told them Kajaki is a garden. You should stop people coming in to ruin it," he said. He convened another gathering of two thousand elders and won promises of support from tribal leaders. Yet as the government's weakness became evident, that support slipped away. Police reinforcements never arrived. The district chief became so cash-strapped he had to borrow money from townspeople. Then the Taliban started laying mines on the roads. Razziq and his men defused a few of them, but one blew up his car just a mile outside his base. No one was hurt, but Razziq lamented it was a sign of his loss of local support. "I was so weak that I could not discover that there was a mine one and a half kilometers away," he told me. Gradually the villages became unsafe for him and his men.

In May 2006, the Taliban mounted another series of attacks in northern Helmand, this time boosted by large numbers of local tribesmen. They besieged Afghan police and threatened to overrun several towns. British troops were just deploying to the province, in what they had planned as a peacekeeping mission, but within days the new governor, Mohammad Daoud, appealed to them to save the towns of northern Helmand from falling. British troops were dropped into the towns of Nawzad, Sangin, and Musa Qala to shore up police defenses, and found themselves fighting off several assaults a day by the Taliban.

In early June, the Taliban attacked Kajaki. The Afghan Army and their French advisors had left. Razziq was alone with his fifty police. Cut off for so long, they were low on ammunition and food. They survived on fortified biscuits donated by the Indian government and intended for the district's schoolchildren. A group of fifty Taliban broke through and seized positions just half a mile to the north of the dam as another group closed in from the south. They pounded the camp with mortars. "We were completely surrounded by the enemy," Razziq told me. "It was a very tough situation, we could not even raise our heads." The Taliban force, which he said included foreign fighters, tried to capture the dam. Seizing such a prime economic asset, destroying it, or shutting down the electricity across the south would have been a political and economic disaster for the Karzai government and NATO forces. "They came very close," Razziq observed.

British troops reached Kajaki later in the summer but could do little more than defend the dam and the camp next to it. All over northern Helmand, their troops were trapped in makeshift bases, often private compounds known as platoon houses, fighting off waves of Taliban attacks through the infernal heat. They fought on through the summer, running low on rations and ammunition as helicopters struggled to resupply them through heavy enemy gunfire, sometimes waiting hours to evacuate the wounded and losing some men because of the delay. They lost thirty-three men by September, a shock to the British public who had expected the mission in Afghanistan to be focused on development and reconstruction.

It was a disastrous policy to use British troops to guard government positions in these small towns. Without enough troops to push out patrols and take the fight to the Taliban, they ended up just battling to defend their platoon houses, while calling in artillery and airstrikes on the destroyed townscape around them. Nawzad, Musa Qala, San-gin, and Kajaki, as well as the southern towns of Garmser and Nawa, became ghost towns as the residents fled and NATO and the Taliban scrapped over the ruins day and night.

President Karzai did little to counter the insurgency and keep the people on his side. He trusted too much in his own popularity — he had won a resounding vote in the 2004 presidential election — and was ill-served by his own officials. Many analysts have blamed Karzai's first appointee as governor of Helmand, Sher Mohammad Akhundzada, and his security chiefs for alienating much of the population through their misrule. Karzai's half-brother Ahmed Wali Karzai, who acted as the president's representative in the south and wielded enormous influence in appointing officials and removing opponents, also left many disaffected. The government should have been as assiduous as the Taliban at wooing the public, countering the Taliban propaganda, and listening to people's grievances. Above all, the Afghan government should have provided a strong defense against the Taliban. Instead, Karzai turned to foreign troops to do the job, which was a fatal mis-take. Using foreign soldiers to defend district towns with inadequate local forces was to use the wrong tool for the job.

Thousands of Taliban fighters and weapons infiltrated into southern and eastern Afghanistan through the spring and summer of 2006. The Taliban was transformed. Until then a shadow guerrilla army, it was now making an ambitious bid to seize control of southern Afghani-stan and stall the expansion of NATO peacekeepers into its traditional heartland. Mullah Dadullah was the mastermind behind the offensive.

He recruited thousands of Afghans from both sides of the border, and met with al Qaeda and Pakistani militant leaders, traveling several times to South and North Waziristan in 2005 and 2006 to sign up additional men, explosives, and trainers.[5]

The previous September, U.S. Defense Secretary Donald Rumsfeld had announced the withdrawal of three thousand American troops from Afghanistan. They were needed in Iraq, where that war was demanding more and more manpower. The cuts were never carried out, since the need for troops grew in eastern Afghanistan, yet the announcement was taken as a sign of dwindling U.S. commitment. It alarmed Afghans, who had been abandoned before in the 1990s after the Soviet pullout, and signaled especially to those living in the south that the United States was not serious about countering the Taliban resurgence. The announcement also affected Pakistan's calculations. The Pakistani military had surmised that the United States could not wage two counterinsurgencies at once, and would withdraw its troops from Afghanistan in order to deal fully with Iraq.[6] Pakistan was happy to see U.S. forces leave the southern Pashtun belt of Afghanistan, which it considered its own back yard. Yet in December, NATO had announced an expansion of its UN-mandated peacekeeping force to southern Afghanistan. Six thousand troops, including British, Canadian, Dutch, and other forces, would arrive shortly.

That was a red rag to the ISI. It pushed the Taliban to give NATO troops, new to the terrain, an unpleasant welcome. It was time, the intelligence agency calculated, for the Taliban to make a lunge for control of the south.

Karzai and his security officials tried to deflect the coming storm. In February, Karzai traveled to Islamabad where he met with General Pervez Musharraf and Prime Minister Shaukat Aziz and gave a speech at the National Defense College of Pakistan. The Afghan president tried to make the case for Pakistan not to support the Taliban. The Taliban government had been a burden on Pakistan, and his new government offered a good business opportunity to its neighbor, he told them. Pakistani exports to Afghanistan during the Taliban rule amounted to only $25 million but had since risen to $1.2 billion. Nurturing extremism and training militants would only hurt Pakistan, he warned. "If anyone thinks that he can train a snake to bite another person, he should know that it is possible at any time for the snake to turn and bite his trainer," he argued. "Terrorism is something like this example. It is nobody's friend."[7] He also took his intelligence chief, the director of the National Directorate of Security, Amrullah Saleh, in to meet with Musharraf. They handed the Pakistani leader a dossier of al Qaeda and Taliban members active in the insurgency, including details of their whereabouts in Pakistan. The first two to three pages of the dossier detailed intelligence that al Qaeda operatives were hiding in safe houses in Mansehra, a hilly area north of Pakistan's capital, adjacent to the towns of Haripur and Abbottabad.

Musharraf was dismissive of the information but uncomfortable at being put on the spot. He shifted in his chair, grasping the arms, almost shaking at the mention of Mansehra. "I did not know then that that was where bin Laden was hiding," Saleh recounted later.[8] The Afghans' effort to share intelligence brought them nothing. Not a single member of the Taliban was detained or handed over.

In Afghanistan, the Taliban began popping up everywhere in numbers never seen before. In April, a force of fifty to sixty Taliban turned up around the village of Sartak, near Mullah Omar's old base of Sangesar. They were moving around on motorbikes and in small cars, keeping away from the main villages. A farmer told us that he saw a group of several dozen Taliban fighters carrying heavy machine guns and brand-new Chinese-made Kalashnikovs. Soon after, the Taliban laid siege to the police force at Sartak, battling them for hours until the police requested help from NATO forces, who called in airstrikes. A young woman was killed, as well as six policemen. Within two weeks, a villager told an Afghan colleague that the Taliban had returned, walking openly in the villages with their weapons and sitting under the trees eating mulberries, one of the Afghans' favorite summer pastimes. The Taliban were demanding food, lodging, and the Muslim tithing, *zakat*, from villagers.[9] Their brazen behavior, and the failure of the U.S.-led coalition to apprehend them, was turning public opinion. People were questioning the seriousness of NATO and the government.

The province of Uruzgan, where tribesmen had been the first to rise up in support of Karzai in 2001, was once more in the thrall of the Taliban. Insurgents had reclaimed the countryside and controlled the main roads, placing the provincial capital, Tarin Kot, in a stranglehold. Security commanders and townspeople warned Lieutenant General Karl Eikenberry, the U.S. commander in Afghanistan, when he visited in April that the town might fall. The map used at a military briefing showed every district of the province as red or amber, indicating instability. A shopkeeper, Haji Saifullah, told the general, "During the day the people, the police, and the army are with the government, but during the night, they are all with the Taliban and al Qaeda." Young men were running to the hills to join the Taliban because they were scared of raids and house searches, another man called Rahmatullah said. Young, unemployed men were going to Pakistan in search of work and being recruited by the Taliban, Mullah Hamdullah, the elected head of the provincial council, explained. "The unemployment rate is very high and the people of Uruzgan are very poor," he warned the general. The Taliban were paying them $175 a month to join up and fight.

The slide in Uruzgan was blamed on the former governor, Jan Mohammad, a grizzled, one-eyed old mujahideen commander and former ally of Karzai's late father. He was sternly anti-Taliban after being imprisoned by them, yet he had alienated his own people by amassing too much power and crushing his rivals, sometimes brutally. Karzai had been forced to replace him with the thirty-five-year-old Maulavi Abdul Hakim Munib, a serious, educated, religious man who had served as deputy minister of tribal affairs in the Taliban government. Yet Munib looked alarmed after barely a month in the job. Sitting on the first floor of the governor's office, he complained to a visiting delegation of Afghan and American officials that security was precarious. A sea of white and pink poppies in full bloom stretched out from beneath his windows to the hills beyond.

Governor Munib said he needed more policemen. The Taliban were several times the strength of the government forces in the province. The government had recently sent 500 newly trained army recruits, yet the police, which were in the forefront of every encounter with the Taliban, numbered only 347, roughly 45 men for each district. That was barely enough to man a single police station. No one really knew how many Taliban there were in Uruzgan, but the lowest estimate was 300. They were certainly better armed than the police.[10] The governors of Helmand and Kandahar had joined Munib in asking the central government for a quadrupling of the forces they had, as well as for more resources and equipment. A deputy interior minister, Abdul Malik Siddiqi, announced to the governor in front of a gathering of provincial elders that the government planned to send 250 to 500 men to each district. Yet outside the meeting the American commander, General Eikenberry, expressed reservations. There were not enough trained men to send to the area, and, more important, there were too few good leaders to control them. The police never arrived in the numbers that had been announced to the elders.

General Eikenberry was the father of the Afghan National Army. He describes himself as arriving a skeptic about the task of building a national, multiethnic army from scratch in 2002, but he became an ardent supporter. A national army, he believed, was the answer to Afghanistan's years of strife.

It was a painstaking business. The first Afghan battalion was deployed outside Kabul in 2003.[11] A year later, 2,500 Afghan soldiers were deployed around the country.[12] By 2006, 14,000 combat troops had been trained, but they were still thinly stretched in a country the size of Afghanistan. Moreover, by focusing on the army, the United States missed entirely the need for a provincial police force not to mention trained civil servants for the regions. The Bush administration was averse to expensive, time-consuming nation-building, and persuaded its NATO partners to share responsibility for different sectors of the reconstruction of Afghanistan. The British took counternarcotics; Germany, the police; and Italy, justice. The United States took the army.

The Germans sent forty police trainers to the Kabul police academy to run a three-year police officer's course for three hundred men. That was the limit of police training in Afghanistan for the first three years after 2001. The United States did not contribute to police training until 2004, when the Bush administration began to understand the security vacuum at the provincial level, starting a $1.1 billion regional training program. The first program, managed by the U.S. State Department and run by U.S. contractor DynCorp International, sent thirty American police advisors to work in pairs in the provinces to run two- to four-week training courses. It was insufficient. Afghan police barely seemed to improve. By 2005, the Defense Department, which had been training the police in Iraq since 2004, took over and expanded the program to hundreds of trainers. The delays, bureaucratic and political, had been disastrous.[13]

In May 2006 the Taliban returned to their offensive along the Arghandab River Valley, southwest of Kandahar city. The districts of Panjwayi and Zhare[14] had been a favorite fighting ground for the mujahideen during the Soviet occupation, and now became a favorite of the Taliban. The area is intensively cultivated, a warren of narrow lanes and walled fruit gardens, fabled for their twenty-eight varieties of grapes and their lush pomegranates. Vines are grown on serried banks of earth, three feet high, fed by irrigation ditches that were ready-made trenches — ideal cover for guerrilla fighters. The vineyards are enclosed by twelve-foot-high walls and dotted with tall, mud-walled barns used for drying grapes. The barns are perforated with narrow air vents to allow air to circulate and to provide props for the drying racks inside. Similar to arrow slits on a medieval tower, the air vents also provided ideal lookouts.

The Arghandab River Valley sits on an infiltration route that crosses the Registan Desert from Pakistan. Insurgents used it to move through the green cover of Panjwayi and Zhare to within striking distance of

Kandahar, the prize for many a conqueror of the region since Alexander the Great founded the city in 330 B.C. It was from the villages of Panjwayi and Zhare that the Taliban first organized their bid for Kandahar in 1994. They were set on reassuming control.

A large group camped in the vineyards on the edge of the village of Zangabad and ambushed a police patrol, sparking off a week of fighting. Taliban fighters swarmed in from all directions to join battle against Afghan police and newly deployed Canadian troops, and then dispersed as quickly through the vineyards. As fighting intensified, a force of Taliban pulled back into the large village of Talokan and occupied some of the houses. Canadian troops called in airstrikes. American bombers hit a number of houses, killing Taliban fighters but also thirty-five civilians.[15] It was the second case of aerial bombardment in two months in the area, and it shook residents. Hundreds of villagers fled their homes and headed for the city. The episode marked the beginning of a catastrophic eight years of war for the two districts that would render them largely uninhabitable and turn their fertile vineyards to dust.

By June, coalition forces were clashing daily with Taliban somewhere in Afghanistan's five southern provinces. The Taliban fielded as many as six thousand fighters, about the same as the coalition forces deployed in the south by then. Although each firefight usually ended with heavy losses to the Taliban, they seemed irrepressible. U.S. and NATO special forces troops reported that the fighters were younger, braver, and more adaptable than before.[16] Reinforcements kept arriving. Reports from Pakistan suggested that hundreds of madrassas in Pakistan's border areas had emptied as students were dispatched to fight jihad. Scores of local Afghans joined the Taliban too, sometimes serving as part-time scouts and guides. Villagers gave them shelter and local assistance.

Afghans were pessimistic. "We told the government for months the situation was bad, that the Taliban were coming and killing people, and that it would get difficult if they became too numerous," a former member of the mujahideen and landowner in Panjwayi told me. He asked not to be named for fear of reprisals. The Taliban were already powerful in his area, and it was dangerous to be seen talking to foreigners. By this time, the Taliban were scanning the international press on the Internet. The landowner came to see me in my guesthouse only because a mutual friend asked him to.

This man, like many villagers, had left his farm and brought his family to the city. "The Taliban could get into the city, if the government continues to sleep," he said. He had seen members of the Taliban he knew walking around in the city center. "I don't think the government can turn it around now."

The Canadian general in command in southern Afghanistan, Brigadier General David Fraser, played down the threat. "The Taliban have this great ability to blend into the villages and towns," he told me in an interview at his headquarters at the Kandahar Airbase in June 2006. "But they are not the superstars people make them out to be. They are capable fighters but defeatable."

Throughout 2006, NATO forces were behind the curve of the Taliban resurgence. Canada deployed 2,200 troops to take charge of Kandahar province but had to send some to Helmand for a clearing operation. Colonel Ian Hope, the Canadian commander of forces in Kandahar, conceded that his forces were too thinly spread there. "It will not occur again, it's dangerous for people to lose confidence in us," he said.[17] But confidence was ebbing fast.

By August, the Taliban had set up a headquarters in Panjwayi and massed one thousand fighters, including hundreds of men from Helmand and a few hundred from Pakistan. The senior commander, Mullah Abdul Rauf, taunted the American military. "Where is the American power? Why couldn't they capture the Taliban and mujahideen in their caves?" he said in an interview with Al Jazeera television network. He predicted the Afghans would break the American superpower. "These people have a history of jihad. You will see this jihad will break [the Americans]."[18] A battle was brewing, but for all his bravado, Abdul Rauf skipped back to Pakistan before it began.[19]

For weeks Kandahar was rife with rumors that the Taliban were going to storm the city. Afghan officials gathered tribal elders and people from the community, urging them to resist. But Afghans had learned how to survive. Many were leaving the districts for the safety of the city, and merchants were already reaching out to the Taliban to ensure protection of their goods if the insurgents stormed the city.

It was not until September 2, 2006, that NATO finally gathered a force against the Taliban and mounted Operation Medusa. The new overall commander of ISAF, the 16,000-strong NATO force, was the British four-star general David Richards. He was determined to show the Taliban that NATO was not a soft touch. "We had to show that NATO can fight," he told me later. "We killed a lot of insurgents and continue to do so — sad in some respects, but that's what the locals, if I have a discussion with the elders, that's what they most want from us at one moment. Followed by proper improvements." He reckoned that 70 percent of Afghans were sitting on the fence, not with the Taliban, but unwilling to support the government either. "That's my main focus at the moment, getting those visible improvements, in security, governance, and reconstruction and development to start happening in the south so that we can persuade that 70 percent that we will win."

Operation Medusa did not go as planned. Canadian forces led a pincer movement on the village of Pashmul, which they knew was a hotbed of the Taliban, but their troops immediately ran into trouble crossing the river. Hit by mines and rocket fire, they called for air support — only to be struck by friendly fire from American planes. Within hours, most of the Canadians were wounded and out of action.

As the Canadian attack floundered, an American unit was brought in to help. Colonel R. Stephen Williams put together a larger combined American, Canadian, and Afghan force for another attempt against Pashmul on September 12. Williams, a forty-six-year-old ranger from Anchorage, Alaska, injected a new style. He blasted the Taliban with rock music across the river valley for six days and pounded them with artillery and airstrikes anywhere enemy movement was spotted. Playing his favorite hard rock tune, AC/DC's "Back in Black"—to hide the sound of the armored vehicles, he said—he crossed the river and drove through the cornfields from the northeast, taking the Taliban by surprise. The fighting was nevertheless intense. The Taliban were well dug in, using irrigation channels and the high mud-walls for cover. "It was Normandy invasion tactics with bunker systems and trenches," Williams said as he walked a few journalists through a battlefield tour a week later. "We found a lot of bunkers, with metal roofs and air-holes with metal pipes running up for ventilation," he added, standing over one bunker that had been blown up by his forces. "They used the canals as trenches and then would pull back to the bunker." The village school, a cluster of white painted classrooms built with American government assistance after 2001, was destroyed from repeated air- and artillery strikes. The colonel estimated they had killed 150 to 200 Taliban fighters in the battle, including a number of commanders.

Colonel Williams tramped around the deserted fields and orchards of Pashmul describing a coalition victory, but Operation Medusa was far from that. The Taliban had been pushed out of Panjwayi, but they escaped west into Helmand province to fight another day. American special forces blocked their route out to the south with some ferocious fighting, but French and Dutch troops failed to set blocking positions to the west, according to the American attorney Gary Bowman, a U.S. Army reservist who wrote a classified military history on the war in southern Afghanistan.[20]

The challenge from the Taliban, with several thousand men massed so close to Kandahar city, had been far more serious than many in the country realized. Kandahar came close to falling that summer, General McNeill told me later. General Richards saw that not only was the Afghan government at risk of losing the south, but that NATO risked failure too. Within a month of taking over, Richards had ordered Operation Medusa to establish NATO's authority in Kandahar. But as the battle unfolded, it became clear that NATO commanders had underestimated the Taliban's strength. "The real story of Medusa is the utter intelligence failure — it is the best example that the coalition did not understand the residual Taliban influence in the south," Bowman told me.

For the inhabitants of Panjwayi, Medusa was just one of a series of heavy battles that summer. The civilian toll from the fighting was high. The United Nations said later that forty civilians had been killed, and Kandahar hospital took in twenty-four wounded civilians. NATO announced the operation as successfully concluded, yet the next day, four Canadian soldiers were killed when a suicide bomber cycled up to their foot patrol and blew himself up. The Canadians had been handing out pencils and notebooks to the village children at the time. Nine children were wounded in the explosion. From that moment, Canadian troops struggled to hold the district and make it secure. Most of the Taliban had departed, but they had left small cells of local fighters who laid mines, set ambushes, and enlisted the help of the local population and so dragged them into the fight. NATO and Afghan units came under repeated ambush and sniping.

Canadian troops camped in a field in the village of Pashmul and set about securing the surrounding area and providing assistance to the farming community. They decided to carve a new road straight down from the main ring road. It would provide Canadian troops with a safer route and allow them to avoid the village road, which snaked through high walls and homesteads where insurgents ambushed them at every turn. It meant destroying houses, farm buildings, and property walls, tearing up orchards and cutting off irrigation channels, which would anger many farmers and landowners. I saw it time and again in Afghanistan: foreign troops taking actions for their own protection, alienating the local population, and thus undermining their security.

A few weeks after Operation Medusa, on October 3, a group of American and Canadian soldiers were working to clear the road. Staff Sergeant Gregory Robinson, a twenty-seven-year-old combat engineer from Rosiclare, Illinois, was standing on the road as his team's bulldozer moved in to demolish a raisin barn and an adjoining wall. The wall was six feet high. As it came down, it was as if the soldiers had cracked open a hornet's nest. The Taliban had been lying in wait and opened fire on the road crew with a hail of bullets, mortars, and rocket-propelled grenades (RPGs). Within a minute, they hit army vehicles and a trailer of demolition explosives, killing two Canadian soldiers and wounding five others. An RPG slammed into a Humvee near Sergeant Robinson, and the explosion threw him into the air. He was injured in the leg, and he lay on the ground as a friend bound up his wounds.

The battle raged over their heads for forty-five minutes until the unit pulled back to Forward Operating Base (FOB) Wilson, still under fire. Two Black Hawk helicopters and an Apache answered the call. Robinson lay on a stretcher on the ground amid the shouting and chaos as the crew ripped out the seating from the Apache to fit in all the wounded. Dead and wounded were loaded up together. "We were packed like sardines," he said. "There was one dead Canadian soldier next to me and when they banked he kind of fell on me. His arm kept falling on me."[21] Robinson's leg was amputated, and he was flown from the U.S. medical center at Landstuhl in Germany back to the United States on a cavernous troop carrier packed with military casualties from Iraq and Afghanistan. The wounded were stacked in berths four rows high for the flight. Medical personnel passed down the aisles among them, stopping to administer medication and change dressings in the hushed gloom. Sergeant Robinson kept floating in and out of consciousness, oppressed by the sense of men close to death all around him. "There was this whole eerie feeling, hearing and seeing people way worse than you," he told me. "That was one of the roughest times."[22]

His ordeal went largely unseen in the turmoil of 2006. American casualties from the wars in Iraq and Afghanistan were hidden from the public since photographs and film of dead and wounded soldiers were restricted by the Bush administration. The war in Iraq had descended into a spasm of civil violence in 2006, and October of that year was the deadliest month for U.S. soldiers since 2001. In Iraq, 111 U.S. servicemen were killed, along with 17 in Afghanistan. If not entirely forgotten, Afghanistan was certainly the lesser concern. The Taliban were close to taking back their spiritual capital of Kandahar and much of southern Afghanistan, and America was looking the other way.

Left in charge of Kandahar province for the next four years, Canadian forces failed to prevent the buildup of the Taliban around Kandahar city. Like the British in Helmand, they were undermanned for the task and quickly forced into a defensive posture. At one point, General Fraser infuriated the provincial governor, Asadullah Khaled, by suggesting his NATO forces pull back into defensive positions and focus on guarding only the city. The implication was they would leave the rest of the province to the Taliban.

Khaled, who had fought with the mujahideen since the age of fourteen when he succeeded his father, a famous commander, as the tribal leader in his native Ghazni, had been urging the Canadians to be more aggressive. He was so incensed by what he heard that he walked out of the room, leaving the general mid-speech. An independent review of the Canadian deployment in Afghanistan, known as the Manley Panel report, concluded in 2008 that at least another one thousand troops — in addition to the force of two thousand Canadians in place — were needed to secure Kandahar province.[23] Canada could not provide that number, and no other NATO force stepped in until the U.S. surge in 2009 and 2010. By then, the Taliban presence was so well entrenched that a combined force of seventeen thousand soldiers and security personnel was needed to clear Kandahar.

The calamities continued. A herders' camp was bombed killing thirty-five men, women, and children. I could feel the frustration mounting in many districts that summer. The mood vacillated as the local populace waited for a sign of strong leadership from the government. I interviewed a nineteen-year-old farmer, Lala Jan, from Deh Rawud in Uruzgan province. "We are going mad now," he said in agitation. "From one side we have the government and Americans, and on the other side the Taliban. When the Taliban come in they enter without asking, and it's the same with the Americans. We cannot tolerate any of them." He said that Taliban forces had entered their village a few weeks before and savagely beaten people they accused of supporting the government. "Half of the people like them, half the people don't," he said of the militants. "Whoever can bring security should do it. One side should be finished, the Taliban or the government, we don't care which."

The population was waiting for the government to act. "If the government enforces security then the people will come alongside," said Abdul Qader Noorzai, the head of the Afghan human rights commission in Kandahar and a well-connected tribal elder. But as the summer wore on, the Afghans saw that the Taliban were more determined than the Karzai government and Western forces. After the United States had defeated the Taliban so decisively in 2001, people could not understand why U.S. and NATO forces were failing to deal with the Taliban this time. They began to suspect a conspiracy.

Compounding the people's sense of insecurity was a vicious campaign of suicide bombing that burst upon Afghanistan in 2006. Unheard of in Afghanistan before 2001, suicide bombings began in a trickle. In the first years, few were even particularly successful, sometimes killing only the bomber. But in 2006, a wave of 119 suicide bombers attacked Afghanistan, nearly one every three days. A high proportion of these attacks occurred in Kandahar. It had seemed as if Afghans had experienced every possible horror of war in the past twenty-five years, but these suicide bombers, detonating their explosives in the midst of crowds of shoppers or crashing into busy traffic, brought a new terror. They stunned Afghan communities, paralyzed the government, and sent NATO forces scurrying for their bunkers.

As in most religions, suicide is a sin in Islam, and so the method of killing was appalling to Afghans, as was the indiscriminate nature of the attacks. The Taliban and its al Qaeda and Pakistani mentors were wielding an instrument of maximum terror to destroy popular confidence in the Afghan government, to chase it from power and chase its Western allies from the country.

A group of us from the *New York Times* had a close encounter with a suicide bomber one day early in February 2006. We had driven up to the central police station in Kandahar, only a few blocks from the hotel where we often stayed. It was mid-morning. A crowd of people, papers in hand, was clustered at the gate. Their bicycles and motorbikes were parked in a huddle across the street. A few off-duty policemen were sitting on plastic chairs warming themselves in the winter sun and chatting with their friends. We pulled up at the barrier. Scott Eells, an American photographer, and I were sitting in the back seat, hidden from view behind black windows. Our Afghan reporter, Ruhullah, had insisted on putting on the black film even though it was illegal. Things had changed in Kandahar, he said. It was not safe for foreigners to be driving around, and for him and our driver to be seen with foreigners anymore. The police were expecting us and waved us through. An aide whisked us into the main building and up the stairs to the police chief's office.

The moment we reached the landing, a wave of air punched the building and the windows shattered on all sides. The crack of a powerful bomb reverberated and made us all duck. We were used to hearing the sound of explosions, but this was very close. Momentarily stunned, I watched the aide in front of me run forward, then run back. I turned and saw Scott and Ruhullah racing down the stairs and followed them. In the courtyard, a policeman, his clothes on fire, was running from the gate and hurled himself into a ditch. The front gate was blown apart, and the ground strewn with burning debris. Bodies lay in awful poses, blackened, naked limbs splayed. Police began to haul them off the ground. The wounded were heavy and stupid with shock. A policeman, blood dripping down his face, stared dumbly as a younger colleague carried him on his back to a car. Two policemen pulled their burned colleague from the ditch. He was dead, his body covered in stinking black slime. Jamshed, our driver, appeared at my side, wide-eyed with shock but unhurt. He had just parked the car across the yard and had watched it all.

The bomber had blown himself up at the gate, in the thick of the crowd. There was a stench of burning. Motorbikes were twisted into tangled heaps. The men pressing around the gate with their papers had taken the brunt of the explosion. They had been thrown in all directions and lay face down in a rubbish heap; in a sewage ditch along the side of the street, some still clutched their documents in their hands. A Kandahari driver we knew, Abdul Hadi, who had been waiting for his boss, was pulled unconscious from behind the wheel of his car. Construction workers building new rooms beside the gatehouse were carrying out dead and wounded coworkers. The police were loading the dead into the back of a pickup truck now. "You see what we are up against?" one said to me. Others howled at the photographers to stop taking pictures of the dead.

Mullah Gul, a tough district police chief we knew well, came out. His clothes were grimy and his eyes bloodshot. "I lost five men and five wounded," he told us as he climbed into the pickup to follow the casualties to the hospital. Two women in blue burqas arrived at the end of the street, screaming for relatives who worked in the police station. The police shouted at them to go home. Emotions were fraying. A police officer slapped a junior policeman across the face for not wearing his cap while on duty. The man's commander started swearing at the official, who was a newcomer to the station.

An investigator wearing plastic gloves was squatting down by the gate examining the ground. "He was a suicide bomber. I found his head on the roof of the factory," he said, nodding at the building opposite. He began explaining that if a bomber has explosives strapped to his chest, the blast usually blows the head clear off the body. "It happened at 10:20 a.m.," he went on. "He came on a motorbike and ran into the people and the police."

A police commander, Habibullah, said he had been on his way to the gate and had seen the bomber, a youth wearing a turban, talking to the men at the barrier before he detonated his bomb. "They are doing it in the name of Islam. They ask us why we have given our hand to non-Muslims," he said. "They say we are the eyes for the foreign forces. So the enemy is saying they want to cut out the eyes, and then the foreigners will not be able to do anything and they will have to leave Afghanistan." He paused. "If the foreigners leave, in three days the Taliban would be back."

We drove across town to the hospital. People were clustered around a list of dead at the hospital entrance. The final death toll was thirteen, with fifteen wounded. Five of the dead were police, eight civilians. One, Najibullah, was only thirteen. They came from different places, in the city and the districts, one from Uruzgan province. Upstairs in the intensive care unit, some of the casualties were badly burned. Slathered in cream, they shivered violently. Our friend, the driver Abdul Hadi, lay motionless in a coma.

8

The Suicide Bomb Factory

"All Taliban are ISI Taliban. It is not possible to go to
Afghanistan without the help of the ISI. Everyone says this."

— *brother of a Pakistani suicide bomber killed in Afghanistan*

2006. Afghan investigators soon discovered that the suicide bombers and the networks supplying them were emanating from Pakistan. In January 2006, the Afghan intelligence service and police
rounded up a group of Pakistanis and Afghans in Kandahar who, they
said, were behind a string of suicide attacks. Three of those arrested
were Pakistanis who said they had been shown jihadi videos and urged
to go to Afghanistan and kill Americans to earn a sure way to paradise.
One said he was a member of Harkat-ul-Mujahideen and had been
through militant training in the 1990s. He was stopped by police in a
car rigged with explosives, which failed to go off.[1] "I think there is a
factory for these bombers," Asadullah Khaled, the governor of Kandahar province, told me.

Khaled had worked in intelligence with the Northern Alliance during their resistance against the Taliban and was no novice when it came
to tracking Taliban activities. Kandahar had received the highest number of suicide bombings of all provinces when Khaled decided to go
public with some of the evidence Afghan intelligence was uncovering.
"Most of the attackers are non-Afghans," Khaled said at a memorial
service for fourteen victims of a suicide bombing in Kandahar. "We
have proof: we have prisoners, we have addresses, we have cassettes."

Over the months the evidence accumulated. Those bombers that could be identified turned out to be mostly Pakistanis or Afghans living in Pakistan. They were being recruited through mosques and madrassas, and some through connections to Pakistan's banned militant groups such as Jaish-e-Mohammad and Harakat-ul-Mujahedin. Others were organized by Afghan groups under the Taliban's operational commander, Mullah Dadullah, and Gulbuddin Hekmatyar, the mujahideen leader of Hesbe-Islami and longtime proxy of Pakistan. These were the groups that forged a coalition with al Qaeda in Pakistan in 2003. Afghan sympathizers were bringing the bombers into Afghanistan, and providing them with safe houses, logistics, and vests and cars primed with explosives.

In Kabul in September 2006, Afghan intelligence operatives caught another suspect, Daoud Shah, a third-generation Afghan immigrant to Pakistan who was part of a suicide cell planning bombings.[2] Daoud Shah was a thin twenty-one-year-old with a black prayer cap and scraggly beard. His father and grandfather were economic migrants from Paktia who struggled to make a living as cloth dealers in Karachi. His father sent his sons to the neighborhood madrassa when they moved there in the 1990s. Daoud Shah entered the madrassa at the age of ten and graduated as a Hafiz, one who has memorized the Koran. He returned to live with his family in a rough tenement in Karachi and earned money selling popcorn from a street cart. But he and his brother kept their ties with the madrassa, and they drifted into Islamist extremism under the influence of their teacher, Maulavi Abdul Shakoor Khairpuri. The elder brother, Zaher Shah, became a member of the militant Pakistani group Jaish-e-Mohammad. He left Pakistan to fight alongside the Taliban in Afghanistan in the 1990s, and was captured and imprisoned by the Northern Alliance.[3]

Daoud Shah underwent weapons training when he was only fifteen years old in a Harakat-ul-Mujahideen camp near Mansehra in Pakistan in 2000, and briefly visited Afghanistan with the Taliban in Kunar province. He went back to his popcorn cart after 9/11 as the militant groups laid low. He married and had two children, and was living at home in Karachi. Then, in 2006, he had a falling-out with his father who yelled at him to find a proper job. He took off soon after for Afghanistan on a suicide mission. His old teacher from the madrassa set it up, giving him a letter for a contact in Kabul and promising to pay his family $1,400 if he was successful. He set off with three others. They traveled by bus via Quetta to Kabul. At the bus stop in Kabul, a man handed them a sack with four suicide vests inside. Soon after that Daoud Shah was detained by intelligence agents patrolling the bus station. One of his companions slipped away and blew himself up outside the Interior Ministry, killing twelve people and wounding forty-two.

Gulbuddin Hekmatyar, the Afghan mujahideen leader who opposed the American intervention in Afghanistan, also organized a group of suicide bombers in 2006. The operation was traced by Afghan intelligence agents to a Hesbe-Islami group in Shamshatu refugee camp, on the edge of the city of Peshawar in northwest Pakistan. Hekmatyar had always been close to Pakistani intelligence and had controlled the Shamshatu camp through his party since the 1980s. Afghan intelligence managed to follow the movements of the bombing cell in 2006, when an informant living in Shamshatu tipped them off and helped thwart at least two suicide bombings and arrest seventeen people. The Afghans listened on the detainees' cell phones to telephone calls from the organizers in Pakistan, who kept calling to urge the cell members into action and demanding why the bombings were not being carried out. NATO officials pressured the Afghans to share their information, but NATO then passed it to the ISI in Pakistan, naively expecting that the police would round up the Peshawar end of the bombing group. The Pakistanis made no move.

Instead, the informant who helped to unlock the entire cell was seized and killed. His body, cut up into eight pieces, was dumped in a black refuse bag in the refugee camp. Afghan intelligence officials accused the ISI of tipping off Hekmatyar's people. "How come Hekmatyar runs bombing cells from the Shamshatu camp?" asked an Afghan intelligence official bitterly. "We strongly think the ISI leaked the information to him."[4]

Taliban spokesmen, who were by now fielding scores of calls from journalists every day, readily claimed responsibility for the suicide bombings. Each time they insisted that the bombers were Afghan, and often gave their names and places of origin. It was propaganda, not always true. We started to hear of memorial ceremonies being held for the "martyred" bombers back home in Pakistan. It was evident too that the organization, recruitment, indoctrination, and funding of the bombers was being done by Pakistan's militant groups.

One Pakistani, who gave his name as Mohammad Sohail, was caught in southern Afghanistan back in 2004 and held at the National Directorate of Security jail in Kabul. He was seventeen, a Pashtun from the Swat Valley in northwestern Pakistan, who grew up in Karachi. He said he had joined up for jihad at his local mosque and had undergone a one-month weapons and explosives training in a camp in Mansehra in northwestern Pakistan, with the group Jamiat-ul-Ansar, a front for the banned organization Harakat-ul-Mujahideen. The leader of the group, Fazlur Rehman Khalil, a notorious militant leader and supposedly a wanted man in Pakistan, gave a speech at Sohail's mosque and personally selected the men to be sent to Afghanistan. "He decides where everyone goes," Sohail said. "He told us: 'Go and fight the Americans.'"

Suicide bombing, unknown in Afghanistan before 2001, seems to have been introduced by al Qaeda, but in the years after, it became a powerful weapon of Pakistan's most extreme militant groups. The first suicide bombing in Afghanistan was the one conducted by two Tunisian members of al Qaeda, masquerading as journalists, who assassinated Ahmed Shah Massoud on September 9, 2001. There were other signs of al Qaeda's involvement in suicide bombings in the years that followed. Afghan intelligence caught an Iraqi with a suicide vest in Kabul in 2002, and a Yemeni man blew himself up in an attack outside an Afghan Army training base in 2005.

The longtime Pakistani trainer and mentor of the mujahideen, Colonel Imam, told me that some of the Arab fighters had wanted to use suicide bombers against the Soviet Army in the 1980s, but that the ISI and the Afghan mujahideen leaders rejected the idea since they thought it would damage the cause with the Afghan people. Pakistan seemed to have dropped that restraint in the ensuing years.

For their part, of course, Pakistani officials denied all knowledge of the suicide bombing networks in Pakistan and dismissed the idea that the attacks were emanating from their country or that they were part of government policy. Yet the Pakistani militant groups that were conducting the first suicide bombings, Harakat-ul-Mujahideen, Jaish-e-Mohammad, and Hesbe-Islami, were organizations that Pakistan's ISI had created and sponsored for years. They were among those that Musharraf had told U.S. ambassador Wendy Chamberlain and Talat Masood that he would not dismantle.[5] Musharraf instead paid off their leaders to go quiet for several years and wait out the U.S. intervention in Afghanistan.[6]

The Afghan Taliban were divided in their support for the tactic of suicide bombing. Mullah Dadullah embraced it, appearing on video with bombers as they made their last vows of faith. Other members of the movement indicated the violence was hurting their cause. Even Hekmatyar tempered his involvement after that first cell, possibly because of the revulsion among the Afghan population.

The Pakistan government did little to investigate the suicide bombing networks organizing in Pakistan. Western officials found that their requests for cooperation were always dismissed. They complained that whenever they asked Pakistani military and ISI officials to arrest members of the Taliban or other figures suspected of orchestrating the attacks, the Pakistanis stonewalled them. A former Western diplomat described the impasse to me. "We would go to them and say: 'We are worried about the Quetta shura,' and they would say: 'How do you spell that?' So we would say, 'Well Quetta, and shura,' and then they would say: 'Could you give us the names and addresses of the people involved?' We were not going to do that, give them our sources." Another frustrated diplomat complained that they would pass on detailed information of the location of a senior Taliban figure in Quetta, down to the street number and color of the gate. "The Pakistanis would come back saying: 'The gate was blue, not green, so we did not go inside.'"

The evidence was piling up, though. There were 119 suicide attacks in 2006, and others that were thwarted. They were not militarily effective, but they were successful at driving a wedge between the people and the government, a United Nations report concluded. The aim was to reinforce the Taliban offensive to retake southern Afghanistan by undermining popular morale, and to turn the Afghan people against the government and Western forces, who were failing to protect them. The plan coincided with that of Pakistan's military, which was to give NATO forces a bloody nose so that they did not linger in Afghanistan.

December 2006. The trail took me back to Quetta. I flew in from Islamabad and met up with a local reporter and photographer. We set out first for Pishin, a farming district that runs to the border with Afghanistan. The population is predominantly Pashtun, and virtually every village in the area had lost sons in the fighting in Afghanistan that year. The two adjoining districts, Qilla Abdullah and Qilla Saifullah, were the same. The landscape is not unlike that of southern Afghanistan — arid, with a narrow strip of irrigated fields, orchards, and mud-walled houses along the valley floor beneath stark, brown mountains.

But this was evidently Pakistan. The black and white striped flag of Jamiat Ulema-e-Islam (JUI-F), the Deobandi religious party of Maulana Fazlur Rehman, flew above the mosques and houses in every village. There were huge brick-and-cement madrassa compounds, incongruous among the small farming homesteads, funded by Arab donors from the Persian Gulf. Someone had painted "Long Live Fazlur Rehman" in large white script across the hillside outside one village. Rehman, a Pashtun from Dera Ismail Khan on the edge of the tribal areas, was one of the most prominent religious political leaders in Pakistan, as his father, Maulana Mufti Mahmoud, had been before him. His party, JUI-F, held seats in parliament, and had been a close coalition partner to Benazir Bhutto in the 1990s. It had also been a strong supporter of the Taliban.

It was from Fazlur Rehman's madrassas that so many students joined to support the Taliban in their grab for power in 1994. Although Rehman had not supported Pakistan's military regimes, he nevertheless came to work closely with the Pakistani intelligence agency in its covert program to supply and train recruits to fight jihad in Afghanistan and in support of the Taliban. He did not stop that support after 9/11.

In Pishin, we found families whose sons had been drawn away to war without their knowledge, and who were grappling with the news that their sons had blown themselves up in Afghanistan. They were shocked at the concept of suicide bombing, and they struggled to explain who had induced their sons to do such a thing. Their loss was compounded by the fact that they had no bodies over which to grieve. No remains of suicide bombers were returned to their families. They were buried in unmarked graves. Some families were not even sure whether to believe news of their sons' deaths, relayed in anonymous phone calls or secondhand, through someone in the community. Most troubling of all, the relatives were scared: scared to talk about their sons' deaths, scared to say who had recruited them.

As we knocked on doors and asked questions, I realized the fear was above all of the Pakistani intelligence service, the ISI. Within a day of landing in Quetta, we were being followed by an intelligence agent on a motorbike, and we noticed that everyone we interviewed was visited afterward by men from the intelligence agency. Most families only spoke to us on condition that we not publish their names.

One mother in Quetta did not dare to open the gate since she was alone. She did confirm through a chink in the door that her son had died a martyr's death in Afghanistan. The next day when we returned, she begged us to leave and said men from the intelligence agencies had visited her and warned her not to talk to us. We quietly left.

A widow in Pishin was too distraught at the loss of her twenty-one-year-old son to meet us, members of her family said. He was her favorite son, dutiful and religious, and she had dreamed of his becoming a preacher. A few months earlier, her son had been studying at a madrassa in Karachi when he told his family he was leaving with a group of friends to go to the annual convention of the Islamic proselytizing group, Tablighi Jamaat. In fact, the group went to Afghanistan. Two weeks later, toward the end of September, the student blew himself up. The others in the group reportedly followed suit. News of their deaths trickled back to their village in Pishin, and neighbors came and told the bomber's widowed mother. Others visited with confusing stories that the group had been killed by anti-Taliban forces. Male relatives went to the madrassa in Karachi to try to find out more, but the clerics were unhelpful and said they had no knowledge of what the group had been doing. The family was too scared to go to Afghanistan or inquire further, the dead man's brother said. "We don't want to get ourselves killed."

With each suicide bomber's story, a pattern of covert recruitment and training emerged. The madrassas were the starting point. Someone there, a mullah or an outsider, drew selected students away on training courses, with the compliance of the clerics running the institutions. It was when the students left for extra study, or training in a camp, that they were led off on a path of extreme militancy. A former madrassa student told me there were teachers who were sympathetic to the militant organizations, and even connected to al Qaeda, in every madrassa. They acted as talent spotters, singling out potential students for jihad training and suicide bombing.[7] A former police official told me the same. "There are vacations in madrassas and students can go home, or go on a specific course, or go and have a look at jihad," he told me. "The militant organizations come and take them off." Some teachers were sympathetic and would pick out students and make the connections, and some students would make their own way and catch a bus to the tribal areas, he said.[8] Both informants asked that their names not be published for fear of repercussions from militant groups and the ISI for exposing the system.

A family in Quetta had lost their eighteen-year-old son in a suicide bombing. The family too asked that their names not be published. Their son had chosen to attend a madrassa in Punjab province for the last few years of his religious education, his father said. His friends were all Punjabis, and after graduating, he left home saying he was going to study with some of his friends. He was gone three months. He called occasionally to say he was moving to another place of study. The last place he mentioned was Chitral, a mountain resort in northwestern Pakistan near the Afghan border. Then a man called to say their son was fine and continuing his studies. He called again two days later to say he had gone on a mission of martyrdom. He told the family they could hold a *fateha,* a ceremony to pray for his departed soul. That was seven months ago. "We are still waiting and wish our brother would come back. Until we bury him with our hands we will not be comfortable," his younger brother said. He said that someone must have forced his brother into undertaking a suicide bombing, that he would never have committed such an act on his own. His father said someone had misled his son — he blamed the Pakistani government. The madrassa was the first point of contact, but he suggested there was a middleman who was paid to lure his son away. The government was protecting the people who were doing it, he added. "We are afraid of this government," he said. "These days people are getting money from somewhere and they are killing other people's children." He said he was scared the same people would come after his other son.

I came across several reports of middlemen, men from the militant organizations who scouted in the villages or madrassas for potential recruits. In one village near Peshawar, a man was even nicknamed "al Qaeda" because everyone knew he was earning money recruiting local boys and inducting them into jihadi training camps. Using a middleman was a convenient cover for any organization to maintain deniability, whether ISI or al Qaeda.

Another family in Pishin explained how their twenty-two-year-old son, Mohammad Daoud, had disappeared a year earlier. He had spent his entire education in madrassas, in Pishin, in Karachi, and latterly in Pashtunabad, a neighborhood of Quetta. Often during breaks he would travel with his teacher to other places to continue his studies. Daoud frequently spoke in support of jihad in Afghanistan; his father, Haji Noora Gul, who did not believe the war in Afghanistan was a genuine jihad, would try to dissuade him. "I used to tell him not to go on this line. He told me: 'Father, you don't understand what joy this is.'" Then, during Ramadan in 2005, someone told his family that Daoud had gone to Afghanistan for jihad. "We searched to know why he went away, and where he went," his father said. "In our search we went to many places and everyone said different things." At the madrassa in Pashtunabad, no one would tell him where his son was. "Even the madrassa people did not know." Noora Gul, a long-distance truck driver, did not mince his words: "I know the mullahs, but I did not see the mullahs doing this kind of thing. If I saw them doing that, I would cut their throats." He was more cautious in talking about the real culprits, the Pakistani militant organizations and their ISI controllers. "Behind the curtain of the madrassa, maybe there are other people who do this. Maybe there are some businessmen who take them." In this case, his son ended up with the Taliban commander Mullah Dadullah. Two weeks after Daoud's disappearance, they received news through a complicated chain of messages that he had died in Afghanistan. The message came via a contact in Hyderabad and from an Internet website, eventually reaching the family. Daoud had blown himself up in the Kandahar area, on the third or fourth day of Ramadan, just a day or two after they first heard that he had gone to Afghanistan. The family held a memorial ceremony for him. Not long after, they learned there was a DVD circulating of suicide bombers taking an oath before Mullah Dadullah. Neighbors told them Daoud was one of the bombers in the video. "Even his mother saw the DVD. He is covering his face in the video, and is preparing for suicide," Noora Gul said. "He says, 'I am fighting for God, and I am ready for this.'"

I asked Daoud's elder brother, Alla Dad, if it was Taliban or ISI who were responsible, and he said they were one and the same thing. "All Taliban are ISI Taliban," he said. "It is not possible to go to Afghanistan without the help of the ISI. Everyone says this."

With so much pain and grief evident, I kept asking people why the Pashtuns allowed so many of their sons to be sent to their deaths. Many families were religious and wanted their sons to be preachers and religious teachers since it was a respected profession, brought blessings on the family, and offered them a chance at a middle-class life in a city mosque. The madrassas also offered free board and lodging to students, which was attractive to all families. These families trusted and followed the mullahs and their teachings, even when it came to jihad. Yet responsibility to family was also of paramount importance to tribal Pashtuns. When I pressed one Pashtun reporter in Quetta about why

Pashtuns were letting their sons be used, he told me there were signs of unhappiness. He knew some Pashtun elders from a village in Pishin near the border with Afghanistan who had come to Quetta and paid a call on the head of the ISI in Quetta some months earlier. They asked for him to return their sons, who had been gone for three months' "training." The elders had decided the village had lost too many sons to the jihad in Afghanistan, and they did not want to lose any more. They were given short shrift. The ISI chief told them to go home and keep their mouths shut.[9]

We visited the neighborhood in Quetta called Pashtunabad, "town of the Pashtuns," a closely knit neighborhood of narrow alleys and high-walled houses inhabited largely by Afghan refugees. Over the years, they have spread up the hillside, building simple one-story houses from mud and straw, the same color as the brown mountain. The people are working class: laborers, bus drivers, and shopkeepers. Members of the Taliban also live here, in larger houses behind high walls, and often next to the mosques and madrassas that they run.

Along the sloping Haji Ghabi Road stands a madrassa, the Jamiya Darul Ulum Islamia. The small, untidy entrance on the street conceals the size of the establishment. Inside, a brick and cement building three stories high surrounds a courtyard with classrooms for 280 students from the neighborhood. At least three of the suicide bombers we were tracing had been students at this madrassa, and there were reports of more. The place was known as a local headquarters of jihadi activity. Senior figures from Pakistani religious parties and provincial government officials were frequent visitors. Taliban would also visit under cover of darkness in fleets of SUVs, including Mullah Dadullah, who called on several madrassas in late 2006. The men running the madrassa were Afghans but naturalized Pakistanis. The head of the madrassa was Maulavi Jan Mohammad. His brother, Mullah Wali Jan, had served as a governor in the Taliban government, and was detained soon after 9/11 by Pakistani authorities and transferred to the Guantánamo Bay detention camp for a period. He lived in a house on the same road as the madrassa. We requested an interview and were told that a female journalist would not be permitted inside. So I passed some questions to the Pakistani reporter with me, and he and the photographer went in.

One of the students from this madrassa was Abdul Sattar, the son of a packer at the fruit market, who lived on the same street as the seminary. It was known in the neighborhood that he had joined up to fight in Afghanistan. A Pakistani neighbor ran into him in a shop near his home one day and asked him how the jihad was going. "It will not stop, this will continue until the day of judgment," he had exclaimed. A few months later, he died in a suicide bombing in Panjwayi bazaar in August 2006, a particularly devastating attack that did not touch any military or government personnel but killed twenty-one civilians, among them several children. Abdul Sattar's family held a *fateha* ceremony for him at their home that was attended by many in the neighborhood and a number of local politicians and religious leaders, including clerics from the madrassa.

My Pakistani colleague did manage to speak to the deputy head of the madrassa, Qari Mohammad Ibrahim, standing in the courtyard. He was curt in his replies. He denied there was any militant or physical training at the madrassa — only "oral" education — or any forced recruitment for jihad. "We are educating the students in the Koran and in the Koran it is written that it is every Muslim's obligation to fight jihad," he said. "All we are telling them is what is in the Koran. Then it is up to them to go to jihad. We don't send them by force." He ended the conversation. Classes were breaking up, and I could hear a clamor rising as students burst out of their rooms. Boys poured out of the gates onto the street. They looked thin, even spindly, in flapping clothes, wearing prayer caps and turbans, but they were cheerful and energetic. They darted off on their bikes or in groups on foot, chasing each other down the street.

The journalist and photographer joined me on the street outside. They told me a large banner was painted across the wall of the inner courtyard praising both its political patron Fazlur Rehman and the Taliban leader Mullah Omar.

Here was the nexus of Pakistani support for the Taliban, the source of the Taliban resurgence that President Karzai and other Afghan leaders had long been warning about. In this nondescript madrassa, in a poor neighborhood of Quetta, one of hundreds throughout the border region, the Taliban and Pakistan's religious parties were working together to raise an army of militants. "The madrassas are a cover, a camouflage," a Pashtun legislator from the area told me. Behind the curtain, hidden in the shadows, lurked the ISI.

Confirming the links between the ISI and the religious parties and Taliban was always difficult, especially when the families involved, journalists, police, and even the Taliban themselves were scared to talk for fear of retribution from the ISI. This was a covert program and designed to be deniable, as one Western diplomat told me. Western officials began to talk of the "S" Directorate of the ISI, which was responsible for Pakistan's covert programs outside the country, namely the proxy operations. One department handled Kashmir, one Afghanistan, and another the Sikhs in India, the former Western diplomat told me. "It is truly deniable. They do not use serving officers," he said.[10] Retired army officers and special forces commandos tend to work for the "S" wing. They are the handlers of the Taliban who meet with the militant leaders and commanders. These are the men who go into the madrassas, meet with operational commanders, and coordinate support for Taliban offensives. They provide the Taliban with fuel, ammunition, and other logistical support, and they hold strategy meetings with the Taliban to discuss when to increase or ease up on operations. The headquarters of the "S" Directorate is in Camp Hamza, the ISI compound in Rawalpindi.

The United States only began watching the links between the ISI and the Taliban in 2007 and 2008. Before that, the CIA had been focused purely on al Qaeda. The United States was tied to Pakistan as an ally in the war on terror, and U.S. officials concentrated on that collaboration. "When you are running a joint project with another country you don't spy on them," the former Western diplomat said. That changed when the National Security Agency began a program of worldwide electronic surveillance from 2007, however, and Pakistan became one of its particular targets.

Despite the signals, at the U.S. State Department, support for the relationship with Pakistan became a mantra. Pakistan complained vehemently about criticism in the press, and American diplomats and administration officials listened. The Bush administration for years praised Pakistan as a stalwart ally in the fight against terror, and never publicly questioned the wisdom or legality of the Pakistani military's role in supporting the Taliban insurgency. The most Western officials asked of Pakistan was to do more to prevent cross-border infiltration by militants, which Pakistan easily deflected by saying it had neither the resources nor the military capacity to do better.

The former Western diplomat complained that nitpicking government officials, whom he described as "stamp collectors," always asked for proof of Pakistan's support for the Taliban, which was difficult to produce. "We were too much like stamp collectors. We should have taken as read that they were playing a dual role," the diplomat said. "We should have not allowed the stamp collectors to keep sending us back for more proof. We should have said: 'They are doing it, they are supporting the Taliban. So what is the policy?'"

For those living in Quetta, journalists, politicians, and activists who saw Taliban leaders coming and going, visiting ISI offices and madrassas, there was no doubt about the close collaboration between the ISI and the Taliban. "The Taliban cannot work for a single day without our patronage, cooperation, and support," Mahmood Khan Achakzai, the Pashtun nationalist leader in Quetta and a longtime opponent of the government's support of Islamists, told me during my visit. "They are being protected here, equipped, and trained here," he went on. Two intelligence departments, the ISI and the Military Intelligence, were organizing the assistance to the Taliban, he said. When I asked how he knew that, he replied, "How do I know you are in this room?"

Even members of the Taliban complained of the pressures of the ISI. An Afghan reporter tracked down for me a former Taliban commander in a poor neighborhood on the outskirts of Quetta. The commander had fled Afghanistan after police detained him there. In Pakistan, he was also arrested. But far from opposing his connection to the Taliban, the ISI agents threatened him with prison unless he returned to Afghanistan to fight U.S. forces. He went into hiding and was eking out a living selling religious amulets. "This is my life now. If I look up, there is a tiger that will eat me. If I look down, there is a river," he said.

Over the years a number of senior Taliban members were detained by the Pakistani authorities in such circumstances, always under secret conditions, with no public judicial procedure and no transparency, which has raised intense suspicions on all sides. The detentions ostensibly complied with U.S. and Afghan requests for Pakistan to crack down on Taliban cross-border activities, but Pakistan never cooperated in handing over the Taliban suspects to the Afghan government or American forces. The detentions were clearly part of a Pakistani program of internal control of the Taliban.

Some, such as the Taliban defense minister Mullah Obaidullah, who was held by the Pakistanis for years without trial and eventually died in custody in 2012, were thought to be detained to prevent them having contacts with the Karzai government. Another younger Taliban commander, Mullah Yassar, a former Sayyaf commander from the eastern provinces, also died in Pakistani custody.[11]

Pakistan's determination to control the Taliban was exposed as U.S. and Afghan efforts to reach out to the Taliban increased from 2009 onward. Pakistan detained several dozen Taliban members that the Karzai government was trying to talk to. Mullah Abdul Ghani Baradar, the Taliban operations chief who was often described as Mullah Omar's second-in-command, was the most prominent. He was seized in early 2010 in a joint U.S.-Pakistan operation. Mullah Baradar had become the man to go to in the Taliban for a growing number of international organizations, from the International Committee of the Red Cross and the United Nations, to other aid groups and Afghan government officials. It was his extensive contacts with Ahmed Wali Karzai, the president's half-brother and representative in southern Afghanistan, that Pakistan most distrusted.

Baradar was a member of the Populzai tribe, the same as the Karzais, and although he seemed to have used Ahmed Wali Karzai and given little in return, the suspicion that he was making his own deals with the Karzai government would have angered Mullah Omar and the ISI. Afghan and UN officials, including Kai Eide, the head of the UN Assistance Mission in Afghanistan at the time, accused Pakistan of coordinating Baradar's detention to prevent peace negotiations. Despite public denials, Pakistani officials admitted to my *New York Times* colleague Pir Zubair Shah months later that they had acted in order to stop Baradar's direct talks with Kabul. Despite repeated requests from the Afghan and U.S. governments, Pakistan restricted access to Mullah Baradar and for years refused to hand him over or allow him to contribute toward negotiations. He was too valuable a player in the ISI's plan to dominate affairs in Afghanistan.

It was only toward the end of the decade that U.S. intelligence and military services began to examine more closely Pakistan's relationship with its militant proxies. As U.S. forces began to monitor the links and level of contacts, and to intercept phone conversations, they came to realize that Pakistan was pulling the strings of the Taliban and actually involved in promoting terrorist attacks.

"We always sensed that they were using the relationship as leverage," a retired senior U.S. counterterrorism official told me. The Taliban were used as leverage against Afghanistan, and the Pakistani militant groups as leverage against India. "Part of it was to keep the situation in Afghanistan off-balance so that Pakistan could play a larger role in deciding what happened ultimately in that part of the world," the official said. "It is something that I came to understand that their approach was not to rely on diplomacy or engagement as the key way to resolve issues. Their approach was to operate using chaos as a principal weapon to try to get things moving in their direction."[12]

9

Militancy Explodes in Pakistan

"We indoctrinated them and told them, 'You will go to heaven.'
You cannot turn it around so suddenly."

— *former Pakistani intelligence official*

2007. After eight years at the helm, President Pervez Musharraf was struggling to hold on to power. He faced legal challenges from the chief justice of the Supreme Court, Iftikhar Muhammad Chaudhry, and massive street demonstrations when he removed the judge from office. He faced political challenges too from Benazir Bhutto and Nawaz Sharif, who both returned from exile to huge rallies of their supporters ahead of the 2008 parliamentary elections. He was further weakened by silent resistance within the army to his long tenure at the top, and a more vociferous opposition from former army officers, including some of those who had helped him to power in the coup of 1999. At this moment of political upheaval, al Qaeda unleashed a deadly campaign of suicide bombings and subversive attacks that shook the country and the armed forces to the core.

One of the most calamitous events of 2007 began innocuously enough that spring. On a leafy street in the heart of the capital, Islamabad, just a stone's throw from the headquarters of Pakistan's Directorate for Inter-Services Intelligence, female madrassa students staged a sit-in at a children's public library adjoining their seminary. Dressed in full-length black burqas with only their eyes showing, the students came from the Jamia Hafsa, a girls' seminary attached to the Red Mosque, a large mosque and madrassa complex known for its jihadist leanings. They were protesting the demolition of several mosques that the city authorities said had been illegally constructed. As the world was to see, this was the opening act in an orchestrated plan. Male students armed with batons appeared to guard the perimeter of the library. The Red Mosque had staged similar protests before, and the government had avoided confrontation, fearing outrage if it used force against female religious students. This time would be different.

The Red Mosque stood at the center of Pakistan's support for jihad in Afghanistan and further afield. It was founded by a famed jihadi preacher, Maulana Abdullah Ghazi, who had enjoyed the patronage of military dictator General Zia-ul-Haq in the 1980s. It had supplied thousands of students over the years for Pakistan's religious establishments and militant groups. Ghazi had also claimed friendship with bin Laden. The preacher was assassinated in 1998, not long after visiting bin Laden in Afghanistan. Al Qaeda blamed the killing on the Pakistani government of the time.

Ghazi's sons inherited the complex and continued its expansion and extremist teachings. The elder son, Maulana Abdul Aziz, served as the chief cleric, delivering fiery Friday sermons in support of global jihad and the Taliban, excoriating Musharraf for his stance in the war on terror, and calling for the imposition of Islamic law in Pakistan. Aziz's wife, Umme Hassan, ran the girls' seminary in a similarly fanatical spirit. The younger brother, Abdul Rashid Ghazi, took over the administration of the mosque. Despite an earlier reputation as a non-religious, secularly educated bureaucrat, the younger Ghazi steadily adopted the same extremist rhetoric of his father and brother. He spoke of undergoing a conversion after meeting bin Laden. He adopted the trappings of jihad, wearing the pakul, the roll-brim wool hat of the Afghan mujahideen, or a checkered keffiyeh over white robes. He even acquired armed bodyguards, who would appear beside him wearing scarves across their faces and wielding Kalashnikovs. By 2007, he never left the Red Mosque compound for fear of arrest. He warned that ranks of suicide bombers would retaliate if the government moved against the students occupying the library.

With such leaders behind them, the students grew bolder. They began staging vigilante actions in the shops and streets around the mosque. They berated owners of music stores for selling movies and pop videos the students deemed immoral. They accused beauty salons of serving as brothels. They began inquiring about the inhabitants of houses in the neighborhood, which alarmed Western embassies that had diplomatic staff living nearby. The students were radical and obsessive. The female students appeared highly emotional, vowing to die rather than give up their protest.

The government's inaction only encouraged them. Male students disarmed and kidnapped two policemen after an altercation in May, forcing the government to send in a cabinet minister to negotiate their release. The following month, a group of female students made a midnight raid on a Chinese massage parlor and abducted several Chinese women, accusing them of running a brothel and taking them back to their seminary in a protest. The workers were released after twenty-four hours only after China made a stern protest to the Musharraf government.

Remonstrations from China, Pakistan's most important regional ally, pushed Musharraf to take action. Police and soldiers moved in to surround the mosque on July 3, with orders to try to prevent further vigilante raids from the students. Army rangers occupied a school across the street, and police cordoned off the mosque entrance with barbed wire. Immediately students rushed the police lines and clashes broke out. Among the students and burqa-clad women who carried sticks, armed fighters appeared for the first time. Their faces hidden behind scarves and gas masks, they carried rockets and assault rifles and took up sandbagged positions on the mosque walls. The mosque loudspeakers told the students that this was the time for bravery. A female student took over the microphone. "Allah, where is your help?" she asked in a quavering voice. "Destroy the enemies. Tear their hearts apart. Throw fireballs on them."[1]

The students set a government building across the street ablaze, and torched cars in its parking lot. An army ranger was shot by madrassa students in a struggle to seize his weapon. In hours of clashes, five people were killed, and thirty-seven wounded.

So began an extraordinary siege in the heart of Pakistan's normally placid capital. Set beneath the Margalla Hills, Islamabad is a green and tranquil home for civil servants and diplomats, but for several days in July 2007, it resounded with gunfire and explosions. Crowds of worried parents arrived from all over the country to try to retrieve their children from the madrassa as the government set up a tight cordon around the complex and enforced a curfew. Over one thousand students filed out of the mosque complex over the next days, but at least one hundred refused to come out, including a group of women and girls. One father from Kashmir had to order his two teenage daughters to leave the complex. The Red Mosque leaders had tried to make them stay. "They said if the women and others die, the people will take their side," he told me. I realized the militant leaders wanted to spark some kind of revolution.

I spoke to a farmer who had traveled from southern Punjab to collect his young daughters. He trembled, uncomprehending, as angry residents lambasted him for supporting militant jihadists and bringing war to their neighborhood. I stopped a woman in full black niqab, only her eyes showing, who emerged from the mosque to ask her about the conditions inside. She demurred, then raised her hand to her face, and I realized it was a male hand. He was in female disguise to evade the police. He walked away with a female relative down a side street and disappeared from view. The chief imam, Abdul Aziz, was caught by police a few days later, also trying to escape in a woman's burqa and was paraded before the television cameras. His wife remained behind with a number of female students. Ghazi stayed to the end, with his elderly mother. He negotiated with government officials by phone, breaking off repeatedly to talk to television stations.

The government insisted it was showing restraint, but the presence of police, rangers, and special forces units kept the tension high.

Musharraf's most senior officials joined a procession of intermediaries to try to negotiate an end to the standoff. The government even brought in the highest religious cleric from Saudi Arabia, the imam of the Holy Mosque in Mecca, Sheikh Abdul Rehman al-Sudais, to appeal to the protestors. They remained intractable.

On the sixth day of the siege, a sniper inside the mosque killed the commander of the special forces unit, a colonel. Ministers made one last effort at negotiations, talking through the night to Ghazi, even promising him free passage to his home village. They gave up on the morning of the eighth day. As they drove out, explosions rent the dawn air. An operation to storm the compound was underway.

It was a ferocious battle. Commandos from Pakistan's elite Special Services Group (SSG) rappelled from helicopters into the mosque and met raking gunfire from militant machine-gun positions inside the compound. Five commandos were cut down before they reached the ground. Perched in the mosque's minarets and throughout the seventy-five rooms of the madrassa, the militants fought for ten hours. They hurled grenades from bunkers and basements, and suicide bombers thew themselves at their attackers. The commandos found the female students hiding in bricked-up spaces under the stairs and led fifty women and girls, including Umme Hassan, out to safety. Ghazi retreated to an underground basement in the women's madrassa with his mother. They both died there as the last surviving fighters battled around them.

Over one hundred people were killed in the seige, including ten special forces commandos. Ninety-three bodies were retrieved from the mosque complex, most of them militants, among them eleven foreign fighters. The Ghazi brothers had turned their mosque into an arsenal rather than a place of worship, with weapons, mines, and suicide vests, and had sheltered scores of trained fighters among their young students.

There is some evidence that al Qaeda had orchestrated the Red Mosque clash in order to precipitate a confrontation with the Pakistani army and start a war against the Pakistani state. Besides the Ghazi brothers' own links to bin Laden, there were people inside the

Red Mosque who were connected to al Qaeda in the tribal areas. One of the most radical people in the Red Mosque was Ghazi's secretary, Abdul Qayuum, seen brandishing a pistol in television footage. He was a disciple of Sheikh Isa, an Egyptian co-conspirator in the 1981 assassination of President Anwar Sadat. Isa had been imprisoned in Egypt with al Qaeda's deputy leader, Ayman al Zawahiri. Along with Zawahiri, Isa aimed to spark a revolt in Pakistan that would allow jihadis to take control of key institutions and use Pakistan to project their dream of global jihad against the West.

Zawahiri was quick to condemn the government's raid of the mosque. He released a video statement criticizing "the criminal aggression carried out by Musharraf, his army and his security organs — the Crusaders' hunting dogs — against the Red Mosque in Islamabad," and calling for retaliation on the Pakistani army.[2] Even bin Laden, who had been more muted in his criticism of Pakistan, added his call for revenge for the Red Mosque martyrs in an audio message released in September.

The aftermath of the Red Mosque siege played out in al Qaeda's favor and was exploited ruthlessly by the organization. Rumors spread that the government had killed far more than the official death toll, and that one thousand students, or even several thousand, had died and been buried on top of each other to conceal the true number. On her release from jail, Umme Hassan claimed that three hundred female students had died, which was blatantly untrue. There were no victims' families or lists of names to bolster her claims, and human rights groups never found proof that the government figures were inaccurate. Yet the Red Mosque battle became a major rallying cry for the religious parties and militant Islamists, and handed them a powerful propaganda tool. It spawned a plethora of tapes, videos, and speeches that circulated the country. Musharraf's use of force against the mosque cost his supporters dearly at the polls in 2008.

The ISI played a strangely ineffective role, failing to prevent the threat from the Red Mosque despite its long relationship with the mosque and its leaders. The ISI had two informers inside the Mosque complex during the siege, and had accurate intelligence on the number of armed militants inside, but does not seem to have used its influence on the Ghazi brothers.[3] In a cabinet meeting after the siege, ministers questioned a senior ISI official about the intelligence service's failure to prevent the militant action in the city. "Who I meet in the evening and what I discuss is on your desk the next morning," one minister told the general. "How come you did not know what was happening a hundred meters from the ISI headquarters?" The general sat in silence as ministers thumped their desks in a gesture of agreement. "One hundred percent they knew what was happening," a former cabinet minister who attended the meeting told me. The ISI could have prevented militants from gathering in the city but had allowed them to do what they wanted out of sympathy for the Ghazi brothers and the militants, he said. "The state is not as incompetent as people believe."[4]

The Pakistani military faced an immediate and vicious backlash from militants. One group struck a convoy of soldiers in the North West Frontier province even as the special forces were still storming the Red Mosque. Another group blew up a military convoy on July 17 in North Waziristan killing twenty-four soldiers. Baitullah Mehsud, the militant leader in South Waziristan, announced he was breaking his truce with the government. In August, he captured and disarmed a convoy of 250 government soldiers passing through his district in a show of power that shamed the army. In September, he announced the formation of a movement called Teherik-i-Taliban Pakistan, joining all the main militant groups across the northwestern region into the Pakistani Taliban. As Ghazi had promised, and as bin Laden and Zawahiri urged people to rise up and avenge the deaths of the faithful, a wave of suicide bombings engulfed the country, striking at government, military, and civilian targets.

On September 13, a suicide bomber targeted the SSG, Pakistan's elite, American-trained special forces, the very commandos who had been used to storm the Red Mosque. The bomber managed to infiltrate the SSG base at Tarbela, fifty miles from Islamabad, and blew himself up in the canteen, killing twenty-two commandos and wounding forty others. The bombings were hitting right at the heart of the army and intelligence services. In November, a bomber attacked guards at the army's General Command Headquarters in Rawalpindi, and another threw himself at a staff bus entering Hamza Camp, the ISI's headquarters in the army town, killing at least twenty-four intelligence workers. The militants were attacking their own masters.

After years of nurturing jihadists to fight its proxy wars, Pakistan was experiencing the ultimate blowback. Its protégés had turned on their creators. "We could not control them," a former senior intelligence official told a colleague and me six months after the Red Mosque siege. "We indoctrinated them and told them, 'You will go to heaven.' You cannot turn it around so suddenly."[5]

Successive Pakistani governments, both military and civilian, had long used a policy of divide and rule over the country's many factions, political, religious, and militant. As the former leader of Jamaat-e-Islami, Qazi Hussain Ahmad, told me, the ISI was always the government's tool of choice, using it to support groups with money, political gerrymandering, and protection from justice. This is the government that famously formed seven different Afghan mujahideen parties to fight the Soviet Union, so that none dominated the resistance. The ISI sometimes encouraged them to fight each other for territory, and assassinate rival commanders to prevent any one group from growing too strong and independent. This is the government that then formed a plethora of Pakistani militant groups, and managed those who became too troublesome by creating splinter groups, detaining leaders, and even assassinating them. The militant groups themselves complain that many of their members have been killed in deadly ambushes by the police. The government of Nawaz Sharif for example targeted sectarian leaders who grew too disruptive in the late 1990s.[6]

Post-9/11, the Musharraf government paid off the leaders of the main militant groups to keep them loyal, asking them to go quiet. Musharraf formally banned most of the groups linked with al Qaeda or the Kashmir insurgency in 2002, but they were allowed to re-form under new names and establish humanitarian and educational wings that could

Taliban prisoners in Shiberghan prison, in northern Afghanistan, after the mass surrender at Kunduz, December 2001. Among them were foreign fighters and survivors of the battle of Qala-i-Janghi. Alan Chin for the *New York Times*

Some of the prisoners inside Shiberghan. The two men wearing embroidered caps appear to be Pashtuns from southern Afghanistan. Alan Chin for the *New York Times*

Village elders in Baghran, northern Helmand province, who were rounded up and handcuffed during a raid on their homes by American troops in February 2003. "We hate them for this," one told us. "In our culture, we hate it when someone enters our house without our permission."
Hiromi Yasui

Shepherds eke out a living with their herds in the most remote corners of Afghanistan. We met these men on a road in Baghran as airstrikes shattered the mountain stillness. During the raid a few days earlier, American jets had bombed a mountain ridge, killing a shepherd and wounding six villagers. Hiromi Yasui

Asaldin, whose son Dilawar died in U.S. military custody at Bagram Airbase in December 2002. Asaldin told his family not to seek revenge against the Americans. "I am angry with them, but this was the will of God," he said. "God is great, and God will punish them." At his home in Yakubi, Khost province, May 2005. Keith Bedford

Bibi Gul receiving government compensation for the loss of her husband and two children when their village, Granai, in western Afghanistan, was bombed by U.S. planes in May 2009. The bombing of Granai, eight years into the war, caused the highest civilian death toll of any single incident, 147 dead. Joao Silva for the *New York Times*

Haji Arbab Daulat Khan inside a classroom that was destroyed during a U.S.-led operation in April 2007 in the village of Parmakan, in western Afghanistan. After meeting resistance in the village, U.S. troops called in airstrikes that night and killed fifty-seven civilians, nearly half of them women and children. Joao Silva for the *New York Times*

Haji Mir Gul seeks treatment at a British army post in Sangin, in southern Afghanistan, for his two-year-old grandson, Bashir Ahmad, wounded in the abdomen by an American airstrike in May 2007. Bashir had been treated in an Afghan hospital, but two months later his health was deteriorating. Joao Silva for the *New York Times*

A policeman carries a wounded colleague from the scene of a suicide bombing at Kandahar police station in February 2006. We narrowly missed the bomber, who blew himself up at the gate, killing thirteen people. A wave of suicide bombers hit Kandahar in 2006, most of them recruited and dispatched from Pakistan. Scott Eells

Hamid Karzai, while interim leader in 2002, meets with tribal elders from the province of Paktia to resolve a dispute between two rival Pashtun clans. A clever negotiator of tribal politics, Karzai nevertheless lost the support of many of his fellow Pashtuns for failing to secure the country. Kate Brooks

Members of the Taliban settled in Pashtunabad, an ethnic Pashtun neighborhood of Quetta, Pakistan, after escaping Afghanistan in 2001. They run madrassas and recruit Pakistani and Afghan boys from the neighborhood to fight in Afghanistan. December 2006.

Students at the Jamia Darul Ulum Islamia, a madrassa run by former Taliban officials in Pashtunabad. Several former students conducted suicide bomb attacks in Afghanistan in 2006. A sign in the courtyard salutes the Taliban leader Mullah Omar and the Pakistani politician Fazlur Rehman, longtime partners with the ISI in running the Taliban movement.

Afghan Taliban supporters, recognizable by their faces and clothes, were a common sight in Quetta by 2006. The town in southwestern Pakistan, near the Afghan border, became the base of the Taliban leadership for the length of the war.

American soldiers with the Psychological Warfare unit speak through an interpreter to a farmer in Khan Neshin in Helmand province, southern Afghanistan, in August 2009. The job of counter-insurgency involved relentless patrolling to provide security and engage communities, but the cultural divide often remained insurmountable. Robert Nickelsberg/Getty Images

A soldier with the 82nd Airborne Division takes up a perimeter position in the mountains above Kandahar against Taliban fighters in the ravine below. The soldier had survived an IED attack on his vehicle two days earlier. Kate Brooks

The son of an Afghan security guard killed on a U.S.-Afghan outpost arrives for the funeral and collapses crying into the arms of an Afghan army soldier. His father, Nezamuddin, was killed in a Taliban mortar attack on Combat Outpost Lowell in Nuristan, northeastern Afghanistan, October 2008. Tyler Hicks for the *New York Times*

continue recruiting followers, running discreet training camps, and raising funds legally. "The ban was for domestic purposes. They were told to lie low but did not really," a former security official told me. Cross-border raids into Kashmir were largely curtailed, and Taliban and Kashmiri militants remember the years after 9/11 as a period of suppression and fear of arrests. Cross-border attacks into Afghanistan were allowed, but terrorist attacks on Western targets inside Pakistan were not acceptable. Those who ignored the rules were detained.

There were seeds of blowback sewn long before the Red Mosque siege. Some of the most dangerous opponents of the Pakistani state seem to have turned against the military after periods in custody of the military or the intelligence service in the years after 9/11. There are blood-curdling stories of the torture and harsh detention that goes on in underground cells in Pakistan at the hands of military and intelligence agencies. Human rights organizations have documented extensive cases of torture and dozens of incidences of people dying in custody. Doctors told me they had seen detainees unable to walk or speak after sleep deprivation, beatings, and the use of drugs, such as powerful laxatives, to debilitate them. Former detainees described being beaten, sodomized, strung up, and held under strobe lights for days on end, in extreme heat or cold. One former detainee, a Baluch rebel commander, described to me being held for hours, handcuffed, with his head encased in a leather hood, in a roasting hot cell that made his brain feel as if it were boiling. Afghans and Taliban militants have also complained of harsh treatment in ISI jails.

In one instance in 2009, General Ashfaq Parvez Kayani handled the militant blowback personally. By then he had been in the top military post, chief of army staff, for two years, having replaced Musharraf in October 2007 (Musharraf remained the president of Pakistan until August 2008). A group of ten militants stormed the General Command Headquarters of the army in Rawalpindi, the base of military power in Pakistan. They used the type of complex attack that was already familiar from attacks in Afghanistan: breaking through outer security with a suicide attack, they shot and blasted their way into the headquarters and stormed an office building, killing and seizing hostages as they went. Within minutes, they had seized over forty hostages, including several senior army and intelligence officers. They killed a brigadier general and several other officers. Led by a fighter called Dr. Usman, they were well armed and wore suicide jackets stuffed with explosives, and began a thirty-six-hour hostage siege. They demanded the release of a long list of Taliban and other militants held prisoner by the Pakistani authorities.

The army brought in one of its favorite mediators, Hafiz Tahir Ashrafi, a famous preacher and former jihadi who has since become a television personality with his own chat show. He is a colorful character of enormous girth and appetite, with a long beard and flowing white clothes. He arranged to meet me for an interview in a gym in Lahore, plopping himself down on a pink leather sofa in the café and dropping three smart phones on the glass coffee table.

Ashrafi cultivates a benign image, making public statements against sectarian attacks and trying to intervene in cases where people have been accused wrongly of blasphemy. Yet he has worked tirelessly to secure the release of militants from jail and remains a fervent supporter of jihad and the jihadi groups. He told me he had helped secure the release of seven hundred Pakistanis held in Afghanistan after the collapse of the Taliban in 2001, including some important militant commanders, who had successfully hidden their real identities from their captors. In 2007, he had been called in to help negotiate with the clerics at the Red Mosque.

Now, Ashrafi worked with senior military officers in night-long negotiations with Dr. Usman, the leader of the militants. They called in the heads of almost every banned militant group to intercede with the militants to release their hostages.[7] Thinking the militants were connected to the vicious sectarian group Sipa-e-Sahaba, the army sent a military plane to fetch its notoriously hard-line leader, Maulana Mohammad Ahmed Ludhianvi, to intercede. When Dr. Usman said he wanted the army to free men from another group, Lashkar-e-Jhangvi, the most dangerous of all, often described as the foot soldiers of al Qaeda, Kayani sprung the group's leader Malik Ishaq from a Lahore jail. Fifty years old, Ishaq was a Sunni extremist and the most notorious of murderers. He had been in jail since 1997, charged with forty-four cases of homicide, mostly for murdering Shiites. Kayani treated him like a valuable mediator. He sent his personal plane to fly Ishaq to Rawalpindi, and promised to free him in return for helping to release the hostages. Meanwhile, the drawn-out negotiations gave the army time to prepare a rescue. Before dawn, SSG operatives stormed the building and killed four of the five hostage-takers.

"We requested time to talk," Ashrafi told me. "We saved forty-two people." Usman nearly escaped by hiding in a false ceiling and was only caught after soldiers realized they had five suicide vests and only four bodies. The militants, however, had shown what they could do. They could kill and take hostages at will, and win at the negotiating table.[8] During their negotiations, the army chief asked Ishaq to "please stop the sectarian killings," but the Sunni extremist and longtime protégé answered, "We are your children, but we will not follow this." Kayani had no response. He remained silent.[9]

The most revealing example of Pakistan's loss of control of its militants came when a splinter Pakistani group captured Colonel Imam, the old ISI controller of the Taliban, in 2010. Now gray-bearded and officially retired, Colonel Imam had remained active in the years after 9/11, supporting the Taliban resurgence and touring Afghanistan. He denied visiting Afghanistan but over the years, I came across several credible sightings of him there, including once at Kabul airport and once in Uruzgan, where he seems to have been reengaging old Taliban supporters.

Colonel Imam traveled into Pakistan's tribal areas in March 2010 with another former ISI operative, Khalid Khawaja; a British-Pakistani journalist; and a local driver. They were detained by a formerly unknown group of militants who called themselves the Asian Tigers. The journalist and driver were released after months in captivity, probably after payment of a ransom, but Khawaja and Colonel Imam were killed, accused of being government and American spies. Despite his long association with generations of militants, and efforts by the ISI to win his release through the Taliban leaders Mullah Omar and Sira-juddin Haqqani, Colonel Imam was shot dead in January 2011. The head of the Pakistani Taliban at the time, Hakimullah Mehsud himself, oversaw his execution, which was filmed and distributed on DVDs. The Taliban movement was devouring its own.

Yet even as the militants were turning against their masters, rather than crush them, Pakistan's generals sought to use them and direct them toward other targets. They were quite literally playing with fire. Pakistan's first female prime minister, Benazir Bhutto, was preparing to fly home from ten years in exile in the fall of 2007. She had forged a deal with Musharraf that envisaged him resigning as army chief but staying on as a civilian president while she served as prime minister. Kayani, who helped negotiate the deal, would take over from Musharraf as army chief. Bhutto's party allowed Musharraf's election to another term as president, and he signed an order to drop all corruption cases against Bhutto and her close associates. Elections were set for early 2008.

Ahead of her return, Bhutto showed her mettle. She spoke out more than any other Pakistani politician about the dangers of militant extremism. She blamed foreign militants for annexing part of Pakistan's territory, and called for military operations into North and South Waziristan. She supported Musharraf's action against the militants in the Red Mosque, and she declared suicide bombing un-Islamic. She seemed to be challenging any suicide bomber that thought of targeting her. "I do not believe that any true Muslim will make an attack on me because Islam forbids attacks on women, and Muslims know that if they attack a woman they will burn in hell," she said in Dubai on the eve of her return. "Secondly, Islam forbids suicide bombing."[10] Religious leaders had been killed for making that sort of declaration in Afghanistan and Pakistan, and usually politicians avoided offering such overt challenges. She also promised greater cooperation with Afghanistan and the United States in combating terrorism, and even suggested in an interview that she would give American officials access to the man behind Pakistan's program of nuclear proliferation,

A. Q. Khan. Such promises would have alarmed many in the military establishment.

Bhutto was taking on two battles in returning to Pakistan, one against extremist Islamism, the other against the military dictatorship in Pakistan. Her opposition to the military went much deeper than the persona of General Musharraf. Bhutto's own father, Prime Minister Zulfiqar Ali Bhutto, had been overthrown and executed by General Zia-ul-Haq in 1979, and she had been imprisoned. In later years, she blamed the military for the murder of her two brothers, and Musharraf for the imprisonment of her husband, Asif Ali Zardari, on corruption charges. Many in the military despised the political class in Pakistan, in particular the socialist Pakistan People's Party and its leaders, the Bhutto family, whom they often criticized as feudalistic, corrupt, and careless of Pakistan's strategic interests.

Powerful figures including Ejaz Shah, the head of the domestic Intelligence Bureau, had voiced the opinion at a government meeting that her return would not be good for Pakistan.[11] Afghan President Karzai and his intelligence service had also warned Bhutto in the months before her return that it had learned of militant plots to have her killed. The Afghans told Bhutto that the Pakistani military knew of the plots but did not intend to do anything to prevent them. The Afghans had learned indirectly through informants that a meeting of the army corps commanders — the army chief, Musharraf, and his ten most powerful generals — had discussed a militant plot to have Bhutto killed. The generals had evidence of a planned wave of suicide attacks on high-level figures, not just Bhutto but also Prime Minister Shaukat Aziz and Interior Minister Aftab Ahmad Sherpao. "They knew there was going to be an attack against her," a senior Afghan government official told me. The army had decided not to let Bhutto back into power in Pakistan, he said. "They were disgusted at the idea of her coming back." Although Musharraf had agreed to Bhutto's return, he was in on the decision to let the militants remove her, according to the official. The information was circumstantial, but the Afghans thought the discussion at such a high-level meeting was so important that they sent word to Dubai to warn Bhutto. "Pakistan has no interest in seeing you alive," she was told by the government official. Karzai urged Bhutto to take extra precautions for her security.

That same month, September 2007, one of the ISI's most favored Pakistani militants, Qari Saifullah Akhtar, was released from three years of ISI protective custody. He was a close associate of bin Laden and Mullah Omar, and had been implicated in a coup attempt against Bhutto in 1995. "On a fine September morning of 2007, a car took him out of the safe house and dropped him near Islamabad motorway," according to a Pakistani intelligence source. One of the most dangerous militants, who was known to hate Bhutto, had just been let loose.

A few weeks later, on October 18, 2007, Bhutto flew into Karachi. I was one of a crowd of journalists traveling with her. She wore religious amulets on her arm and round her neck, and offered prayers as she stepped onto Pakistani soil. She was trusting in God. Hours later, as Bhutto processed in an open-topped bus through streets of flag-waving, chanting supporters, two huge bombs exploded close to her vehicle, tearing police vans, bodyguards, and party followers into shreds. Bhutto survived the blast, but 149 died, and some 400 were injured. The explosions were set off by two suicide bombers mingling in the center of the celebrations. The bombs were filled with ball bearings and spewed lethal shrapnel into the crowd. Each tiny ball was as deadly as a bullet, a senior Karachi policeman said afterward. One of his officers was slain by a single ball bearing in the head. Bhutto put Musharraf on notice after that attack. She accused people in his government and the militant leader Qari Saifullah Akhtar of being behind it. She told people that Musharraf had threatened her directly. She demanded better security. Karzai again urged Bhutto to take more precautions and asked his intelligence service to arrange for her an armored vehicle with jammers to block cell phone signals, often used to detonate bombs. They started working on it, but the Afghans did not have left-hand-drive vehicles for Pakistan nor time to train vehicle operators. Undaunted, Bhutto pressed on with a busy schedule of campaigning ahead of elections in January. She insisted on greeting waving crowds of supporters from an open-topped car.

Bhutto had ruffled Musharraf. The Supreme Court was also threatening him as it adjudicated on the legality of his election to the presidency. Musharraf made a last startling lunge to hold on to power, declaring martial law on November 3, suspending the constitution, and placing most of the Supreme Court justices under arrest. Yet his grip on power was unraveling. Despite their agreement, Bhutto began campaigning against Musharraf. The Bush administration made it clear it felt let down by Musharraf's dictatorial turn. The general was forced to allow his greatest enemy, Nawaz Sharif, whom Musharraf had ousted from power in 1999, to return from exile on November 25 for the election campaign. Under the combination of diplomatic pressure and growing protests in the streets, Musharraf resigned from the post of army chief on December 3. Without the army position, his power withered, and he was forced out of the presidency eight months later. General Kayani, the former ISI chief, was now the man in charge.

It would make no difference for Bhutto. A group of militants, including two teenage boys trained and primed to commit suicide bombings, arrived at the Haqqania madrassa in Akora Khattak in late December. The madrassa stands near the famous Moghul fort of Attock, where the two great watercourses join, the Kabul River from Afghanistan and Indus River descending from the Himalayas. Attock is the point where the Pashtun lands end and the Punjab begins. It was a good staging place for the travelers, halfway between the tribal areas and their destination, Rawalpindi. The Haqqania madrassa is a notorious establishment; it follows the fundamentalist Deobandi sect and is often described as the alma mater of the Afghan jihad since it has trained generations of students over three decades for war in Afghanistan. It is run by Maulana Sami-ul-Haq, head of his own religious party and close supporter of Zia-ul-Haq. The madrassa houses three thousand religious students from Pashtun areas, Afghans and Pakistanis, in large, white-washed residence blocks built around a series of courtyards. Ninety-five percent of the Taliban fighting in Afghanistan had passed through its classrooms, a spokesman for the madrassa, Syed Mohammad Yousuf Shah, proudly told me.[12]

Their most famous graduate is Jalaluddin Haqqani, the veteran Afghan mujahideen commander, who took his name from the madrassa and won renown as a ferocious warrior against the Soviet occupation. During that time, he forged strong ties with Arab groups, including bin Laden's, and the ISI. He served as a minister in the mujahideen and Taliban governments, and remained an important ally to Pakistan, with control of a large section of eastern Afghanistan. That did not change after 9/11. He continued to head a network of commanders known as the Haqqani network and became the main protector of al Qaeda in North Waziristan. His long and close ties to the ISI and to Arab groups has been the critical element in creating a safe haven in the tribal areas for the Taliban and foreign militants. It is Haqqani who is the linchpin for the entire ISI operation in the tribal areas. He is the most powerful commander who oversees all the other groups. Now elderly, he has passed daily operations to his son, Sirajuddin. Born of an Arab mother, Sirajuddin Haqqani is known as the Khalifa, or Caliph, to his followers although he does not have a high religious standing. He derives his power from his military clout and mafia businesses. His network has become the main instrument for ISI-directed attacks in Kabul and eastern Afghanistan.

The visitors who stopped for a night at the Haqqania madrassa in late December included two young followers of Baitullah Mehsud, leader of the Pakistani Taliban and the country's most wanted man by this time. They stayed with a cleric who was resident at the madrassa. Among the small group that met that night was a student of the madrassa who had been reconnoitering the election rally venue at Liaquat Bagh, a park in Rawalpindi where Bhutto was due to speak. He escorted the teenagers to Rawalpindi and handed them on to another cell in the city.

Bhutto had already changed her schedule in Peshawar to avert one threatened attack on December 26. The next day, December 27, she attended the rally in Liaquat Bagh. As her motorcade left the park, it slowed so she could greet supporters in the street. From the crowd a suicide bomber fired a pistol at her, and then detonated his vest of explosives. Bhutto was standing in the roof opening of an armored SUV. She ducked into the car at the sound of the gunfire but not in time. The power of the blast threw the car forward, slamming the hatch opening into the back of her head with lethal force. Bhutto slumped down into the car, mortally wounded, and fell into the lap of her confidante and constant chaperone, Naheed Khan. The bomber was one of the two teenagers, younger than sixteen years old, a Mehsud tribesman from South Waziristan named Bilal. The other teenager, Ikramullah, was waiting at the second entrance to the park in case Bhutto's convoy had exited by that gate. He left the scene without detonating his explosives.

The bombers were part of a small cell that had formed to avenge the Red Mosque siege. The two leading figures in the cell were a taxi driver and his cousin, both from Rawalpindi. The taxi driver, educated in a madrassa, had lost a close friend in the siege. The group had planned several attacks in and around Rawalpindi, including hits on a minister in Musharraf's cabinet, a colonel working at the military General Headquarters, and Tariq Aziz, Musharraf's chief civilian aide. When they failed to reach those targets, the group was assigned the task of assassinating Bhutto.

It was another terrifying blast amid a crowd of Bhutto's supporters. Twenty-four others were killed in the bombing and over ninety wounded. Political mistrust was running so high at the time that few of Bhutto's supporters accepted the theory, put forward by the Musharraf government, that the Pakistani Taliban leader Baitullah Mehsud was behind her assassination. Several subsequent investigations, including one ordered by Bhutto's own party once it took power, found, however, that he did play a role.

Baitullah was a flamboyant, long-haired Pashtun tribesman. Only thirty-three, he was already the most successful leader of the Pakistani Taliban, having united militant groups the length of the tribal areas. By 2007, he commanded thousands of tribesmen, ran training camps, and mounted cross-border operations into Afghanistan. He had an off-again-on-again relationship with the Pakistani military, entering several peace agreements with them then breaking them off in spectacular fashion, kidnapping soldiers or staging splashy attacks. Baitullah was officially branded a dangerous outlaw, yet the ISI maintained contacts with him throughout and worked with him on projects that suited their agenda, American and Pakistani officials told me. American officials noticed that the Pakistani military never moved aggressively against the Pakistani Taliban and never sought to kill or capture Baitullah. His was another proxy force that the ISI tolerated and used for its own purposes, for leverage against Afghanistan or India, to keep some kind of order over the thousands of militants in the tribal areas, and even to use against its own people. The relationship was such that it is not inconceivable that Baitullah could be tasked with arranging attacks on Bhutto and others inside Pakistan, these officials told me.

As Bhutto had long warned, a conglomeration of opponents wanted her dead, and were all linked in some way. They were the same forces behind the insurgency in Afghanistan: Taliban and Pakistani militant groups, al Qaeda, and the Pakistan military establishment, which included top generals Musharraf and Kayani. A United Nations Commission of Inquiry into the circumstances of Bhutto's death found each group had a motive and merited investigation.[13]

Pakistani prosecutors later indicted Musharraf for being part of a wider conspiracy to remove Bhutto from the political scene. There was "overwhelming circumstantial evidence" that he did not provide her with adequate security because he wanted to ensure her death in an almost inevitable assassination attempt, the chief state prosecutor in her murder trial, Chaudhry Zulfiqar Ali, told me.[14] Musharraf had directly threatened Bhutto during a telephone conversation, he added. A hard-working, hard-charging man, Chaudhry succeeded in having Musharraf arrested and was pushing to speed up the trial when he was gunned down on his way to work in May 2013. His friends said he had begun receiving threats as he pressed the Musharraf case.

For Afghan security officials watching from Kabul, Musharraf's failure to provide security was beside the point: "If your intelligence service wants to get rid of you, no amount of security will protect you," a senior Afghan security official told me.[15]

Chaudhry had no doubts that the mastermind of the plot to kill Bhutto was al Qaeda, which he told me included Baitullah Mehsud. "It was because she was pro-American, because she was a strong leader and a nationalist," he said. A Pakistani security official who interviewed some of the suspects in the Bhutto case and other militants detained in Pakistan's prisons came to the same conclusion. The decision to assassinate Bhutto was made at a meeting of the top council of al Qaeda, the official told me. Mehsud was present at the meeting, as was Abu Ubaydah al-Misri, the operational chief of al Qaeda in Pakistan and Afghanistan at the time.

The morning after the assassination, Pakistani authorities intercepted a telephone call between Baitullah and a senior cleric from his tribe. Baitullah used to make calls from a public phone in Kaniguram, a town in South Waziristan, and the Pakistani authorities had a permanent tap on the phone, the security official told me. A transcript released by the government reveals the two men discussing the bombing and congratulating each other over it. The cleric, just back from a trip, confirms that two of their men, Bilal and Ikramullah, did the deed. Baitullah thanks him for the news. "Great job done. They were brave boys that killed her."

10

The Taliban Close Their Grip

"The Taliban, when they say something, they do it. They
threaten to kill people and they do it. But when we say
we will protect you, we often do not."

— *Jelani Popal, Afghan government official*

August 2008. A container truck lay on its side, burning. Its cab was
empty, the driver nowhere to be seen. Further ahead, the rest of
the convoy was pulled up at the side of the road. Armed men
stood in the road, assault rifles in one hand, walkie-talkies in the other.
Their commander wore sunglasses and a checkered scarf tied untidily
around his head. He shouted a stream of orders at his men and into
his cell phone in one breath. One of his men stood guard, a heavy
machine gun with a tripod slung across his body, a ribbon of bullets
looped around his shoulders. The men were agitated, high on drugs or
adrenaline.

They were members of a private security company guarding a convoy carrying food, water, and other supplies to a string of U.S. military
bases south of Kabul. I was out reporting with the Afghan National
Army when we came across them. The next stretch of road would be
the most dangerous, they told us, where they often came under ambush from the Taliban.

This was Highway One, the main Kabul-Kandahar road that links
the Afghan capital to the south. Restoring it had been a prize project
of the Bush administration, demonstrating America's commitment to

rebuilding Afghanistan and helping it get back on its feet. In 2001, the road was a rutted, dusty track, pockmarked with craters and blown-out bridges. The journey to Kandahar took us sixteen hours by car in those days. I would travel with a small team, a driver, translator or local reporter, sometimes a photographer too. We would stop in a teahouse for the night to break up the journey. By the end, the sinews in my neck ached from holding my head straight in the constant jarring.

President Karzai saw the road as a critical artery that literally would hold the country together, tying the restive south to the commercial north, uniting the Pashtuns, who had largely made up the Taliban, with the northern tribes that had opposed them. Karzai had lobbied Bush personally to have the road rebuilt. It took two years and cost roughly $1 million a mile — making it one of the most expensive pieces of road anywhere in the world — and spawned multiple security problems, including repeated attacks and kidnappings of construction engineers. By the end of 2003, all three hundred miles from Kabul to Kandahar were asphalted, cutting driving time to six hours and bringing the prices of goods down dramatically.

Yet within months highwaymen and insurgents began plaguing passengers on the road. In the ensuing years, as the insurgency advanced up the country, government officials, assistance organizations, and foreign workers risked kidnap and death traveling on Highway One.

By 2008, the road had become an example of the government's and America's failure to thwart the Taliban. The rejuvenated Taliban were closing in on the provinces around Kabul, trying to enforce a stranglehold on the capital by targeting strategic roads and districts, undercutting the country's economy and communications. Highway One had become a dangerous gauntlet of mines, roadside bombs, and ambushes. The U.S. military contracted Afghan security firms to ferry their nonlethal supplies around the country, and we had come across such a group in Wardak province, fifty miles south of Kabul.

The convoy could not risk delays or being split up so when a truck broke down, the drivers abandoned it and set it on fire. The men were gathering themselves for the drive through the most dangerous stretch of road south of Saydebad and into Ghazni province. Taliban gunmen always opened fire in the town of Salar, where houses climbed the hills on either side of the road. The governor of Ghazni had been ambushed there just a few days earlier.

The worst attack had occurred on June 24 at Salar, when fifty fuel tankers and food trucks were ambushed. Insurgents knocked out the lead vehicles, blocking the way, and then set the convoy on fire, the convoy commander told me. Seven drivers were dragged out and beheaded. The insurgents singled out the drivers of the refrigerated trucks because the vehicles looked more obviously foreign, he said. Troops from FOB Airborne, the American forward operating base in Wardak, responded when they saw the attack. "There were multiple plumes of smoke for five to six kilometers down the road," an American officer serving in the area told me later. It took eight days of operations to recover all the burned vehicles. They had to lift some of the wrecks with cranes where they had burned holes through the asphalt.

Wardak is a hard-bitten place. The men are as obdurate as the stony hillsides. But the fighting in Wardak degenerated in the summer of 2008 into something vicious. There were reports of foreign fighters in the province, training local men to make roadside bombs and undertake suicide attacks. Two days after the drivers were beheaded, on June 26 a small convoy of American soldiers was bumping along a dirt road through the Tangi Valley, a narrow verdant line running east from the highway. They were in three armored Humvees, part of a reconnaissance team from the New York National Guard, heading back to their base in the adjoining province of Logar. A marine from special operations command was along on the patrol with them, as was an Afghan interpreter.

As they approached Tangi village, forty minutes from the main highway, one of the vehicles hit a mine or roadside bomb. The others tried to drive through the ambush but came under fire from small arms and rocket-propelled grenades. A second truck was hit and disabled. One Humvee caught fire and burned so ferociously that the trees along the floor of the valley caught fire. The Afghan interpreter never managed to get out of his seat. He died in the vehicle, his body burned beyond recognition. Taliban were firing from tall cornfields below the road, hidden from view by thick vegetation. The soldiers tried to fend off the ambush from behind the cover of the vehicles. One of them sent a text message on his cell phone back to FOB Airborne. It was an SOS, sent in the last few minutes of his life.

Troops on Highway One rushed to help the men at Tangi but hit another mine on the way. They pushed on, found the ambushed vehicles still on fire, and began a search for survivors. There was no one around; the villagers had fled or hid. Bullet casings were scattered all around the vehicles where the men had made a last defense. A military rucksack lay ripped open, its belongings scattered about.

One Humvee had made it out with survivors, but three men were dead at the scene and two more were missing. Search parties scoured the area for the rest of the day. Just before dark they came across the remains of one of the men. He had been dragged nearly a mile from the ambush site, and his body had been mutilated. His arms had been cut off, and someone had tried to carve out his heart. The search went on through the next day, but the units only ever found parts of the other soldier.

The Tangi Valley became notorious for its ambushes. Taliban there shot down a Chinook helicopter full of American and Afghan Navy SEALs and special operations commandos in 2011, killing all twenty-seven on board. The mutilation of victims, which was not often revealed to the public, was a particular horror for the men serving in Afghanistan, a sign of the brutalizing effects of the war. It was a grim burden for those who encountered it and led to acts of retaliation on both sides.

Two weeks later, Taliban seized positions on a craggy mountainside above the road beside the village of Durrani. Their target was a convoy of seven fuel tankers. The fireball was so enormous it set fire to roadside shops and civilian cars. Twenty-two civilians were burned alive.

As we saw in Wardak, the Taliban had swarmed right up to the gates of Kabul by the summer of 2008. They did not control any major towns but had gained such influence in the countryside that they had freedom of movement throughout the south and east of the country. Their target was increasingly Kabul and the faltering Karzai government. The Taliban began to hit right into the heart of the capital with a series of spectacular attacks aimed at grabbing headlines and vaunting their power.

In January 2008, a pair of suicide bombers wearing police uniforms attacked the Serena Hotel, the only five-star hotel in Kabul, just yards across the street from the presidential palace. One blew himself up at the gate, opening the way for the second to break through to the lobby of the hotel. He fired on guests and staff in the lobby, then turned down a corridor to the gym where he shot more people. He telephoned his controllers — in Pakistan — fourteen times during the attack, then hid his weapons and clothes and tried to escape among employees evacuating the building. Police picked him out of the line.

In April, gunmen made an assassination attempt on President Karzai. They attacked a national parade to commemorate the mujahideen's defeat of the Communist government in 1992. One group of gunmen hid for days in a locked city hotel room. They opened fire from the window with a heavy machine gun while another group fired mortars smuggled into a nearby restaurant. The attack killed two legislators in the viewing stands and caused a stampede of diplomats and soldiers from the parade ground. The gunmen hiding in the hotel texted their commander in Pakistan, and he was urging them on, right up to the last minute, investigators found from the gunmen's cell phones.

Then, in July, a suicide bomber drove a car packed with explosives into the gates of the Indian embassy in Kabul, across the street from the Interior Ministry. The bomber killed the Indian military attaché and another diplomat driving into the embassy at that moment, but the real slaughter occurred on the street where Afghans were queuing up for visas outside the embassy or walking to the ministry opposite. Fifty men, women, and children were killed and scores more injured in the carnage.

The Taliban, five years after starting their insurgency, were striking at will in the heart of the nation's capital.

• • •

Sometimes the attackers resorted to indiscriminate slaughter, slaying bank customers in Jalalabad, supermarket shoppers in Kabul, and restaurant guests at the Qarga lakeside resort outside the capital. Other attacks were carefully targeted against the Indian and American embassies, and NATO military bases and vehicles. One suicide bombing in the capital was aimed at the Baluch rebel leader Brahumdagh Bugti, who had sought refuge from Pakistan with the Afghans. Bugti was not a target of the Taliban, but the Pakistani military certainly wanted him dead.

The U.S. military called these incidents "complex attacks" because they involved multiple attackers and weapons. Suicide bombers would often breach the outer security of the target, then gunmen and more bombers would rush in behind. The attacks showed a degree of expertise and planning not seen before with the Taliban indicating military training. But they did not seem to be driven by al Qaeda. There was growing evidence of a Pakistani agenda in the attacks as they expanded to targets in eastern and southern Afghanistan and even further afield to Mumbai, India, in November 2008. A team of Pakistani suicide gunmen attacked multiple targets in the city, killing over 160 people over a period of 48 hours. They used an attack plan originally drafted by the ISI.

Once again, intelligence officials of Pakistan were clearly collaborating with the militants and suicide bombers attacking targets in the Afghan capital. Almost every attack was traced back to Miranshah, the capital of North Waziristan, to the Haqqani network and Lashkar-e-Taiba, the two militant organizations operating there with the closest ties to the ISI. As investigators pieced together the attacks, they discovered a pattern. "Once again our country was attacked from Pakistani soil," Amrullah Saleh, the head of the National Directorate of Security, said at a joint news conference with the defense and interior ministers a few days after the assassination attempt against Karzai. "This is as bright as the sun, and we have all the evidence to show that."[1] The Serena Hotel attack revealed a possible al Qaeda connection. Arabs in Miranshah planned the operation, and an Afghan based in an Arab country supplied the money for the attack, Afghan intelligence found. The operator on the ground, an Afghan called Homayoun, organized that attack and the next one, the assassination attempt on the parade ground, traveling back and forth from Waziristan in Pakistan. Personnel inside the Afghan Interior and Defense Ministries had helped them obtain weapons and access, but the plot was hatched in Pakistan.

Homayoun escaped to Pakistan the day of the Serena Hotel attack but called his wife from there the next day. Afghan officials who tracked the call passed his number to Pakistani officials. The Afghans later complained that no effort was made to find him, and he was able to return to Kabul for the parade attack. He was preparing yet a third suicide bombing attack with two foreigners, a couple with a child, three days later when police surrounded their house and killed them all in a firefight.

The Indian embassy bombing revealed the clearest evidence of ISI complicity in its planning and execution. American and Afghan surveillance intercepted phone calls from ISI officials in Pakistan and heard them planning the attack with the militants in Kabul in the days leading up to the bombing. At the time, intelligence officials monitoring the calls did not know what was being planned, but the involvement of a high-level ISI official in promoting a terrorist attack was clear.

The evidence was so damning that the Bush administration dispatched the deputy chief of the CIA, Stephen Kappes, to Islamabad to remonstrate with the Pakistanis. The bomber struck, however, before Kappes reached Pakistan. Investigators found the bomber's cell phone in the wreckage of his exploded car. They tracked down his collaborator in Kabul, the man who had provided the logistics for the attack. That facilitator, an Afghan, had been in direct contact with Pakistan by telephone. The number he had called belonged to a high-level ISI official in Peshawar. The official had sufficient seniority that he reported directly to ISI headquarters in Islamabad.[2] The embassy bombing was no operation by rogue ISI agents acting on their own. It was sanctioned and monitored by the most senior officials in Pakistani intelligence.

The choice of attack was also revealing. An attack on the Indian embassy and the military attaché, longtime foes of Pakistan, could be explained away by Pakistan as stemming from sixty years of antagonistic relations. But this was not a subtle attack needling an old foe. It was a massive car bomb detonated in the center of a capital city, designed to cause maximum injury and terror. The plan was also to terrify and undermine the confidence of the Afghans and their government, sending a message not just to India but to the forty-two countries that were contributing to the NATO-led international force to rebuild Afghanistan. The aim was to make the cost too high for everyone to continue backing the Karzai government. The ISI wanted them all to go home.

The Afghans recognized the overall strategy. It was the same they had used as mujahideen against the Soviet occupation: placing a stranglehold on the capital by ambushing the roads and running a campaign of sabotage inside the city to undermine the government and sap the morale of citizens.[3]

As it investigated every attack, Afghan intelligence and police officials became convinced that the ISI was working with al Qaeda, the Taliban, the Haqqanis, and Pakistani groups such as Lashkar-e-Taiba, which was behind most of the attacks on Indian targets. "You think after so many years of this we don't know who our enemy is?" a senior Afghan security official retorted when I questioned his findings. His American counterparts knew as well but just could not admit what Pakistan was doing, out of hubris, he said. "They always have the evidence, but they think the viability of Pakistan is more important."

Pakistan denied all this. In every interview, officials insisted that they wanted a stable Afghanistan and were working to defeat terrorism. But Pakistan's actions tell a different story. Even as its militants at home were surging out of control, and the cost in lives and stability to Pakistan was becoming exorbitant, Pakistan's military leaders continued to pursue a policy of using the Taliban to attack the Afghan government and NATO forces in Afghanistan. One obvious reason was to deflect the militants' lethal energy away from home. Another was as General Ashfaq Parvez Kayani had expounded: the Taliban, or specifically the Haqqanis, were an asset that Pakistan needed to keep in order to have a strong ally in Afghanistan when the American and international forces left.[4] At the core of Pakistan's thinking was an obsessive desire to dominate Afghanistan in order to protect its own rear flank from India. In that way of thinking, the Taliban were guarantors of Pakistan's national strategic interests.

As the Taliban expanded their insurgency northward, security deteriorated. Despite the newly paved highway, we ceased driving down to Kandahar or out to Khost in 2006 because the roads had become so dangerous. The provinces ringing the capital started to slide out of control. By mid-2008, the decline seemed unstoppable. The Taliban were growing in numbers, and their resurgence was accompanied by a campaign of terror that magnified their influence. They had dispensed with the niceties of their propaganda campaign of 2006, when the mullah-commanders in the south had called people to the mosques and persuaded them to join the jihad. Instead, they increasingly used retribution for those who did not cooperate. We began to hear more accounts of torture and mutilation: truck drivers who had their ears cut off or their throats slit for carrying supplies for American forces. The campaign paralyzed local government as police, judges, provincial councillors, and teachers began abandoning their jobs and moving to the cities for protection.

The mayhem in Wardak forced the Afghan government to deploy units of the Afghan Army to defend the road. Soldiers of Afghanistan's 201st Corps occupied old hilltop positions that the Soviet Army had used in the 1980s, surveying the road and the green side valleys that provided easy cover for the insurgents. It was an irony that the Karzai government was now deploying its army in former Soviet positions, against insurgents who were using the old mujahideen tactics. Karzai understood the incongruity. For a long time, he refused to refer to those fighting as Taliban or insurgents, calling them simply the enemy, and terrorists. He did not want to be on the wrong side of a popular war. Increasingly, the people were siding with, or at least not opposing, the Taliban.

As soon as they arrived, the Afghan Army units found themselves in daily firefights. A unit we found camping in a school building in

Salar said they had been called out the previous day to help the police, besieged in a station just two miles down the road. The commander, Captain Gul Jan, told us they had run into an ambush almost immediately and battled for three hours before they could even reach the police station. The local police were woefully outmanned and outgunned, and would not have survived much longer without the army, another officer, Captain Mohammad Zaman, told us. His platoon had set up camp in Durrani just after the conflagration there. "If there was no Afghan Army here, it would be too difficult to secure the road for one hour," he said. Camping in the open, he had minimal defenses and was worried about Taliban mortar fire. Coordination with American forces in the area was so poor that a passing American military convoy had fired on Zaman's positions just five days earlier and wounded one of his soldiers in both legs. Another group of Afghan soldiers, in an old Russian hilltop post, was more upbeat. "We can beat the Taliban conclusively when we build up our manpower," said First Lieutenant Rahmatullah Minallah, who commanded a post overlooking the Tangi Valley, where the Americans had died. "I have fifty men here now. When I have one hundred men, I can leave fifty here and go and clear out the village." Individual Afghans were often impressive, but the government always seemed to fall short.

Wardak was just one frontline province that needed urgent attention. At least half of the country had security problems. The United Nations was reporting that 20 percent of districts were off limits to their workers because of insecurity in 2008. Even Afghan government officials were unable to travel to 10 percent of districts.

Every Afghan I interviewed complained above all about the lack of security. Yet many in the international community decided that it was the lack of services that disaffected people from the government. Foreign governments talked of providing better healthcare, education, and other services to win hearts and minds. They pushed for more educated governors who understood human rights and how to implement assistance programs. The U.S. military beefed up its own assistance programs, allowing commanders on the ground to spend

millions of dollars building schools, government buildings, police stations, and jails. One international idea was to improve the coordination between the central government and the provinces by supporting
a new agency, the Independent Directorate of Local Governance. The
directorate, working directly under President Karzai, was to oversee
the appointment of governors, police chiefs, and district administrators, and ensure a more effective management of provincial affairs.
Jelani Popal, the experienced manager of an Afghan aid organization,
was chosen to run it. A Pashtun, he had spent many years working
in the southern provinces on assistance projects. He knew the people
and their needs. He saw the dangers of letting the insurgents grow so
strong that only a full-blown military offensive could dislodge them,
and he wanted to attend to provinces that might be targets of the insurgents before it was too late.

He quickly discovered the police chief in Wardak was a source of
intense unhappiness in the community. Popal removed him. He found
that, although there were 1,100 policemen on the books in the province, two thirds were phantom employees and only 400 were actually
working. The salaries of the remainder were being pocketed by police
bosses. Popal's directorate was designed to streamline support for the
provincial governments, and he saw it as critical that the government
delivered on its promises. "The Taliban, when they say something,
they do it," he explained in an interview early in 2008. "They threaten
to kill people and they do it. But when we say we will protect you, we
often do not."

Popal made sure the government supplied equipment and cars, increased salaries, and paid them on time to police and district officials.
"We put the government in a very strong position," he noted. They
also removed several mullahs who were preaching antigovernment
sermons. The population remained indifferent, however, so he began
organizing councils of elders to try to engage the communities and
address the grievances of the population. "If the community is organized and not indifferent to the government then they can make it very
difficult for the Taliban to come," he said. "We have to empower communities better to defend themselves, not with weapons but with or-

ganization." Yet the plan soon faltered. It was too dangerous for elders to attend government meetings or be seen to be cooperating with the government. The Taliban were far from popular, but the people would not risk their lives to work with a government they did not trust. Lack of security was still the overriding problem.

East of Wardak, also on the doorstep of Kabul, sits the province of Logar, another important gateway to the capital. Just a short drive from the capital, in the provincial capital, Mohammad Agha, the Taliban began driving around and delivering threats in broad daylight to anyone working for the government.

A judge from Logar spoke to us after resigning his post in July 2008. He was too scared to allow his name to be published. He had been working for six years in Logar without mishap. Then the Taliban came. They had begun some months earlier leaving night letters, warning that anyone working in the government, the police, or the intelligence agency should leave their jobs or be killed. The judge knew what the Taliban were capable of. A fellow judge, his former classmate, had been killed by the Taliban in the southeast. The threats became more frequent and more overt. The judge's two brothers abandoned their police jobs and left Logar. He began receiving daily threats, by telephone and then one day in person.

A large group of masked gunmen came to his home. They said their top leader had ordered the judge to be killed because he was working for the Americans. The proof, they said, was the weekly directive that he received from the Supreme Court in Kabul. After seven years' service, six of them in Logar, on a salary of forty dollars a month, the judge was giving up. "I have old parents and young children," he said. "I cannot work anymore, the situation is getting worse and worse." The government had to fight the Taliban with toughness and use of intelligence but was failing at every level, he said. The police chief was a thief. The governor was weak. The government intelligence department caught a suicide bomber, but he was released, almost certainly through bribery, the judge went on. The foreign military presence in Logar consisted only of a Czech Army provincial reconstruction team, which focused on civil affairs projects. People were disheartened by the widespread government corruption, and angered by the raids by foreign forces, which often targeted innocent people. Some Afghans were using the foreigners as a way to attack their enemies. "If the situation goes on like this, I see the Taliban growing day by day," he concluded.

Militants were appearing in large numbers in the remoter districts. American forces, which had maintained a consistent presence in the eastern provinces along the Pakistani border and steadily built up their bases and numbers since 2001, had pushed out to the more remote provinces of Kunar and Nuristan in the northeast since 2006. Yet the insurgency grew faster, and the entire eastern border region became restive, infiltrated by Taliban and pockets of Pakistani and al Qaeda fighters. In July 2008, a mass of insurgents came together in an attack in Wanat, in the far northeastern mountains of Afghanistan. Hundreds of militants, including foreign fighters and members of Lashkar-e-Taiba, attacked and nearly overran a patrol base there. Nine American soldiers died in a frantic defense of the base. More were wounded.

An army investigation found the base was ill-positioned and poorly protected. Nevertheless, the attack showed the buildup of extremist militants in the north of Kunar and Nuristan. The remote mountain valleys had drawn Arab Salafists to Nuristan and the upper reaches of Kunar since the 1970s, and they had been able to maintain a presence in the most remote reaches throughout the Soviet occupation and the years after. Afghan officials told me that Islamist groups from Pakistan had been building up a new presence in the area since 2005. "The ISI has expended a lot of money and work," an elder from Nuristan, a former mujahid, told me.[5] Like most of the mujahideen, he had been trained in the Pakistani militant camps and knew the leaders behind the resurgence.

Yet if a local leader stood up against the Taliban, the government often failed to protect him. One example was a widely respected religious elder from Barg-e-Matal, a district of Nuristan that borders Pakistan. The elder, Fazle Ahad, presided over a large gathering of tribal elders and dignitaries brought together in Barg-e-Matal by the government.

He spoke passionately, urging people that it was not the time for jihad and that they should work instead to rebuild the country.

The Taliban killed him soon after. They tortured him first, breaking his hands and shooting out his eyes. The provincial government traced the killers to a district in the neighboring province, but the central government did nothing to pursue them. The killing caused outrage among the local people, and they were ready to retaliate. The failure to act by the central government left people disillusioned, the Nuristani elder told me.

The Taliban were much sterner masters. They rewarded their men for successful attacks, paying sums of money for every government official or American soldier killed. They punished or executed those who transgressed their rules. The Taliban also strongly supported their fighters. If one of their men was captured by the government, they would kidnap someone in order to exchange him for their man. It was a time of greatest need in the provinces, but in Kabul and Western capitals, there was a sense of drift.

General David D. McKiernan, who had commanded all allied forces in the 2003 invasion of Iraq, took over command of the NATO-led force in Afghanistan in June 2008. More than any commander of the entire war, McKiernan was hampered by the lack of forces at his disposal. He was struck by how few men he had in Afghanistan — 35,000 U.S. troops in 2008 — compared to commanders in Iraq who had 160,000 that year to cover roughly the same size population. Every day after he arrived, his forces came under attack from insurgents crossing the border from Pakistan. The lack of troops forced him to use more airpower, and casualties were rising on all sides. American military casualties in Afghanistan since 2001 passed the five hundred mark in July 2008. For the first time, in June and July of that year, more American soldiers died in Afghanistan than in Iraq.

McKiernan put in requests for more troops, appealing to European nations that already had forces in Afghanistan to boost their numbers. By November 2008, he had realized that his NATO partners were not going to increase their forces. He turned to the Pentagon, requesting twenty thousand additional U.S. troops. Well aware of the war still ongoing in Iraq, he nevertheless urged leaders in Washington to consider sparing some forces from Iraq to prevent Afghanistan from failing. "A country that is one-third smaller in size than Afghanistan, has far less fighters — whether they are insurgents, foreign fighters, whatever groupings, criminals, narco-traffickers, far less — and between them the Iraqi forces and international forces number 800,000," he told me. In Afghanistan, facing the insurgents, McKiernan had a combined force of NATO and Afghan Army and police forces of no more than 200,000. "It is time to have to take some risks in Iraq, and boost forces in Afghanistan."

In February 2009, the newly elected President Barack Obama announced seventeen thousand extra American troops would be sent to Afghanistan. One of their tasks would be to improve security for Afghan presidential elections in August 2009. Already by then it was not enough.

By the spring of 2009, inside the Kabul office of the Afghan interior minister, Hanif Atmar, a map showed that nearly half the country was a danger zone for his officials. Ten of Afghanistan's 364 districts were colored black, meaning they were wholly under Taliban control, and 156 were colored red or amber to indicate high-risk areas for officials or anyone associated with the government.

The instability not only meant it would be physically difficult to run the elections, but they might also be skewed politically. The north was more stable. There, voters were agitating for a change from the Karzai government. The population in the south and east, subsumed in violence, was so despairing that few said they would go and vote. Yet the south and east was Karzai's main constituency. Without their participation, Karzai would be robbed of the bulk of his support and could lose the election. More important, without Pashtun participation in the election, the country could break apart and the south slide away entirely into the arms of the Taliban, al Qaeda, and Pakistan. Despite their reservations about the security situation and about Karzai's leadership, Afghan officials bent to the task of opening as many polling stations as possible.

Diplomats briefed journalists on the electoral process, laying out a timeline with willful optimism. They delayed the election until August, illegally extending Karzai's constitutional mandate and ignoring the evident security problems, not to mention disaffection in the south and signs of fraud in voter registration.

In the south, the population was cracking. Hundreds of families displaced by the fighting filled the main towns. On three occasions that summer of 2009, I watched grown men break down and weep in the middle of interviews. The usually resilient and self-reliant Afghans were showing signs of desperation. People kept asking me why, if the United States could spot a four-inch-long speck with their satellites, could they not find the Taliban?

A tall, thin man stood and talked to me at an election rally in Kandahar city. He was forty-five, a laborer who had fled his home in the western province of Farah three months earlier when fighting had flared. The Taliban had moved into his area, and the Americans were bombing, he told me. "We cannot even step out of the house," he said. He began to cry. He had come to see Karzai's main rival in the election, Abdullah Abdullah, because the country needed new leadership. "We need a change because we have been broken."

Others wanted nothing to do with the whole process. A farmer who had fled the fighting in Panjwayi with his family to live in Kandahar city said he could not bear to vote. "What can I say? We are living in destitution. We have lost every single thing we had. To tell the truth I will not participate in presidential election, even though I have a registration card, my mind doesn't allow me to use it, my heart and my feelings are crushed."[6]

On August 20, few people turned out to vote in Kandahar or anywhere in southern Afghanistan. Observers estimated turnout was no higher than 15 percent in the southern provinces, and in some places in the single digits. The Taliban had warned of harsh penalties if anyone voted — threatening to cut off fingers of those who had the telltale inked digit. They attacked a number of polling stations and ordered a curfew, forbidding villagers to go out. "No one voted, no one could dare go out of their house," Haji Abdul Majid, a prominent elder from Arghestan district, told me.[7] It was not only fear that kept voters away. Even in heavily guarded central Kandahar, voters stayed at home out of disgust for the government and the whole Western experiment in Afghanistan.

As the votes came in, so did allegations of massive fraud. The absurdity of holding an election in the middle of a losing war was revealed to all. Officials in southern Afghanistan, led by the president's brother Ahmed Wali Karzai, the strongman of the south, forged hundreds of thousands of votes in Karzai's favor. Their reasoning was that it was too dangerous to leave the Pashtuns disenfranchised, and given the chance to vote, the Pashtuns would have chosen Karzai anyway. They were right — but the fraud was too blatant for one American diplomat, posted as a deputy head of mission at the United Nations office in Kabul. Peter Galbraith blew the whistle, busting open the mess of the election and Western efforts to show that the Afghan mission was on track.

Despite Karzai's insistence that he won a fair election, one of his political supporters told me several years later that officials had stuffed ballot boxes for Karzai in both the 2004 and 2009 presidential elections. "I helped Karzai and I campaigned for him," Samad Zazai, a businessman from Paktia, told me. "I myself stuffed boxes for Karzai in both elections." When I asked him if the palace had known what he was doing, he answered, "If we did not have support, no one would have dared do that. There were people in Paktia, Paktika, and Khost provinces who did not let their wives and daughters vote, so we did it for them. I don't know exactly if Karzai knew, but people in power in all the three provinces where we worked all knew. We had meetings about how to do it all."[8]

"Karzai is the president of Afghanistan now, and not a single Pashtun can relax in his home," complained Mohammad Haq Jenabi, an elder in a black turban from Kandahar city, just after the election. "The Taliban are more and more powerful and officials are living in bunkers and building security fences. What kind of system is this?" he went on. "We need a favor from the international community. If they could bring giant airplanes and take all the Pashtuns and drop us in the ocean, then we would get rid of this situation. Every day, every night we are in pain."[9]

11

Karzai's Turn

"For how long will you be attending funerals and shedding
tears? You are the president. Change the situation."

— *elder in Nangarhar to President Hamid Karzai*

October 2009. President Karzai had aged in just a few weeks. The
bags under his eyes were deeper, his skin was sallow, and his eyes
showed hurt. It was the face of humiliation that appeared at the
podium before the world's press. He whispered something in the ear
of U.S. Senator John Kerry, who looked sharper and healthier than the
Afghan president despite his nonstop shuttle diplomacy of the last five
days. Karzai, usually so ebullient and breezy at news conferences, was
curt and humorless. He read a short statement. The election commission had announced the presidential election would go to a second
round; the decision was legitimate, legal, and constitutional, he said.
He was conceding that he had failed to win the election. He had fallen
short of the necessary 50 percent in the first round and would have to
contest a second against the runner-up. Kerry, who had spent twenty
hours of meetings in five days with the Afghan president to win this
concession, congratulated him for showing statesmanship. He was
strengthening the country by embracing the constitution and the rule
of law, Kerry said.

Karzai did not believe any of it. He did not believe the Independent
Election Commission's tally of the results giving him only 49.7 percent
of the vote, when his own finance minister had leaked early results

showing he had won 54 percent. He did not believe that accepting the election commission's count, which had canceled 1.3 million votes in his favor on the grounds they were fraudulent, made him anything like a statesman in the eyes of the Afghan people — or the world.

Above all, he did not believe anymore that the United States was a genuine partner. He had watched American officials court his rivals, and he felt betrayed. He was convinced that the accusations of fraud, delaying for two months the results of the August 20 vote, and leaked by the American diplomat at the UN mission, Peter Galbraith, had been engineered to remove him from power. His acceptance of the result was a charade, since no one in the international community wanted to go through the immense logistical and security effort of a second round of voting. Sure enough, Karzai's challenger, Abdullah Abdullah, pulled out of the second round days later, citing fears of fraud and conceding the presidency to Karzai. In their hours of talks and long walks in the palace gardens, Kerry had told Karzai about his own 2004 election defeat. "Sometimes there are tough things," the future U.S. secretary of state said.[1] Kerry was off the mark. Afghans could take losing. It was public humiliation that they could not stand. As I watched Karzai's face that day in the palace with Kerry, I knew he would not forgive America for the humiliation.

Karzai's honeymoon with the United States had been over for a while, but this was the moment that broke the relationship. It would never be the same. The brave and charismatic hero who had risked his life to persuade tribesmen to rise up against the Taliban in southern Afghanistan seemed to have been forgotten by the United States. The "best-dressed world leader," a label given him in 2002 by former Gucci designer Tom Ford for his lambskin hats and striped, silk coats, had worn out his welcome. His fluency and persuasiveness, which impressed Western audiences, were no longer convincing foreign governments. Afghans had long wearied of his speeches and promises, since he had failed to meet their expectations. Western nations increasingly found his blithe statements infuriating and disingenuous. His commitment to the war on terror and his strong opposition to al Qaeda and the Taliban, which brought him a standing ovation in the U.S.

Congress in 2004 and a Camp David visit with President Bush in 2007, were no longer enough. Now the war in Afghanistan was turning bad.

By 2009, as U.S. and NATO forces were facing the prospect of defeat by the Taliban, recriminations grew on both sides. Western leaders blamed Karzai for poor leadership, for losing the support of his people by running a shambolic, corrupt administration, and failing to lead the fight against the Taliban. "President Karzai was not an adequate strategic partner," Ambassador Karl Eikenberry, formerly the U.S. military commander in Afghanistan, stated in a diplomatic cable that was leaked to the *New York Times*.[2] Ambassador Francesc Vendrell, the long-serving European Union ambassador in Kabul, had earlier predicted that Karzai would be made a scapegoat as Western governments, anxious to find an exit from Afghanistan, sought to lay the blame elsewhere.

Others warned that he was still better than the alternatives in Afghanistan. "President Karzai is a much better man than he is made out to be," the former British ambassador to Kabul, Sherard Cowper-Coles, said in testimony to a parliamentary select committee in the United Kingdom in 2010. "He's gone from hero to zero, but the truth is somewhere in between. He's a great king, but a poor chief executive."[3]

Karzai, conscious he was being made a scapegoat, lashed out with increasingly harsh complaints and accusations over cultural blunders and civilian casualties. He repeated his usual refrain: the United States and its coalition were failing to tackle the insurgency at its source in the training camps and ISI offices in Pakistan. It was a disastrous falling-out, when the war was at its most dangerous point. The Taliban and Pakistan were able to press their advantage.

Karzai had seemed at first an ideal candidate for leader of Afghanistan. He was from the largest ethnic group, the Pashtun, but a nationalist, anti-Taliban, and accepted by the northern factions. He had a long record of work in the Afghan resistance to the Soviets, still essential for any leader of Afghanistan, but he had no blood on his hands. He was educated, a fluent English speaker, pro-American, and a moderate who supported a constitutional monarchy and democratic system for

Afghanistan. His early speeches of unity and peace genuinely inspired many of his countrymen across ethnic and geographic boundaries. I met people all over the country, even herders high up in the Wakhan corridor, the furthest sliver of Afghanistan reaching toward China, who spoke approvingly of his message for unity. Everyone was weary of war.

Karzai was one of the privileged class in Afghanistan. Born in 1957, he came from a prominent landowning family in the village of Karz, just outside Kandahar city. His father and grandfather were both members of Afghanistan's National Assembly, his grandfather served as deputy speaker of the Senate, and his father, Abdul Ahad Karzai, was deputy speaker of the lower house. They came from the Populzai tribe, a minor tribe but part of the dominant Durrani tribal confederation that has ruled Afghanistan for over two centuries. Karzai attended high school in Kabul and went on to college in India, completing a degree at the University of Simla, the former summer capital during the British Raj. The Soviet invasion of Afghanistan occurred when he was in India. His family left for Quetta, and Karzai began life as an exile. He was lucky by Afghan standards in that he was able to complete his studies. He then moved to Pakistan to work beside his father.

Karzai's brothers had emigrated to the United States where they ran restaurants. Yet he chose from the beginning to stay and work for his country, which was then under foreign occupation. Early influences that were to color his career in politics included Mahatma Gandhi, who led the movement for Indian independence from British rule, and Abdul Ghaffar Khan, the grand old Pashtun nationalist leader from India's northwest frontier and senior member of Gandhi's Congress Party.

Abdul Ghaffar Khan followed Gandhi's philosophy of nonviolent resistance, an unusual move for a Pashtun whose culture is steeped in war and blood feuds. He is famous among Pashtuns for his opposition to the creation of Pakistan. The British had divided the Pashtun tribal lands in order to defend the empire's northwest frontier, and Pashtuns had never accepted the artificially drawn Durand Line. The creation of Pakistan in 1947 absorbed a large part of the Pashtun lands, reinforcing the division. Roughly 26 million Pashtuns now reside in Pakistan and 14 million in Afghanistan. Ghaffar Khan opposed the partition of India and wanted an autonomous Pashtun state within an independent India, if not full statehood separate from Pakistan. He persisted with his campaign despite repeated spells in prison under the British and Pakistani governments. Karzai knew Ghaffar Khan, who died in 1988 in Peshawar at the age of ninety-eight, and admired his stance. It is one of the reasons Pakistani military leaders always mistrusted Karzai.

The invasion of Afghanistan by the Soviet Army in 1979 brought war to his country, and nonviolence no longer seemed an option. Karzai began to work for the Afghan resistance. He joined his father and worked for the Afghan National Liberation Front, one of the seven mujahideen parties. It was led by the widely respected religious scholar Sibghatullah Mojaddedi, who headed the first mujahideen government in 1992 and became leader of the Senate after the fall of the Taliban. His party was traditionalist and promonarchist but considered one of the more moderate. Karzai helped raise funds and channel weapons to the mujahideen, and acted as a liaison between the mujahideen and intelligence officials in the CIA, ISI, and security organizations from other countries. He became a spokesman for the party and worked with the Western journalists who traveled through Pakistan to cover the war in Afghanistan with the mujahideen.

Toward the end of the decade, when the Soviet Army withdrew from Afghanistan, Karzai became more and more involved in political affairs. He lived in Peshawar, the northwest frontier town that was the main hub of mujahideen activity in the 1980s. He used to visit the Pearl Continental Hotel to swim lengths in its pool and meet with Western aid officials, journalists, and diplomats. He was never a fighter but made occasional forays into Afghanistan with the mujahideen. He was a genial, well-spoken figure and popular among Western journalists, not least because of his easy English and relaxed manners. Few imagined him as a future president.

In 1992, when the mujahideen overthrew the government of the Communist leader Najibullah and took power in Kabul, Mojaddedi became interim president and Karzai joined the new government as a deputy foreign minister. He survived barely two years in the job as the mujahideen factions began tearing the government and capital apart. The ISI's favorite commander, Gulbuddin Hekmatyar, was firing rockets from his base on the south side of the capital in anger at having failed to seize control in Kabul. Karzai tried to mediate between Hekmatyar and those in government in Kabul.

Karzai came under suspicion for his efforts and was detained by intelligence officials. Only when a rocket slammed into the building where he was being interrogated did Karzai manage to escape. One of the intelligence officials interrogating him was Mohammad Qasim Fahim, a compact, thuggish Panjsheri commander, whom Karzai chose later to serve as his vice president. It was only one of the many ironies of Afghan political life. That early encounter was indicative of the future relationship: Fahim was the man with muscle, Karzai the fast talker.

Karzai abandoned his job and left for Pakistan in 1994. Disillusioned with the factional fighting in Kabul, he was drawn to support the Taliban when they first emerged in southern Afghanistan that same year. He knew many of the men who started the movement since they were mujahideen from his own province of Kandahar, and they seemed to want to end the violence and lawlessness. He supported them with money and even considered taking the post of ambassador to the United Nations representing the Taliban government — until he was deterred by atrocities committed by the Taliban and the growing influence of Pakistan's ISI over the movement. Karzai turned to work on a political plan with Abdul Haq and supporters of the former monarch to call a loya jirga, a grand tribal assembly, to reinstate King Zahir Shah as leader of Afghanistan.

The plan was not new, but as the Taliban campaign grew increasingly bloody, the group worked to raise support with several international conferences through the late 1990s. When Karzai's father was assassinated in 1999, some of his associates thought the younger Karzai had been the real target of the Taliban. By now he was the more politically active member of the family. Karzai was undeterred. He spoke out against the malign influence of the ISI and Arab fundamentalists, who were increasingly dominating Afghanistan. He journeyed north to talk to Ahmed Shah Massoud and consulted him about raising a resistance force in southern Afghanistan. His work brought him into disfavor with the ISI. Just days before the 9/11 attacks, Karzai was informed by the Pakistani authorities that his visa allowing him to reside in Pakistan would not be renewed.

Karzai showed a sure political touch in the days after 9/11. He spoke often to the world media, denouncing the attacks, railing against the Arabs and al Qaeda that had hijacked his country, and calling on his people to reject their extremist agenda. Karzai knew he had to be among his people after 9/11 and persuade them to work with the United States and the world community, and to rise up against the Taliban. His understanding of how to manage an uprising was dangerously limited, but his political instincts were sound. Thanks to his visits with Massoud in the north, with the former king Zahir Shah and his circle in Rome, as well as with tribal and mujahideen leaders all over the country, he was known and accepted by the various parties at the United Nations–sponsored Bonn conference, which agreed on a transitional process for the post-Taliban era. The most powerful faction in the north, the Northern Alliance, recognized that a Pashtun leader would be more acceptable to the majority of Afghans, and saw Karzai as someone they could work with, perhaps because he was not a powerful figure. When he was named the leader of the interim government in December 2001, most ordinary Afghans had never heard of him, but he was familiar to all the political and mujahideen leaders as well as to Western diplomats and intelligence agencies.

He arrived in Kabul on December 13 by American helicopter with his uncle and a small entourage of unarmed men. "We did not even have a knife," Hafizullah Khan recalled, so strict were the American flight rules. The Kandaharis had offered to muster thousands of armed men by road to provide him with protection, but Karzai had declined, aware that the Northern Alliance, led by his former interrogator, General Fahim, had taken control of the capital. "He said if we go there with this force there will be some unfriendliness," Hafizullah Khan said. "He did the right thing. Fahim controlled everything, and there was no way there would not have been clashes between us. We did not bring anything with us and in the end we got all the weapons and planes for the government. This also brought unity among Afghans." The passengers felt some nervousness stepping out to greet the Northern Alliance, but the welcome was effusive. "The Northerners were *so* happy. They welcomed us and Karzai sat with the leaders and we sat with others."

Karzai undoubtedly smoothed the transition of late 2001 with his diplomacy. He shuttled around the city calling on the various United Front leaders who had already taken over ministries and barracks in the capital to enlist their support. He soothed those who were unhappy at being excluded from the Bonn conference, not least President Burhanuddin Rabbani, who was being made to step down in favor of Karzai. The two men lived uncomfortably alongside each other in the presidential palace compound, Karzai in the courtyard of the former royal palace and Rabbani in the more modern president's residence, until Karzai's inauguration. Yet it was to Karzai's credit that he kept Rabbani on his side. The elder statesman became a source of advice and support to Karzai over the next ten years, until his assassination by a suicide bomber in 2011.

Karzai's great strength was personal relations. He spent hours and hours receiving tribal delegations from all over the country, which in the Afghan tradition came to show their respect and loyalty to the new leader. They urged him to keep the foreign peacekeeping forces in Afghanistan and even to expand them across the country, to ensure stability and prevent a return to civil war. He balanced the mujahideen factions, which had reasserted themselves after the collapse of the Taliban, dividing government and security posts to give each ethnic group a share of power. Many Afghans have criticized Karzai and his Western backers for bringing back the warlords and commanders, men who have been accused of human rights abuses. Yet the Bush administration saw the coalition as important for stability. They did not want Afghans fighting each other. It became Karzai's signature approach to politics. He wanted to represent all Afghans, including the Taliban, and he wanted to bring them inside the tent. It was a form of tribal politics, something he had learned at his father's knee, a consultative system designed to keep the peace between conflicting interests. It was as much about his own survival as that of the country. Karzai parceled out cabinet posts, governorships, and security positions in Afghanistan's provinces, and even created two extra provinces to please the Hazaras and Panjsheris, both powerful mujahideen factions. This was where Karzai excelled — at internal politicking. He worked tirelessly at it, paying great attention to detail. "He was probably the best tactician I have ever seen in negotiating his way around, even in hard negotiations and getting his own way," a former cabinet minister told me. Karzai never showed the same interest in managing the country, the minister bemoaned. "He never had time for details on governance, rule of law, security, but he always had time for details on politics."[4]

Karzai often promised too much, and supporters fell out with him when he did not fulfill his promises. Yet he survived by keeping the most powerful factions on his side, working with him for more than a decade. He deflected all challengers to his position as president and avoided any internal coup, which, considering the short tenures and brutal ends of most of his predecessors in the Arg, the former royal palace, was something of an achievement. Virtually every Afghan leader in the twentieth century had been forced from power, overthrown, or assassinated.

Karzai undoubtedly drew strength from having the most powerful players at his back, the U.S. Army. They helped remove some troublemakers and bring others to heel. The powerful warlord Ismail Khan, who ran western Afghanistan as his own fiefdom, was undermined by a local uprising and then persuaded to accept the offer of a cabinet post in the capital, which removed him from his stronghold. Afghans understood that the United States had orchestrated his fall. The leaders of the uprising told me later that they were doing the bidding of the United States. I was sitting with the American ambassador Zalmai Khalilzad when Ismail Khan called him in the middle of the crisis to ask him what he should do.

Karzai kept unsavory characters close because he needed the political and militia power they commanded as faction leaders. Abdul Rasul Sayyaf was one such person. Sayyaf was an imposing Pashtun, over six feet tall, with a broad chest and terrifying reputation for the slaughter committed by his mujahideen. Human rights groups accused his forces of mass murders in the 1990s. A professor of Islamic law who trained in Egypt and speaks Arabic, he was one of the founding members, along with Burhanuddin Rabbani, of the Islamist movement in Afghanistan in 1973. He had close ties to Arab groups but was threatened by the Taliban and fought against them. After 2001, Sayyaf won a seat in parliament from his native region of Paghman, west of Kabul. Karzai often consulted him and other jihadi leaders on important political issues, such as relations with the West and negotiations with the Taliban. Karzai has been much criticized for giving Sayyaf respect and influence when he has been accused of land-grabbing and mafia-like criminality since 2001. Critics charge that the influence of such warlords has prevented any form of transitional justice for all the war crimes committed over thirty years in Afghanistan. Far from committing to reforms to prevent such impunity and corruption, legislators passed an amnesty law for Afghan political leaders that Karzai later approved.

Sayyaf was at the forefront of pushing the amnesty bill through. His command of language and erudition in the Islamic faith were far higher than that of the president, and he could usually persuade the younger Karzai. In the larger scheme, Sayyaf commanded a powerful constituency of supporters, and was important to Karzai's hold on political power, human rights notwithstanding.

For the same reason, Karzai brought Marshall Fahim back in as a running mate for the 2009 elections. Under international pressure, Karzai had dropped Fahim in 2004 because of his links to armed militias. By this time, though, the two families had business ties. Fahim's brother, Haseen Fahim, was a business associate of Karzai's brother, Mahmoud Karzai. They were shareholders in the Kabul Bank, which became the center of the country's biggest financial scandal in 2010 when hundreds of millions of dollars went missing. Before the scandal broke, while business was still good, Mahmoud Karzai persuaded his brother to ask Fahim back to be his vice presidential candidate for the 2009 presidential elections. Despite his unpopularity with many Afghans, Fahim still possessed enough political clout and money to deliver votes for Karzai and dilute support for the main Northern Alliance candidate, Abdullah Abdullah. Even more important for Karzai, Fahim had proved that he could cause more trouble for the president left out of power than in.

A woman candidate for parliament told me she had asked Karzai why he had chosen to bring Fahim back in as vice president after he had been successfully sidelined. Karzai replied that many of Fahim's jihadi supporters had been upset at his removal and caused trouble. Certainly crime, kidnapping, and riots had all risen sharply in the capital in the years that Fahim was out of power, and they largely subsided after his reinstatement. Karzai was bringing his rivals inside the tent, but he was sullying his own threshold by doing so.

Karzai also arranged the return of General Abdul Rashid Dostum, the most brutal of all the warlords, to ensure the support of the Uzbek and Turkmen vote. By 2008, Dostum was a dissolute and sick man, a diabetic and alcoholic who had beaten and abused political rivals and even his own officials, in order to retain dominance of his political party, Junbesh-e-Milli, and the Uzbek ethnic minority. When he nearly killed a political rival in his house in Kabul, and police surrounded the marble-clad mini-palace, Turkey offered to take him abroad to dry him out and keep him out of Afghanistan to defuse the situation. Karzai did not want to arrest Dostum, but he had gone too far, too many times, for Karzai's Western allies and United Nations officials.

Karzai brought Dostum back days before the 2009 election, just in time to announce his return and to tell his followers to vote for Karzai. He was given the symbolic post of chief of staff for defense to the president, and an office in the palace that he barely ever used. There was little protest from the U.S. administration. Turkey, a loyal and useful partner in the U.S.-led coalition, had lobbied for it. Although their militias had been disbanded, figures like Sayyaf, Dostum, and Fahim could rely on an army of supporters — former fighters, students, party workers — who could cause trouble but also deliver votes. Karzai needed these men politically, and he did what he felt he had to do in order to survive. It helped to secure his election though he lost the support of the educated elite and reformers, and the growing middle class.

For many of his own supporters, Karzai's greatest failing has been just that: He has allowed some of the worst war criminals and mafia bosses access to power. Members of the Afghanistan Independent Human Rights Commission, which is independently funded though the commissioners are appointed by the president, blame Karzai for not having the vision to remove the warlords and institute a process of transitional justice to bring accountability for the decades of war crimes in Afghanistan. The Afghan people have suffered massacres, disappearances, summary executions, and indiscriminate bombardments for thirty years. The period after 2001 offered a unique chance to break the cycle of violence that has wracked Afghanistan since the Communist revolution of 1978. Yet apart from bringing freedom of speech and opening up education, the Karzai era has made poor progress in advancing human rights and justice. Simar Samar, the founder and head of the human rights commission since 2002, said Karzai would complain that he did not have the power to move against the warlords. She never accepted that, and told me that both Karzai and the Bush administration had lacked the political will to prosecute war criminals. "The situation wasn't easy. We all know that," she said. "And there was not enough support from the international community for transitional justice." But Karzai could have done more, she said. "I think he should have used his own power and that of his office."[5]

In the end, though, Karzai decided not to fight the strongmen, and chose to tolerate the corruption that swelled to obscene proportions under his administration. Even his close associates agreed that Karzai had been too soft. His foreign minister, Rangin Dadfar Spanta, told me once that corruption could be controlled with a firmer hand. Hedayat Amin Arsala, who has served at minister level in all of Karzai's governments, concurred: "A stronger, willing hand, yes." Of the president he said, "At times he is too nice a person."

With those who were less threatening, Karzai showed a deft political hand. He undermined parliament to ensure it did not become a base of opposition to him. He co-opted parliamentarians, buying some, side-lining others, and ignored the votes that did not suit him. He retained ministers even when parliament had voted against their appointment, and it was common knowledge that he or his ministers paid bribes to legislators to win the confirmations he wanted. According to several Afghan officials, the going rate was ten thousand dollars per legislator per vote by 2012.

In 2009, with the presidential elections approaching, forty candidates entered the race against Karzai. Most had no hope of winning but wanted a moment of fame or to pull themselves up the career ladder. Democracy might be new to Afghanistan, but politics was as old as the hills. "Politics runs in their blood," Richard C. Holbrooke said admiringly in the run-up to the election.[6]

Karzai sought reelection by doing what he knew best, working his form of tribal politics. Not only did he choose Fahim to be his running mate to split the Tajik vote, but he induced at least six candidates to withdraw from the race in his favor. He persuaded a likely formidable opponent, the powerful governor of Nangarhar, Gul Agha Shirzai, against even entering the race. Shirzai was the man who had seized control of Kandahar in 2001 against Karzai's wishes, and he was now preparing to run against Karzai for president. He came from a large Pashtun tribe, the Barakzai, and his candidacy would have been very damaging to Karzai. On the eve of the deadline for nominations, Karzai wooed his rival. He invited Shirzai to the palace and played on his Pashtun sensibility. We should not divide the Pashtuns at this critical time, and not split the Pashtun vote and let a Tajik win the presidency, Karzai told him. We should stay together and keep the Pashtun strong. Then Karzai pulled out his trump card. Karzai's wife entered the room with their young son Mirwais. She placed the child on Shirzai's knee.

Would Shirzai turf her and little Mirwais out of their home? she asked. Shirzai never registered his candidacy.

Karzai refused to form his own political party or to allow party lists in elections. He did not even build a team around him, preferring to keep vertical relationships with his ministers and officials so that they relied only on the president for their position. The presidential palace became a place of intrigue and suspicion. His concentration on internal politics came at the expense of any strategic vision, one of his former ambassadors said. "He kept a tribal strategy of having no strategy and defeating everyone," said Sayed Tayeb Jawad, who served as Afghan ambassador to the United States for seven years from 2003.

Unfortunately, Karzai cared only about tactics, not strategy, in everything, including foreign policy and directing the country, Jawad said. Ten years after taking power, Karzai was still focused on tactical issues, denouncing every night raid and every incident of civilian casualties but offering little in the way of strategic thinking. Discussion around the withdrawal of NATO troops in 2014 was reduced to a purely tactical target of timing and numbers, he added. Karzai had retained aides with a similar narrow vision who see relations with Iran and Pakistan through the old prism. "They think that if the U.S. leaves Afghanistan, Iran and Pakistan will treat us better. That's not true. Only if we have strong relations with the U.S. will they treat us better," he said.[7]

For all his skill at politics, Karzai proved a poor administrator. Problems were already emerging in his first term. The public was disillusioned with the growing insecurity and lawlessness, the creeping corruption and general impunity. The abject poverty of the Taliban years had been alleviated with the end of the war, the influx of food assistance, and health and employment programs, but social problems were aggravated by a growing disparity between the rich and poor.

"He's a horrible manager," one military commander told me of the president. A foreign advisor assisting with palace media communications said to me that he had never seen a more dysfunctional government office. The president issued orders, and his staff simply ignored them. Western diplomats and military commanders all saw the problems and tried to devise ways to mitigate the malfunctions. Zalmai Khalilzad, U.S. ambassador from 2003 to 2005, was described as "Karzai's CEO" by my *New York Times* colleague Amy Waldman, because of his assiduous guidance of Karzai's agenda, decision-making, and public appearances. The British helped set up and fund Karzai's National Security Council in the early days of his administration. Yet when British General David Richards arrived to command NATO forces in 2006, he described the lack of coordination among the Afghan government, the foreign military, and Western donors as "anarchy."

General Richards decided that Karzai needed a war cabinet. He formed the Policy Action Group, comprising the top Afghan and Western figures on intelligence and security, to provide "joined-up, timely, and coordinated government action" on crucial issues.[8] It was designed to help Karzai, but it was a symbolic rebuke. After Richards departed in 2007, the group fell by the wayside because it, too, had become unwieldy and inefficient.

Karzai became a micromanager, personally appointing district administrators and security officers, and even selecting the principal of a Kandahar high school. He often managed the provinces through his own allies, undermining appointed officials. He was constantly in touch with tribal elders and other contacts. Once I was interviewing a provincial governor when President Karzai called to tell him there were forty members of the Taliban sheltering in a school in a village in his province, ordering him to take action. The governor had not even been informed about the Taliban sighting, but the president was already exercised over it. Karzai also fell into the trap of favoring his own tribe, the Populzai, for appointments. When the head of Kandahar's education department, a Populzai, was removed because his claim of a master's degree was revealed to be false, he appealed to Karzai who promptly made him head of the transport department, a lucrative job for a dishonest official.

Reformists in the government and among foreign donors tried to instill a system of merit and appointments according to qualifications, but it was an uphill battle in Afghanistan, where ministers and department heads often gave jobs to people from their own faction and tribe, following the lead of their president. As the favored few became rich and powerful, social problems became aggravated. There were grotesque displays of wealth in the gaudy villas built on prime government land that the cabinet doled out to themselves. The land grab happened early in Karzai's administration when he was out of the country one week. The area, called Sherpur, soon became the butt of jokes, nicknamed Sher Chur, which means "Lions' Loot." Yet it encapsulated what was going wrong in Karzai's Afghanistan. When he returned, he was urged by a member of the cabinet to reverse the decree that handed out the land. It had been approved by the cabinet and signed by Vice President Marshall Fahim at a cabinet meeting. Yet Karzai preferred to avoid conflict. He persuaded the ministers to make a nominal payment for the land instead. Only three of them had declined the offer of land.

The resentment among the wider public over such illegal appropriations — which were happening all over the city and country — exploded one summer's day in May 2006. The brakes of an American military truck failed on a steep hill at the northern entrance to Kabul, sending it plowing into cars and people at a busy intersection. The American soldiers tried to help the wounded, but an angry crowd gathered and the military convoy pulled out, firing into the air, then into the crowd. It all happened in the working-class district of Khairkhana, populated by northerners from the Panjsher Valley and the Shomali Plain. They were not generally anti-American, but many were poor and jobless. The incident unleashed tremendous anger and pent-up resentment of the foreign presence and Karzai government. Crowds of men rioted across the city, looting foreign relief organizations and offices, smashing government billboards and police kiosks, and chanting "Death to Karzai" and "Death to America." The police melted away rather than fight the crowd. One group of armed men made it all the way across town to Pashtunistan Square and fired shots at the presidential palace. Finally, the defense minister ordered the army into the streets. By then the rioters had exhausted themselves, and the spasm came to an end. The rampage was a warning for many that the people's patience with the government was running out, but Karzai suspected a conspiracy.

Corruption was fast becoming the issue that most angered the public in the Karzai era. There had always been an element of what Westerners considered corruption in Afghan society. This was a society that functioned on patronage, a duty to help your relatives and clan, and the everyday use of bakshish — whether a tip or a bribe. Yet the combination of Karzai's poor management and the influx of vast sums of assistance, often poorly administered by donors, created the most corrupt regime Afghans had ever seen. The mujahideen commanders who came into government brought an unbridled sense of entitlement to take property, ministries, and jobs. There were plenty of honorable mujahideen, but after so many years of hardship, fighting to free their country, many believed they deserved some reward. Afghans returning from abroad after twenty years as refugees showed a similar desire to make money. While many returned from America and Europe to help their country, there were also opportunists who abused their positions of power to get rich.

By Karzai's second term in 2010, Afghanistan ranked as the second most corrupt country in the Transparency International Scale, tied with Myanmar. Only Somalia was lower. The amount of money floating around Kabul was extraordinary. When the biggest financial scandal in Afghanistan's history erupted, the numbers were barely comprehensible to ordinary Afghans, whose average income was just two dollars a day. Kabul Bank was suddenly missing over $900 million in loans, most of them unsecured. Karzai's brother, Mahmoud Karzai, a shareholder in the bank, and family members of Karzai's vice president, Marshall Fahim, among many others in the inner circle of power, were directly involved in taking millions of dollars in loans from the bank. As customers began a run on the bank, the Afghan government, which could not even support its own budget, had to delve into its reserves to shore up the bank. Three years later, only between $200 and $400 million had been recovered. A number of bank officials were found guilty of mismanagement, but the shareholders and defaulters who had stolen the money were never charged with any crimes.

Karzai's supporters say the president is not personally corrupt. Yet he has tolerated and benefited from crooked dealings. His brothers, and indeed loans from Kabul Bank, bankrolled his election campaigns. He has shown leniency to members of his administration accused of corruption. He has sprung people from jail to serve his political interests.[9] In some cases, Karzai does not even seem to see it as corruption. When U.S. officials leaked to the *New York Times* that his chief of staff, Umar Daudzai, was receiving bagfuls of cash from the Iranian government for the presidential palace, Karzai brushed it off as a necessary way of doing business in his cash-strapped country. He added that the United States also gave him money. Three years later, he admitted to having received bags of cash from the CIA for over a decade. The presidential slush fund — millions of dollars — was used to maintain the political support of all manner of groups and factions, and to secure Karzai's two elections.

The issue that consumed Karzai more than any other in his second term was the Taliban. He hated the term "insurgency." At first he also refused to call insurgents "Taliban." He did not want to believe they were the rump Taliban movement. He referred instead to terrorism, and to people sent by the ISI and al Qaeda from outside, to attack his country.

His government had always invited former Taliban members to return home. Afghanistan was their country, and they had a right to live there in peace. The former president Sibghatullah Mojaddedi ran a reconciliation commission to enable them to return, though few ranking figures took up the offer. Karzai maintained contacts with a number of Taliban figures and supporters. By 2008, he had begun more serious efforts to make peace with the Taliban. Two things influenced him. Gulbuddin Hekmatyar, the renegade mujahideen leader who was close to the ISI and had been allied to the Taliban, sent Karzai two letters offering peace negotiations. The former president and deadly enemy of Hekmatyar, Burhanuddin Rabbani, advised Karzai to explore the offer. The Americans gave the go-ahead for talks, too, even though Hekmatyar was on their list of wanted terrorists. Hekmatyar's forces were small, with influence in the northeastern provinces of Kunar, Laghman, Baghlan, and Kapisa, but they were enough of an irritation to make the overture worth pursuing.

Then in July 2008, American jets accidentally bombed a wedding party in eastern Afghanistan. It was one of the most shocking bomb- ings of the war: a village wedding in the mountains, on a summer's day, in a remote, sparsely inhabited area close to the Pakistani border. The whole village, one extended family, was traveling on foot, accom panying the bride from her mountain hamlet to her new home in the groom's village. They had stopped to rest on a grassy slope when U.S. jets bombed them. The planes first hit a group of children who had run ahead, then circled back and hit the main group of mostly women and children, the bride among them. She escaped injury and fled, only to be struck down and killed by a third bomb. The U.S. coalition in- sisted it had struck a group of insurgents, but a government investiga- tion found forty-seven civilians, all from one family, had died in the bombing.

Karzai rarely traveled around the country, but he flew to the village of Deh Bala and spent two hours with a gathering of one hundred elders and grieving relatives. It was there that a mullah spoke out, re- minding the president that the job of the Caliph or ruler was to protect his people. Then a tribal elder stood and addressed Karzai: "For how long will you be attending funerals and shedding tears? You are the president. Change the situation."[10]

Umar Daudzai, the president's chief of staff, was with Karzai that day and said the villagers' admonitions hit home. From that moment, Karzai hammered the United States over civilian casualties. His pro- tests became more and more strident. He began to demand Afghan control over detainees, night raids, and armed security companies. In 2013, he banned Afghan forces from requesting NATO air support while on operations.

Karzai became convinced that the United States was not going to win the war against the Taliban. He had long realized that no administration in Washington was going to make Pakistan cease its support for the Taliban. Pakistan continued to ignore U.S. requests that it do more against the militants on its soil, and the United States was evidently not prepared to use greater pressure. Pakistan was, after all, a nuclear-armed country of 180 million Muslims, and in the scale of things more important than much smaller, impoverished Afghanistan. In 2006, a Western diplomat in Kabul told me how bitter Karzai felt because the Bush administration had promised to handle Pakistan but never had. "Karzai has been let down. He was told two to three years ago to pipe down on the Taliban, that the U.S. would ensure that cross-border diversions and cases of insurgency were dealt with, and the international community would ensure it would not get worse. Two years later things are a lot worse," he told me.[11]

By 2009, Karzai had come to the conclusion that peace was the only way forward — peace with the Taliban and with Pakistan.

Summer 2009. Shortly after General Stanley McChrystal took over as commander of coalition forces in Afghanistan, Ambassador Eikenberry went with him to see President Karzai. The Taliban's growing control over large areas of Afghanistan was reaching crisis proportions. President Obama would soon trigger a three-month review of strategic options, and General McChrystal wanted to argue for a substantial increase in U.S. forces. McChrystal's assessment was that if they did not stop the Taliban's momentum, in a year the war would be unwinnable. He was proposing the introduction of a new operational culture, that of a counterinsurgency campaign as opposed to the more narrow focus on counterterrorism. Counterinsurgency would mean flooding southern Afghanistan with tens of thousands of extra troops and police to tamp down the violence, break the Taliban's intimidation of the population, and give the government and the people enough security and confidence to get to work. But it would dramatically scale up the war.

Karzai was reluctant. He disliked the idea of counterinsurgency. To him, the answer was not more fighting in Afghan towns and villages.

The answers were at the source of terror in Pakistan, in the sanctuaries, training camps, and madrassas that were motivating young men to take up arms, and in the offices of the ISI that were sponsoring them. Moreover, if he faced an insurgency, that meant Afghans were rebelling against the government, and against him. Bringing in more foreign troops to counter the insurgency would further undermine the legitimacy of his government. His administration would be seen as a puppet government, and the Taliban would be seen as fighting on the right side, for independence and religion. The Taliban had long labeled Karzai a puppet and likened him to Shah Shuja, the Afghan king who had served under British patronage in the nineteenth century. The counterinsurgency would only reinforce that image.

Karzai and his staff proposed an Afghan solution to dilute the Taliban influence by working to reinstate traditional tribal leadership through development and employment programs. They wanted $25 million for a pilot project. Karzai also mistrusted McChrystal's plan to arm local militias. "He was ready to listen," Umar Daudzai told me. "But he asked: 'It was a surge for what, and to kill whom?'"

General McChrystal worked hard to gain Karzai's trust and eventually won his agreement for a surge and counterinsurgency campaign. McChrystal was the only ISAF commander who told Karzai that he felt he had two commanders in chief, President Obama and President Karzai. He did a lot to mend the broken relationship. McChrystal wanted Karzai to join him in leading the fight against the Taliban and turning the population away from the Taliban and toward a shared future, much as he had done in 2001.

But this time Karzai was a reluctant commander in chief. Publicly he barely supported the tough fight ahead, nor did he offer much support to his own troops. He rarely if ever visited Afghan troops or police, and rarely commended them for their bravery. He became increasingly distressed with each new case of civilian casualties and railed against the bombardments and night raids that caused them, even though McChrystal did more than any other commander to reduce civilian casualties. Karzai continued to call for peace, just as his soldiers and police were mobilizing for their biggest effort since 2001. He even went through a phase of appealing to the Taliban to put down their arms, addressing them as "Talib Jan" or "Dear Talib," until the fierce anti-Taliban jihadi leader, Abdul Rasul Sayyaf, told him to stop using the epithet.

Karzai was stuck. He was dependent on American military power for his own survival and now needed another influx of troops to prevent his government from being overrun. Vulnerable, ineffective, he lashed out in increasingly outspoken diatribes, often against his foreign backers. On one occasion, he burst into tears during a speech. On another memorable instance, he threatened to abandon the fight. "If you and the international community pressure me more," he told members of parliament, "I swear that I am going to join the Taliban."[12]

In 2009, Richard C. Holbrooke, the special envoy for Afghanistan and Pakistan, began the first diplomatic efforts to open back-channel contacts with the Taliban. He tasked the German diplomat Michael Steiner, who had worked with him on the Dayton peace talks that ended the Bosnian war, to make the first contacts. Steiner succeeded in holding several meetings with Tayeb Agha, a young, English-speaking assistant to Mullah Omar. Steiner brought American officials in on at least one of these meetings. He was offering no quick fix. His working theory was that it took the Soviet Union five years of secret contacts with the mujahideen in order to negotiate the safe withdrawal of its forces from Afghanistan.

When I asked Holbrooke to describe the U.S. strategy for Afghanistan — was it doubling up the war effort with a surge or going for peace talks? — he told me it was both. "It's jaw, jaw, war, war." He was intentionally mangling Winston Churchill's famous phrase that it was better to talk than wage war. Holbrooke added that when the United States was negotiating an end to the Vietnam War, negotiations that he took part in as a young diplomat, the fighting continued apace and U.S. casualties were at their highest, even as peace talks were underway. Well aware that the war in Afghanistan was running out of time, he was working hard to push through trade and political agreements between Afghanistan and Pakistan that would bind the two countries together and encourage peace.

Holbrooke was one of those who understood the wider diplomatic conundrum that Karzai was driving at. It was not peace between Kabul and the Taliban that was the key, but peace with Pakistan. When discussing the Western campaign against the Taliban with British Foreign Secretary David Miliband and senior diplomat Sherard Cowper-Coles, Holbrooke summed it up in typical blunt fashion: "We may be fighting the wrong enemy in the wrong country."[13]

12

Obama's Surge

"We don't trust foreigners. Their friendship lasts
only until the end of the afternoon."

— *Afghan landowner*

August 2010. The Taliban were at their zenith. News spread like wildfire that Taliban fighters had slung a chain across the road on the south side of Kandahar city and were stopping cars. For months, the insurgents had been steadily encroaching on the city from the surrounding districts. They roamed freely in the semirural suburb of Mahalajat just to the south, and were running checkpoints there in broad daylight, searching people and cars coming from the city. Now in the most brazen manner, the Taliban were operating inside the city.

Mahalajat was the Taliban's springboard into the city. It was from this suburb that a massive tanker bomb had entered Kandahar the previous summer an entire block of houses and shops and leveled, killing forty people. The blast resounded through the whole city and struck working-class families as they were sitting down to the evening meal to break the Ramadan fast. A second truck bomb exploded a few weeks later in a cemetery in Mahalajat, apparently also on its way toward the city. Kandaharis had suffered scores of horrific suicide bombings for three years, but this was a new level of calamity and made them despair.

By August 2010, the government seemed almost defeated. Parliamentary elections were just a month away, and life around Kandahar was paralyzed. The Taliban crept closer to the provincial capital, flaunting their presence in the surrounding districts more aggressively than ever before. Fighters were so confident that some of them were dropping in from Pakistan for a few months, to make some easy money before returning home, a resident told me. They demanded contributions from wealthy families, extracted protection money from security contractors, who paid them for safe passage for their supply convoys, and kidnapped people for ransom.

In December 2009, President Barack Obama had announced that the United States would send 33,000 extra troops to Afghanistan. The influx would be similar to the surge that President Bush had sent into Iraq in 2007, when the insurgency there threatened to engulf the country. Afghanistan was on an equally dangerous trajectory. Eighteen months had passed since military commanders had first flagged the need for more forces to stem the Taliban resurgence, and General McChrystal had been warning that the war would be unwinnable if they waited any longer.[1] Despite his campaign promises to put in the resources needed to win in Afghanistan, Obama was reluctant to send more troops when the crunch came. When he did send them, it was only just in time.

By August 2010, all the extra troops had arrived, but the surge had yet to make an impact in Kandahar. U.S. Marines had been operating in Helmand since the spring, but they seemed a whole planet away. American forces had been deploying over the summer months into Kandahar province, but they had not changed the status quo. Troops on forays from FOB Wilson on the main road of Kandahar were attacked every time, often within minutes of emerging from their base. Stryker Brigade units in Arghandab had been taking some of the heaviest casualties of any unit in Afghanistan, blown up by enormous roadside bombs that demolished their fighting vehicles. Afghan forces did conduct an operation to search Mahalajat in July, and NATO forces rounded up some Taliban suspects in a burst of heavy fighting in early August. Yet they had not dented the Taliban's persistent pressure on the city.

Nine years after they were chased from power, the Taliban were poised to overrun their old capital. Several hundred armed men ranged around Mahalajat, walking in the open with weapons. White Taliban flags appeared on houses just a few blocks from the district center. The government was barely functioning. Officials and police did not dare enter the twisting lanes and clustered hamlets of the neighborhood beyond their compound, for fear of ambushes and mines.

The chain-link roadblocks conjured up old fears for the civilians of the area who had lived through the lawless years of the civil war when gunmen stopped cars and killed people at will. Villagers and farmers visiting their fields, many of them former mujahideen themselves, described how they had to stand in silence as teenage Taliban fighters searched their pockets, smashing their cell phones and calling them spies. The Taliban often accused villagers of using the phones to tip off NATO forces about Taliban presence. They held the population in thrall. If they regained control of Kandahar, they would dominate southern Afghanistan once more.

Taliban fighters had moved into positions close to two police stations on the edge of the urban area, likely targets for attack. Families were packing up and leaving Mahalajat for the city. Townspeople had for months recognized members of the Taliban walking in the streets, and heard talk that known commanders were back in the area. They braced for an attack.

For the provincial governor, Tooryalai Wesa, the news that the Taliban were operating a roadblock inside the city was alarming. A ponderous, Westernized bureaucrat, he had spent much of the previous twenty years in Canada working in development. He was no fighter. He called the person who was really in charge in the south: Ahmed Wali Karzai, the president's brother. Together they called President Karzai to ask him to order NATO to intervene in Mahalajat. Karzai's chief of staff, Umar Daudzai, was with the president when the call came through, and told me about it.

"How many Taliban are there?" Karzai asked.

"Probably thirty to forty."

"How many bodyguards do you have between you?"

"Maybe a hundred."

"Well, how come you cannot move against them?" the president asked.

It was typical Karzai, giving orders almost blithely. Yet what happened next dealt the Taliban a body blow across southern Afghanistan from which they would not recover.

Goaded into action, the governor first ordered police to move against the Taliban checkpoint. Karzai had recently given his provincial governors the power to order operations by Afghan security forces in this kind of emergency. But the police soon ran into difficulties. Five policemen were killed by mines as they were returning to base.

The president's brother then turned to a loyalist strongman, the thirty-two-year-old commander of the border guards, Abdul Razziq, asking him to come up from his base at Spin Boldak on the Pakistani border. Razziq was the boss of the border. With his tribesmen border guards, he dominated the trade and smuggling business at the busy border crossing of Spin Boldak. He was an unruly but formidable enemy of the Taliban. He was the son of a mujahideen commander killed by the Russians, and nephew of the commander Mansour Achakzai, whom the Taliban had hung from a tank barrel in 1994. It was Mansour who had famously pulled the beard of the ISI operative Colonel Imam when he tried to lead a Pakistani trade convoy into Afghanistan. Razziq was open and friendly and enthusiastically pro-American. He wore a glittering skullcap and shalwar kamize, and proved as fierce and flamboyant a character as his father and uncle — and a vengeful opponent of the Taliban and Pakistan.

Under his leadership, Spin Boldak swelled and prospered despite frequent suicide attacks. Razziq's rule was so strong that the Taliban were kept at bay at the border, even as they encroached on the city of Kandahar. Part of Razziq's success was that his border police force was a mujahideen-type militia force — the only one of its type left in Kandahar. It had survived the disarmament program and been trained into a border force by the U.S. contractor Blackwater, by then renamed Xe Services.

Razziq's men, from the Achakzai tribe, fought and thought like the Taliban, and so were much more effective in combating the insurgents than other police forces. The Achakzai tribe lives on both sides of the border. Thanks to his tribal contacts in Pakistan, Razziq had accurate information about the movements of the Taliban and their leadership in exile in Quetta. He once told me he knew the houses and cell phone numbers of most of the Quetta shura, and I believed him. The pieces of information he gave me usually checked out. The American trainers put his men in uniforms and put them to work at customs at the airport, but at heart, Razziq and his force were still mujahideen. His men were mountain tribesmen, more familiar with guns and fighting than school or rulebooks. They lived by their own tribal code, and they hated the Taliban. They also were intent on reassuming their dominance of the border region and oppressing the Noorzai tribe, their rival in the region, which had prospered under the Taliban regime. The Karzai government understood Razziq's value and kept him on, even after an ugly incident in which he pursued a group of Noorzai all the way to Kabul, where he had them abducted and killed. Razziq has always insisted that the group were Taliban and were killed in a firefight on the border. He and his men were ruthless. A member of the Taliban told me once that they did not fear capture by NATO or Afghan forces, since they could usually bribe their way out within weeks or months. It was Razziq they feared. He did not take prisoners; he fought to the death.

When Ahmed Wali Karzai called in Razziq to help clear the Taliban in Mahalajat in late August, Razziq burst into the neighborhood with just a hundred men and routed the Taliban in five days. He said his men killed two Taliban fighters in the whole operation, and only one of his men was injured in a mine blast. Residents from Mahalajat said the death toll was much higher.

Rumors flew that Razziq had hanged two Taliban members from a tree. Razziq said it was the Taliban who did the hanging, killing two employees of the government.[2] He recounted with a grin that the Taliban had rigged a stolen police car with explosives; the bomber hid above it in a mulberry tree ready to pull the trigger. Suspicious, Razziq's men fired on the car, blowing it up, and the bomber dropped out of the tree and was also killed.

The Mahalajat operation sealed Razziq's reputation as a fearless conqueror of the Taliban. At last the Afghans were seeing their own government grasping the insurgents by the throat and forcing the Taliban into retreat. NATO commanders, for their part, especially the Canadians who had failed to keep the Taliban out of Mahalajat, were astonished at Razziq's success.

Home to 1.2 million people, Kandahar was critical to the stability of the whole of southern Afghanistan. With only two thousand troops, the Canadians had failed to control the insurgency in the province since 2006. Extra British and American units since then had only brought temporary help. The McChrystal counterinsurgency plan was on an altogether different scale. It swelled coalition forces in the south to 24,000, and tripled the size of Afghan Army forces. Police forces in Kandahar city were increased fivefold, to guard the entrances to the city and comb neighborhoods to stamp down on assassinations and suicide attacks. American troops moved into the districts around Kandahar through the summer of 2010, north into Arghandab, west into Zhare district, and into Dand to the southeast. The Canadians were able to draw back and concentrate all their forces on one district, Panjwayi. For the first time in Kandahar province, there were enough forces to conduct operations into all the districts around the city simultaneously and cut off the Taliban's infiltration routes. The Taliban had been used to escaping operations by moving into a neighboring area. Like a balloon, when squeezed in one place they would pop up in another. But this time they were feeling the squeeze in every quarter and finding their usual supply routes blocked.

Razziq's border guards spearheaded offensive movements into the districts, routing Taliban in Arghandab in September, and in the western districts in October, but he could not sustain long operations. Each time, after a few days, he would pull his forces out. The hard grind of counterinsurgency, securing and holding the districts from small outposts and with relentless patrolling, was left to the American forces and smaller units of the Afghan Army.

In the late summer, troops from the 75th Cavalry Regiment, part of the 2nd Brigade Combat Team of the 101st Airborne Division, made a slow, deliberate maneuver into Zhare, west of Kandahar city. It was a district infested with Taliban where coalition convoys and patrols had been repeatedly ambushed. The operation had been delayed for two months, partly because of Karzai's reluctance, but that had given the troops time to train with their Afghan counterparts and study the lay of the land and Taliban movements. When they did move in September, they executed one of the most exemplary counterinsurgency operations of the war, targeting Taliban defenses they had earmarked from their surveillance and clearing half the district within days. There was significant structural damage but hardly a single civilian casualty, since the population had left the area.

Zhare stretches south from the main highway west of Kandahar down to the west bank of the River Arghandab, a densely cultivated patchwork of walled gardens and fruit farms. The district includes Sangesar, the home village of Mullah Omar, where the Taliban first formed and made a bid for power. Taliban fighters had filtered back into the area soon after the heavy battles of 2006, and for the last four years had enjoyed almost complete freedom of movement funneling fighters and weapons further north and into the city. Most of the population had left, except the poorest sharecroppers. The Taliban built a sophisticated defense system through the area, with command posts, weapons depots, and safe houses that they used to ambush convoys along the main highway.

The place was teeming with fighters. Canadian forces had an outpost at Pashmul but came under attack driving in and out. As they pushed south from the road and set up combat outposts, U.S. patrols ran into persistent firefights. "If you stopped, within five minutes they would come and attack," Captain Matthew Crawford, an intelligence officer with the 101st, told me. The Taliban had scouts everywhere and were canny fighters. "They had a very early warning system, it was impossible to work undetected," he said. "They had good fighting positions and were unbelievably quick at getting their wounded out."

The Taliban used the terrain cleverly. They had built a layered defense, so they could pull back from their fighting positions through the gardens and vineyards to a cache where they would drop their weapons, and then fall back further to a safe house. But the 101st had been watching them for weeks, and as they fought their way down from Highway One, the main highway running due west, they targeted the Taliban safe houses and escape routes.

Within days the ambushes ceased on the main highway and traffic surged anew along the road. In mid-October, hundreds of American and Afghan troops made an air assault into the horn of Panjwayi, south of Zhare, seizing the region that served as the Taliban's rear base adjoining the desert. Razziq and his border guards blasted into the Taliban's last supply base at Bandi-Temur, on the edge of the Registan Desert, breaking open their jail and freeing a number of prisoners and kidnap victims. After a month of fighting, the Taliban pulled out entirely, escaping to Pakistan and ceding the area to the Americans. They told local residents they would wait out the surge and reinfiltrate fighters when the pressure was reduced.

U.S. forces were planning a different scenario, however. For the first time, they were moving into Kandahar's districts with an intent to stay and hold them with large numbers of security forces. Their plan was to stake a permanent presence in a series of combat outposts along the river valley and through the most populated areas, and build up the Afghan Army and police to take over security of the region. By destroying Taliban bases and weapons caches, deploying police and army, and strengthening the government, the U.S. and Afghan forces would render the area inhospitable to a Taliban return, General McChrystal reasoned.

The Taliban had nevertheless left behind a horrendous offering. Threaded throughout the lanes, orchards, and homesteads were hundreds of mines and improvised explosive devices, which the military called IEDs. They planted yellow plastic jugs full of fertilizer linked up to antipersonnel mines or homemade detonators. They rigged them with long-life batteries or even sponges to lie in wait until a soldier or villager came walking along and stepped on the trigger. They booby-trapped houses, doors, and gateways, outhouses, and even overhanging trees. Patrolling on foot, the daily business of a counterinsurgency campaign, was a grim and dangerous job. Soldiers would cut across country to avoid obvious routes, climbing twelve-foot mud walls rather than going through gateways, and wading through irrigation channels and newly dug fields to avoid walking on the well-trodden paths the insurgents expected them to take.

I went on patrol with a unit in Arghandab with photographer Joao Silva. We scaled fifteen walls in less than two hours to avoid paths and gateways that could be booby-trapped. I shredded my hands, wedging fingers and toes into footholds in the walls to haul myself up. I realized why most soldiers were wearing gloves even in the sweltering Kandahar heat. Joao was always ahead, taking photos, making light of the work despite his heavy camera gear. The toll from IEDs was heavy. The 101st's 2nd Brigade lost fifty-nine men in seven months in Kandahar, an officer told me. To save lives and time, units fired dozens of mine-clearing line charges, a rope loaded with explosives that is fired into a minefield to blow the mines for a one-hundred-yard stretch. In Arghandab, one commander called in airstrikes to level three villages, rather than risk his men's lives clearing them on foot. The villages were empty of civilians but sewn with mines and booby traps. The strain the mines were taking on the troops was evident. "From this door to that you might find four to five IEDs," one commander told me. "It's been scouts, infantry, cooks, everyone, walking to try and find mines with our feet." Added to that, they had the strain of not doing anything to hurt the local Afghans. "We walk around on eggshells, in case we might do something and get investigated," he said.

We too were walking on dangerous ground. A few days after climbing all those walls, Joao stepped on a mine during a patrol. I was on the road just outside the compound when I heard the explosion and shouts for a medic. Then they shouted that it was the photographer that was down, and I cursed. They carried him out to the road. His legs were mangled but he was still conscious. He grabbed the satellite phone from me and called his wife. Joao survived but lost both legs and spent the next two and a half years going through multiple operations alongside American soldiers at the Walter Reed Hospital in Washington, D.C., an ordeal that taught us all firsthand the horrific legacy of IEDs.

To bolster the surge operations, NATO commanders drew from old mujahideen and tribal networks in Arghandab with local knowledge of the Taliban in their area. General Khan Mohammad, an uneducated Alokozai tribesman from Arghandab who had become the most powerful mujahideen commander in Kandahar in the 1990s, was brought back from Kabul, where he had been sidelined in an obscure police job, and made Kandahar's provincial police chief. His thirty-two-year-old younger brother, Niaz Mohammad, was made police chief of Arghandab district. Another Alokozai mujahideen chief was tasked with raising a local police force of tribesmen to defend the villages. It represented a 180-degree turnaround from the years under the Karzai government during which mujahideen commanders had been made redundant and Kandahar's most powerful tribes sidelined.

The president's brother had concentrated on removing all challengers to his power in the south in the years after 2001. He had divided and weakened Kandahar's strongest tribes. He had had repeated clashes with the most powerful commanders of the Alokozai tribe, and had had two of them, serving police commanders, Khan Mohammad and General Akram Khakrezwal, removed and posted elsewhere in the country. Khakrezwal and a number of other influential Alokozai commanders were later assassinated. Their supporters pointed the finger at Ahmed Wali Karzai. One commander, Haji Granai, survived long enough to tell friends who rushed to his side that his attackers had been Ahmed Wali's men. One of those friends, who gave me his account, was later gunned down himself. Supporters of Ahmed Wali blamed the Taliban, pointing out that the Taliban, al Qaeda, and the ISI were skilled at exploiting divisions within the government and the tribes to weaken their opponents. That was true, and the Alokozai men were the Taliban's greatest opponents, but somehow Ahmed Wali survived and his rivals were conveniently removed.

The combination of the international community's demands for changes in government appointments and Ahmed Wali Karzai's machinations in the years after 2001 had been disastrous for Kandahar and much of the south. Many of the appointed officials had been too weak to perform their jobs, and the manipulation and fracturing of the tribes and society opened the way for the Taliban to exploit public grievances and make a comeback.

An effective counterinsurgency campaign demanded good and effective government alongside the military campaign. The first recommendation of General Stanley McChrystal's review was to remove the worst offenders among local officials, including Ahmed Wali Karzai. But the British commander in southern Afghanistan, Major General Nick Carter, wanted to work with Ahmed Wali rather than fight to get rid of him. "We agreed to hang out some red lines and sought to co-opt him into the framework," he said later.[3] General Carter also saw that former mujahideen commanders, such as Khan Mohammad and Abdul Razziq, however unsavory, were needed for the bravery and leadership they possessed. Bringing them in brought their tribes — and some of the most formidable fighting men in the province — with them. "It is about trying to be more inclusive because so much of what breeds insurgency is the 'haves' and 'have-nots.' So you need to have people in the tent if you can," Carter told me in an interview at his headquarters in the middle of the campaign. "By this stage of this insurgency you cannot afford not to get the help of everybody. Where the Taliban of course have been very clever over the last four or five years is to kill and intimidate the elders to such a degree that you do not have that glue that holds it together at the village level. And some of these guys have probably got the clout to be able to encourage elders to be braver, and we need to do that."

Within weeks of operations in Arghandab, the mujahideen police chief Niaz Mohammad was confident that the tide had turned against the Taliban. "We have broken their neck," he told me. Only small remnants remained in the district, and he said he did not expect them to regroup. The Taliban were tired from the fighting. They had also lost the support of the people. In previous months, their fighters had been preying on the farming population, demanding food twice a day and taxing all produce. When the tide turned against them, the local people supported the clearing operation.

Afghans were telling me all over the province that the Taliban had been dealt a debilitating blow, that their intimidating hold over the people was broken. It was still too dangerous for us to drive around the province and for Afghan reporters to be seen working with foreign journalists so I traveled mostly with the military, as an embedded reporter, traveling to the districts by helicopter or on armored convoys. I would go independently into Kandahar city and stay in a hotel for a few days to do interviews there. For the local Afghans, the province was suddenly open again, and they were able to move around. Haji Agha Kaka, a village elder and former mujahideen commander who lived at Kukaran, a village a couple of miles west of the city, had not even been able to attend his village mosque or walk to the end of the street for the last two years because of the threat of assassination by the Taliban. They had been using the area as a staging post to make attacks in the city. Now he had a base of Afghan and American soldiers on his doorstep, and tables had turned. "If the Taliban come to our village now they come like thieves. We saw one the other day and he ran away," he said.

For those of us who had been reporting in Kandahar since 2001, the surge represented a major shift. The Taliban had been thoroughly routed, and this time there was a plan to build and maintain strong security. Military commanders were cautious. The job of consolidating the Afghan forces and persuading people to support the government was going to be a long, slow process, they warned. Not everyone welcomed the new forces. When we went on a patrol through Kukaran, a local youth jeered at the Afghan soldiers, asking them why they had joined an infidel army. Haji Agha Kaka acknowledged the difficulties. Families were divided and took sides to settle scores. "These days you have to be careful of even having an argument with your own son, because he can just go off and join the Taliban," he said.

Nevertheless, the Taliban had taken heavy losses. The U.S. soldiers had intercepted radio calls from insurgents on the battlefield refusing help to each other, and complaining that the local population were no longer cooperating and were refusing to give them food and bury their dead.

U.S. troops had also received intelligence that Taliban commanders were resisting orders to return from their sanctuaries in Pakistan to fight. Some of the Taliban were even talking of joining the government's reconciliation program. With NATO's backing, President Karzai had revamped the program, creating a High Peace Council to encourage high- and low-level Taliban to give up the fight with offers of amnesty and jobs. It never secured significant defections from the Taliban, but the peace commission did successfully disseminate the message of a peaceful solution across Afghanistan, which helped undermine the Taliban cause.

By November, American commanders in Zhare were finding further signs that the insurgents were feeling insecure. The Taliban were no longer threatening with night letters but using them to beg for help from the community instead. "They became pleas to not cooperate in the cash-for-work programs, and pleas to give them food and a place to sleep," Captain Crawford told me. He knew local loyalties were not easily won. The people had told him they would wait to see if the Americans still controlled the area in two months. "That was four months ago." By January, the commander of the troops in Zhare, Lieutenant Colonel Tom McFadyen, said he sensed the fear in the community was beginning to subside, and people were starting to cooperate with his forces. Hundreds of laborers had come forward to work on community projects, and a fledgling local government was starting to function.

January 2011. In the wake of the surge, townspeople in Kandahar were saying that a lot of Taliban had slunk into the city and gone underground. Taliban fighters often moved into the cities for the winter, when the mountains were too cold and valleys devoid of green cover made it too difficult for fighting. They would stay with old friends and pick up daily laboring work. Some would carry out bombings and assassinations. This winter they did the same, but their mood was low. They were badly depleted and feeling hunted. They turned to old contacts for protection. An Afghan colleague came across an old acquaintance this way. The man was a mid-level Taliban commander and had sought shelter with trusted friends. It was never easy to meet or interview members of the Taliban, since for a long time the movement had had a policy of kidnapping or killing journalists either for political or financial gain. But in the changed circumstances in Kandahar after the surge, it seemed feasible. When I asked if the Talib would give an interview, the answer came back yes, since it was an old friend asking. I agreed not to publish his name or take his photo. He asked that I report his words truthfully.

We met on a construction site on the edge of Kandahar. The commander looked like any other poor Afghan laborer from the countryside, tall, thin, and bearded, a strong, bony face beneath a black turban, a cotton shawl wrapped around his upper body. He wore leather shoes with no socks, despite the near-freezing temperature, and sat down without hesitation on the cold concrete floor of the half-built house where we met for the interview. He was forty-five, a native of Kandahar province. He had been a fighter all his life. He joined the mujahideen at seventeen to fight the Russians, and joined the Taliban at its inception in 1994. He had been disgusted at the mujahideen leaders who were fighting each other for power, and blamed them bitterly for causing years of war, including the rise of the Taliban. He had been badly wounded in northern Afghanistan on the frontline in 2001 before 9/11, and convalesced for several years in Pakistan.

He rejoined the insurgency around 2004 or 2005 in a command and logistics role, drawn in by his brothers who were already fighting. Since the latest fighting around Kandahar, he was living in the city but moving all the time, not staying more than one day in the same place.

He said he passed through military and police checkpoints without difficulty.

The commander conceded that the Taliban had taken a battering and forfeited virtually all of the territory they had held in Kandahar province. The loss of bases in Panjwayi, their provincial headquarters, and of positions in Mahalajat so close to the city, were the worst blows. They had also ceded control of their main staging post at Bandi-Temur on the edge of the Registan Desert, which had been a base for the last eight or nine years. But he made light of the territorial losses. The Taliban would return in time, he said. "This is our country, these are our people, and we have only to retreat and wait and use other tactics." His words reminded me of Mullah Omar's comments on the Taliban's fall in 2001, when he said they would pull back and fight in a different way. They had done as he said.

Yet this commander admitted that some of the Taliban forces were losing heart, not only because of their heavy losses but because the mood of the people had changed. Some commanders now in Pakistan were reluctant to return to Afghanistan to fight. There were disagreements between the leadership and the field commanders about that. "Compared to two years ago when people were willingly going to fight, that mood is reduced," he said. "We are tired of fighting and we say this among ourselves." Taliban commanders were even discussing the option of peace talks and a power-sharing deal, but, he said, they would only negotiate with the Afghan government after foreign forces leave. "This is our vow, not to leave our country to foreigners," he told me.

He gave some stock answers that were nevertheless revealing. The Taliban leader, Mullah Omar, kept in touch with his followers through audiotapes passed from hand to hand, and recently exhorted his men to keep fighting. He encouraged them with an unlikely story, swearing that he had been searched three times at checkpoints in Afghanistan by Americans who did not know who he was. He promised to take revenge on those who had betrayed the Taliban in the heat of the battle. "This is an emergency situation and we will remember those who do ill to us," the commander quoted his leader as saying. The sound of his voice on tape had a very powerful effect on them all. "A lot of us have never seen Mullah Omar, but his order is everything," the commander said. "We obey his orders, every Talib does, and we believe in him."

Taliban casualties had been lower than claimed by NATO forces, he also noted. He had had two groups of twenty to thirty men under his command and had only lost four men in the last year with six wounded. Most of them had pulled out to Pakistan. He said they were ready to return, but he had advised them to wait and prepare for an offensive in the spring, when the weather would be warmer and the trees provide cover. "It will not be difficult," he said. "We have a lot of brave fighters." He added, "We do not bring in tanks and heavy equipment. What we bring is very light and simple."

U.S. forces were set on preventing their return by building up a strong Afghan security force that would then in turn persuade the people to reject the Taliban. But people would take some convincing. They knew U.S. forces would not stay forever, and they doubted that the Afghan government could protect them from the Taliban when the fighters returned.

One farmer and landowner who lived near Mullah Omar's home village told me as much. "We don't trust foreigners. Last time they came and then left, and left us to the Taliban. So we are careful. Their friendship lasts only until the end of the afternoon," he said. "The Russians were the same."

The Taliban commander voiced the same undeniable logic. "The Americans have promised a lot to the Afghan people, but they have not fulfilled their promises. They have forgotten what they said last year. They promised a good administration, and we have seen they empowered the people who we opposed: Gul Agha Shirzai; the ethnic groups; Abdul Rashid Dostum — they brought him specially back and everyone knows what he did to us. They have empowered those who were against us, and the people were against them. That is why we started the movement against them. We will never stop fighting them," he continued. "The whole administration, and the bad American system, is driving us."

By pulling out, the Taliban were counting on the Americans to alienate most Afghans, as they had done repeatedly over the last decade. "We are benefiting from this whole operation. Go to the districts, the Americans have destroyed the farms, they are killing innocent people, putting bags over people's heads, the troops with them are stealing from the people. This operation will show the people how bad they are," he said. "That's why we left, to show the people what it will be like under the Americans, and that it was better with us."

The commander looked at me directly with his black eyes. He was a man of flint. He never fidgeted from the cold or the hard floor. He barely moved at all. He said the loss of popular support was not as serious as in 2002 and 2003, when the Taliban were at their lowest ebb. "In the early days, when there was a drought and poverty, and the foreigners were promising a lot, that was when we did not have support of the people." Some of that was occurring in the days after this operation. "People are tired and are thinking like that. It was a big operation," he said of the surge. Yet there remained a base of support. "Some people are still helping us because they are scared, but some are doing it for religious reasons, and some because they hate this government." And, he added, Afghans would never let go of their desire for revenge.

At the end of the interview, when my notebook was closed and we were chatting before saying goodbye, the commander explained how the Taliban maintained its control over the rural population: "We just have to kill two people, and the village is in our hands."

The Taliban's capacity for ruthlessness was undimmed, but would it remain a winning formula, I wondered. It was clear to me that the surge had dealt a potentially fatal blow to the Taliban. It would take them years to regain the position they had held in Kandahar in 2010. Would the Taliban return from this setback, or would the Afghan government be able to hold them at bay this time? I asked the man who had helped to arrange the meeting, a trusted acquaintance who was from the area and knew the Taliban and the local people intimately. Would people start helping the Taliban again? I asked. "No," he said. "It's over."

• • •

There remained, of course, the other great question mark, that of the other enemy, the one behind so much of the insurgents' power. As the landowner from Sangesar, Mohammad Nabi, told me, it all depended on how strongly America wanted to defend Afghanistan. "If the Americans leave now it will be a big mistake. If in two years they leave and the Afghan security forces are not ready, we will see the Taliban back," he told me. Above all, he worried that America was not putting pressure on Pakistan, and Pakistan was not giving up its support for the Taliban. When Taliban fighters escaped to Pakistan during the surge of 2010, Pakistan forced them to go back into Afghanistan to continue fighting. "Still now the Pakistanis are very serious."

· 13 ·

Osama's Safe Haven

"In a Pakistani village, they notice even a stray dog."
— *Ejaz Shah, former domestic intelligence chief*

When he was about to deploy as the chief U.S. military representative to Pakistan in 2006, Major General James "Ron" Helmly called on a senior military officer for a chat. The officer explained to him that Pakistan was no conventional ally. If Osama bin Laden walked into President Musharraf's office to give himself up, the officer told Helmly, the Pakistani leader would excuse himself and call the American ambassador and tell him, "Come quick, I am having a bad dream." General Helmly's face twisted when he told me that story several years later. It was hard for a military man to accept that your ally would rather not capture your enemy for you.

Pakistan had often complained that America was a fickle friend, showering it with financial assistance and military cooperation when it needed something but then cutting off the aid and slamming on sanctions when it did not. That is certainly true. The United States should have built a relationship with Pakistan for the long term that encouraged democratic and economic development. Pakistan was the junior partner in the relationship but no less fickle, even while receiving billions of dollars of aid and enjoying the status of major non-NATO ally. For surely the ultimate test of loyalty is this: Are you harboring my enemy? Are you trying to hurt me?

An extraordinary test of Pakistan's relationship with America surfaced suddenly in public when the world learned where Osama bin Laden had been hiding. To the end of his life, bin Laden had been trying to organize plots against the United States, urging militant leaders not to attack Pakistani targets but rather focus their energies against America. So, did Pakistan knowingly shelter Osama bin Laden?

May 2011. The road was sealed off by the army, so we left the car and walked down a side street. The dirt road wound past several walled houses and a small village corner shop where we bought some cartons of fruit juice. It was early summer, but the weather in Pakistan was already hot. Police stopped us as the road opened out into fields, so we took another side street and crossed an open plot of land, walking a plank to pass over a stinking drainage ditch. We were in Bilal town, a neighborhood on the edge of Abbottabad, where new houses were going up piecemeal on agricultural land fringing the town. The roads were unpaved and houses were dotted unevenly among fields of young wheat and vegetables.

We walked along a track and there it was: Osama bin Laden's house, not a palace as we had been told, but a utilitarian, three-story concrete building, mostly concealed behind a twelve-foot-high gray cement wall, topped with rusting strands of barbed wire. The upper floor was visible but gave away few secrets. There were only a few, tiny windows, and the top terrace was closed in with a cement wall. This was where bin Laden had been hiding for nearly six years, cloistered in seclusion with three of his four wives and over a dozen children and grandchildren. Here, in a top floor bedroom, U.S. Navy SEAL commandos had shot him dead thirty hours earlier.

A police officer stopped us from approaching the house. We stood around chatting with him. He was as intrigued as we were about the whole event. The police had received calls from people living near the compound on the night of May 2, he said. They reported explosions and shooting, but the commanders had ordered the police to stand down and let the army deal with it. Yet army and intelligence operatives arrived too late to catch the U.S. SEALs during their forty minutes on the ground. The officer said that if the police had acted on those first telephone calls, they could have reached the scene while the American commandos were still there.

We were pondering this when suddenly the cordon was lifted, and the officer led us up to the walls of the house. The compound was still out of bounds, but the people living in the surrounding houses had been allowed out of their homes for the first time since the raid. They were agog with the news of their notorious neighbor.

After ten years of reporting in Afghanistan and Pakistan and tracking bin Laden, I was also fascinated to see where and how he had been hiding, just forty miles from the capital, Islamabad. He had dispensed with the large entourage of Arab bodyguards and mujahideen that had surrounded him in Afghanistan. For nearly eight years, living in the nearby town of Haripur and then Abbottabad, he had relied on just two trusted Pakistanis, Abrar and Ibrahim. American investigators described them as a courier, Abu Ahmed al-Kuwaiti, and his brother. Both men lived in rooms in the same compound with their wives and children, providing the cover of a typical extended Pakistani family.

Inside these walls, bin Laden lived a strange life, cut off from his war comrades, surrounded with women and young children and only his adult son, Khalid, as a male companion. He had spent hours ensconced in a small room with computers and a television but no Internet or phone lines. He continued to lead al Qaeda but mostly at one remove, sending messages that were stored on flash drives and computer disks, carried out by his courier and passed on and disseminated by others. He followed world events on a satellite television and through information brought back on flash drives by the courier.

American officials released a video found in the house of bin Laden sitting on the floor wrapped in a blanket, a wool cap on his head, watching videos of himself on a small television set. The officials said that he seems to have spent hours on the computer reading news and information about the world outside, and drafting letters and directives to militant leaders around the world. A billionaire's son, he had always tended toward the ascetic life, but he ended up living very modestly, with sixteen family members sharing ten cramped, cheaply furnished rooms. The man who had relished riding horses and hiking trails with the mujahideen in Afghanistan had been confined to pacing in the small kitchen garden planted with poplar trees. He was fifty-four at the time of his death. He had married five times and divorced once, in keeping with Islamic law that allows a man to have four wives at any one time.

Three of his wives were living with him in Abbottabad in 2011: Khairiah, Siham, both Saudi nationals, and Amal al-Sadah, a twenty-nine-year-old Yemeni, twenty-five years his junior, whom he married in the months before 9/11. His family had scattered after 9/11, but I was surprised at how many relatives bin Laden had around him. His first wife, his Syrian cousin Najwa, who bore him twelve children, had left him in the days before 9/11 and returned to Syria. His second wife, Khadijah, a well-educated Saudi, had requested a divorce in the mid-nineties when they had lived in Sudan.[1] Three of his grown children were also in the house, twenty-four-year-old Khalid who was killed in the raid, two daughters, and at least nine smaller children, five of them born to Amal in Pakistan since 9/11.[2] They had lived frugally, and Pakistani investigators said the children were hungry and poorly clothed when they took them into custody after the raid.

The courier, al-Kuwaiti, had bought four adjoining plots of land in 2004 and 2005, and built the house over the next year. He chose well. Abbottabad is a quiet town, surrounded by green hills and favored by Pakistanis for retirement and vacation homes because of its pleasant climate. Founded by a Major Abbott in the time of the British Raj, it is home to the elite Kakul Military Academy, Pakistan's equivalent of West Point, as well as several army battalions. Because of its military institutions and secret nuclear installations nearby, military security was always high in the town. The town was out of reach of U.S. drones, which were not permitted to fly beyond the immediate border areas.

Bin Laden and his couriers practiced careful operational security. The house had no communication lines that could be tapped, and he used no satellite or cell phone to contact al Qaeda members that could be traced through global positioning. Al-Kuwaiti only ever switched on his cell phone after driving an hour away from Abbottabad, to avoid being traced to the town, American intelligence officials later said. The family had other cell phones in the house for everyday use, however, and Pakistani intelligence picked up one phone call from the compound in 2004, which it passed on to U.S. investigators. At the time, the Pakistani officers thought it was connected to Abu Faraj al-Libi, al Qaeda's operational chief, who they suspected was in the area. (They captured al-Libi in Mardan, a town not far away from Abbottabad, in 2005.) Two cell phone calls were made to Saudi Arabia from the house, which Pakistani officials appear to have ignored, Afghan intelligence officials told me. Afghan intelligence had also been tipped off about the house and alerted their American counterparts. They thought that Mullah Kabir, a prominent Afghan Taliban leader, lived there.

The courier and his brother provided good cover for the larger bin Laden family hidden inside. They were known to their neighbors as Arshad and Tareq Khan, and they often strolled along the street in the evening with their small children, chatting with neighbors. They were friendly and courteous. They attended the local mosque and funerals in the neighborhood, but otherwise kept to themselves behind the high compound walls. Their children rarely played outside, unusual in a country where children spend most of their time running around in the streets and neighborhoods unsupervised. Women living nearby told me that when neighborhood boys let a ball fly into the compound by mistake, the owners gave them fifty rupees, less than a dollar, to buy a new one rather than let them in to retrieve it. Even when the boys started throwing balls in on purpose, the owners kept paying, one young woman told me, laughing.

The strict seclusion of the family was accepted by the neighbors. Pashtuns, especially from the tribal areas, are known to guard their privacy fiercely, and often have mortal enemies from a family or tribal dispute. "We thought maybe they had killed someone back in their village or something like that and were therefore very cautious," said a neighbor, an engineer who gave his name only as Zaheer. The brothers, both in their thirties, offered various explanations to the neighbors about their comparative wealth, once saying their uncle had a hotel in Dubai, another time that they worked in a foreign exchange business. They said they came from Charsadda, in Pakistan's North West Frontier province.

The courier and his brother were in fact protégés and friends since childhood of Khalid Sheikh Mohammed, one of bin Laden's senior lieutenants and the chief plotter of 9/11. They were raised in the same Pakistani immigrant circle in Kuwait as he was. Originally from Shangla, high up in the Swat Valley, the family were members of the Muslim Brotherhood affiliate Jamaat-e-Islami. Their father, a Muslim cleric known as Manjawor Khan, had emigrated to Kuwait in the 1970s. The brothers worked with bin Laden and Mohammed in Afghanistan and Pakistan in the years before 2001. When Ibrahim married a girl from Shangla in 2001, the wedding was held in Mohammed's house in Karachi. The two brothers, and Abrar's wife, were killed in the raid.

The house had a telling nickname. It was known as the Waziristan *haveli,* or Waziristan mansion, a house where people from the tribal region lived or congregated. It was said that wounded fighters were brought from Waziristan to recuperate there. I was told this by Musharraf's former civilian intelligence chief, Ejaz Shah. Ejaz Shah himself has been accused of having a hand in hiding bin Laden in Abbottabad. He denied any involvement. But he did not absolve local intelligence agents who, he said, would have certainly checked the place in order to know who was inside and who was being treated there. All over the country, Pakistan's various intelligence agencies, the ISI, the Intelligence Bureau, and Military Intelligence, keep safe houses for undercover operations. They use residential houses, often in quiet, secure neighborhoods, with discreet security, high walls, and armed guards, where they lodge people for interrogation, investigation, or just enforced seclusion. Detainees have been questioned by FBI officials in such places, and sometimes held for months. They are provided relative comfort compared to a jail cell: often a bedroom and attached bathroom but no legal rights or judicial procedure. Leaders of banned militant groups are often placed in protective custody in this way. Others, including the Afghan Taliban leaders who took refuge in Pakistan after the fall of their government in 2001, lived under a looser arrangement, in premises with their own guards but known to their Pakistani handlers, former Pakistani officials told me. Because of Pakistan's long practice of covertly supporting militant groups, the police have learned to leave such safe houses well alone. Police officers were warned off or even demoted for getting in the way of ISI operations.

The ISI was also compartmentalized. I gained some insight when reporting on the ISI with a colleague, David Rohde, in 2007. A former senior intelligence official who had worked on tracking down al Qaeda members after 9/11 told us that one part of the ISI was engaged in hunting down militants, while another part continued to work with them. He described how, when arrests were requested, the police refused to carry them out in some cases until they received written orders, believing the militants were still protected by the ISI, as they had been for years.

The Waziristan *haveli* was not an ISI safe house as such — it would have had armed guards, and bin Laden would have been under strict control, a retired ISI official told me. Bin Laden's house operated more like a militants' safe house, with the inhabitants managing their own security inside but covertly protected. A signal from someone inside one of the intelligence services that it was a safe house, to be left alone, or simply the *presumption* that it was by police and local officials, would have been enough to prevent closer inspection.

Almost incredibly, bin Laden's house stood within a few hundred yards of the brick perimeter walls of the Kakul Military Academy. Few in Pakistan therefore believed that the military did not know who was living in the house, or that the military could have slept through the raid on the night of May 2, 2011, and failed to apprehend the Americans during their forty minutes on the ground. The army chief attended officers' graduation parades there twice a year. Military cadets used to pass near the house on regular marathon runs. Pakistani helicopters sometimes flew straight over the house. Militant attacks on military personnel, including on training facilities and a cadets' parade ground, had grown so frequent that all the houses in the surrounding area were checked before each such event. Police and intelligence agencies have informers on every street in the vicinity of the military installations, people who watch for unusual comings and goings. A legislator from Abbottabad told me that the military would send plainclothes agents to check on every house before the visits of the army chief. Yet they would not usually enter houses and search them, unless there was reason to suspect anything untoward. They would rely on paid informers, or interview householders or their staff about who was inside or if there were new arrivals.

There can be no doubt that if there were local rumors about the Waziristan *haveli,* and if it housed wounded militants, local security officers would have had wind of it. That they did not check on the inmates was almost certainly because someone from within the security agencies vouched for the place. An ex-military officer once explained to me how to deal with the ISI: you just need to have one person inside the agency looking out for you, and that protected you from all others. Taliban and others who fought in Afghanistan, and in Kashmir, had always received protection and medical treatment in Pakistan with the tacit approval of Pakistani state agencies. There is a hospital, called the Imdad, in Quetta where wounded Taliban fighters are treated. It is a large, prominent building, known to everyone. The place is guarded by private guards. Members of the public are not permitted to enter. Men from Waziristan who had been wounded in Afghanistan would be afforded the same protection.

Still, in trying to prove that the ISI knew bin Laden's whereabouts and protected him, I initially struggled to do more than piece together circumstantial evidence and indirect suppositions from sources who had no direct knowledge. Only after badgering everyone I met did I finally uncover a bombshell. According to one inside source, the ISI actually ran a special desk assigned to handle the al Qaeda leader. It was operated independently, headed by an officer who made his own decisions. He did not have to pass things by a superior. He handled only one person: bin Laden. What he did was of course wholly deniable by virtually everyone at the ISI. Such is how super-secret intelligence units operate. But the top bosses knew about the desk, I was told.[3]

This revelation explained a lot. For example, there were things that did not make sense about bin Laden's hideout. He had no escape route or priest's hole to hide in, in case of a search party or raid. He was slow to react to the explosions in the house. He never reached for his guns or at least never fired them. From the accounts of the women in the compound, he knew from the instant it started that it was an American raid and, if anything, seemed resigned to the fact. In his correspondence, he had warned colleagues of betrayal by Pakistan. He relied on Pakistan to hide him but knew it could not last forever.

CIA officials thought of the same thing. As they watched his compound, they realized there was no back door, no tunnel. They concluded bin Laden was relying on being forewarned to evade capture. It was one of the reasons they decided not to bring the ISI in on their planning for the raid.[4] I realized U.S. officials had come to the conclusion that someone in the ISI had been protecting bin Laden too. "It is likely that 'someone' in ISI knew of UBL's residence in Abbottabad," General Helmly wrote to me in an email two years after the raid. (He used the military's standard acronym for bin Laden.) "It was most likely," he continued, that the army and intelligence chiefs "did not wish to know of this."

A string of prominent Pakistani officials have been linked to the possible installation of bin Laden in Abbottabad in 2005. Again, there is no hard evidence against them. Retired General Ziauddin Butt, who served as director general of the ISI in the government of Prime Minister Nawaz Sharif from 1998 to 1999, insists that someone in power had to have known when bin Laden was ensconced behind those high walls. He said he thought General Musharraf and Ejaz Shah had arranged for bin Laden to move into the safe house. "Since it was the Musharraf era and he was very well informed, he would have known," Butt told me. Shah was very close to Musharraf and "did everything" for him, Butt added. His theory is that they hid bin Laden in order to keep the war on terror on the boil and U.S. financial assistance flowing, while continuing to cooperate by capturing and handing over lesser al Qaeda figures. Butt was certainly qualified to know how such things were done in Pakistani intelligence circles, but he did not provide any proof for his claims, and he clearly had an axe to grind since he was removed from his post when Musharraf seized power in 1999 and jailed for two years. When Ejaz Shah threatened to sue him, he retracted his claims.

Ejaz Shah insists that everyone in Pakistan was genuinely appalled by the events of 9/11, and that no official would have hidden bin Laden. Yet even Ejaz Shah, who headed the Intelligence Bureau, Pakistan's equivalent of the FBI, from 2004 to 2008, agrees that someone had to have known. "Nobody can believe he was there without people knowing," he told me. "In a Pakistani village, they notice even a stray dog."

Another senior official who would have known of bin Laden's presence in Abbottabad was Lieutenant General Nadeem Taj, a former military secretary to Musharraf and relative of Musharraf's wife. Taj served as head of both Military Intelligence and the ISI during the years bin Laden moved to Haripur and then to Abbottabad. Taj also served as commandant of the Kakul Military Academy for a year in 2006, and so had lived and worked within a mile of bin Laden's house just when he was moving in. The chief of army staff, General Ashfaq Parvez Kayani, who served as ISI chief from 2004 to 2007 before succeeding General Musharraf in the top military post, also would have known. As did his successor at the ISI, Lieutenant General Ahmad Shuja Pasha, and his successor, Lieutenant General Zaheer ul-Islam, who served as the ISI's number two under Pasha, in charge of internal security.

I received another bombshell. A Pakistani official told me soon after the raid on bin Laden's house that the United States had direct evidence that the ISI chief, Pasha, had known of bin Laden's presence in the house in Abbottabad. The information came from a senior U.S. official, and I guessed that the Americans had intercepted a phone call of Pasha's or one about him in the days after the raid. "He knew of Osama's whereabouts, yes," the Pakistani official told me. The official was surprised, and said that the Americans were even more surprised. General Pasha had been an energetic opponent of the Pakistani Taliban, leading operations in Swat, and had proved an open and cooperative counterpart at the ISI. "Pasha was always their blue-eyed boy," the official said. But in the weeks and months after the raid, Pasha, and the ISI press office, strenuously denied that they had had any prior knowledge of bin Laden's presence in Abbottabad.[5] Yet Pasha's demeanor had been revealing. For the first time ever, the ISI chief was called on to testify before parliament. "Pasha's attitude was a mixture of threat, a mixture of bluster, and a mixture of intimidation, and then a lot of hyper-nationalistic talk about sovereignty," the Pakistani official recounted. It was because he had been caught red-handed. There was no proof that his boss, the Army Chief Kayani, knew anything, however. Kayani, the quiet general, was far more careful. Yet American officials suspected he also knew. The relationship between the two went back so far in the military that they considered there was nothing Pasha would do of which Kayani would not be aware.

Colleagues at the *New York Times* ran this information past U.S. officials in Washington, but suddenly everyone clammed up. It was as if a decision had been made to contain the damage to the relationship between the two governments. "There's no smoking gun," officials of the Obama administration began to say.[6]

The haul of handwritten notes, letters, computer files, and other information collected from bin Laden's house during the raid revealed regular correspondence between bin Laden and a string of militant leaders, Pakistanis and Arabs, who must have known that bin Laden was living in Pakistan. American investigators going through the load found correspondence with Hafiz Saeed, the founder of Lashkar-e-Taiba, the pro-Kashmiri group that has also been active in Afghanistan. Bin Laden had likewise maintained correspondence with Mullah Omar. Saeed and Omar are two of the ISI's most important and loyal militant leaders. Both have been protected by the agency. Both cooperate closely with it, restraining their followers to coordinate with Pakistan's greater strategic plans and never attacking the Pakistani state. Any correspondence the two men had with bin Laden must surely have been known to their ISI handlers.

There were other connections to Pakistani militants. The courier al-Kuwaiti's cell phone, which was recovered in the raid, contained contacts to the militant group Harkat-ul-Mujahideen, which had been the closest Pakistani group to bin Laden in the 1990s and also a long-time asset of Pakistani intelligence. In tracing the calls made by the Harkat contacts, American analysts found that the militants were also in touch with, and had even met with, ISI handlers.[7] The ISI has often explained that it needs to maintain contacts with Afghan Taliban and members of banned Pakistani militant groups as part of its basic intelligence gathering.

Western officials have grown weary of this excuse. The high level of those involved on both sides of these meetings means the interactions are far more serious than a general debriefing, one Western diplomat in Islamabad told me. Other correspondence revealed that bin Laden and his aides were discussing the idea of a deal with Pakistan in which al Qaeda would refrain from attacking Pakistan in return for protection inside the country. Some of the correspondence dated from the last year of his life.[8] The correspondence does not prove that bin Laden was in touch with the Pakistani officials about any deal, but Pakistani journalists and some former security officials say it matches their understanding of bin Laden's relationship with the ISI. They believe bin Laden was supportive of Pakistan, whereas his deputy, Zawahiri, was not.

Bin Laden did not only rely on correspondence. There were occasional comings and goings from the Abbottabad compound, and he did travel to meet his aides and fellow militants. "Osama was moving around," one Pakistani security official told me, adding he heard so from jihadi sources. Bin Laden would travel "for inspiration," he said. "You cannot run a movement without contact with people." He traveled in plain sight, relying on contacts seeing him through any checkpoints. In the same way that police gave a wide berth to militants' safe houses, so too did they let VIP convoys pass through highway check-points, no questions asked. In 2003, bin Laden traveled with a small group of men and women from Peshawar to the Swat Valley where he stayed for six to eight months. Bin Laden had shaved off his beard, and was with his youngest wife, Amal, and their small daughter. The courier Ibrahim and his wife, Maryam, accompanied them. A driver and a man in a police uniform escorted the group.[9]

In 2009, bin Laden was reported by Pakistani intelligence to have vis-ited Kohat, in Pakistan's tribal areas, to meet with the Pakistani mili-tant leader Qari Saifullah Akhtar. Akhtar was the commander accused of trying to kill Benazir Bhutto on her return in 2007. Often called the "father of jihad," Akhtar is considered one of the ISI's most valu-able guerrilla assets. A Pashtun born in Waziristan, he was a graduate of the Binori madrassa in Karachi, infamous for its extremist, sectar-ian teaching. He founded one of the first Pakistani militant groups, Harkat-ul-Jihad-ul-Islami, or HUJI. After years in Afghanistan, he was close both to Mullah Omar and bin Laden. He is the person credited with driving Mullah Omar out of Afghanistan on the back of a mo-torbike in 2001, and moving bin Laden out of harm's way just minutes before U.S. missile strikes on his camp in 1998.[10] After 2001, he was detained several times in Pakistan. Yet he was never prosecuted and was quietly released each time by the ISI.

At his meeting with bin Laden in August 2009, Akhtar reportedly requested al Qaeda's help in mounting an attack on the Pakistani Gen-eral Army Headquarters in Rawalpindi. Intelligence officials learned about the meeting later that year, from interrogations of men involved in the attack who were detained afterward. The information on the bin Laden meeting was compiled in a report seen by all the civilian and military intelligence agencies, security officials at the interior ministry, and U.S. counterterrorism officials. The report was leaked to the Paki-stani newspaper *The Daily Times* in May 2010. It is the only recorded episode showing that bin Laden's presence inside Pakistan was known to Pakistani intelligence agencies.[11]

At the meeting, bin Laden rejected Akhtar's request for help on the

headquarters attack and urged him and other militant groups not to
fight Pakistan but to serve the greater cause — the jihad against America. Bin Laden warned against fighting inside Pakistan since it would
destroy their home base: "If you make a hole in the ship, the whole ship
will go down." He told Akhtar that he did not want to allow U.S. forces
an easy exit from Afghanistan. He wanted Akhtar and the Pakistani
Taliban to accelerate the recruitment and training of fighters, so they
could trap U.S. forces in Afghanistan with a well-organized guerrilla
war. Bin Laden said Pakistan, Afghanistan, Somalia, and the Indian
Ocean would be al Qaeda's main battlefields in the coming years, and
he needed more fighters recruited from those areas. He even offered
navy training for militants, saying that soon the United States would
exit Afghanistan and then the next war would be waged on the seas.

Akhtar, in his mid-fifties by 2013, remains at large in Pakistan. He
is still active in jihadi circles and running madrassas. Pakistani intelligence has also established that he has been in contact with Zawahiri
and Mullah Omar since 2010. He is an example of a militant commander whom the ISI has struggled to control, yet who is too valuable
for them ever to lock up or eliminate. They keep trying to bend and
use him, instead.

The ties between Pakistani militants and al Qaeda were undeniable,
but even as the Musharraf government arrested al Qaeda figures, it
always sought to cover up the extent of the links with Pakistani groups.
The top al Qaeda figures caught in Pakistan after 9/11 were found in
homes of Pakistani Islamist supporters, far from the border with Afghanistan. Abu Zubaydah was caught in the house of a worker of
Lashkar-e-Taiba in the Punjabi town of Faisalabad. Lashkar-e-Taiba
was a favorite group of the ISI and continued operating throughout
the decade after 9/11 despite evidence that it was behind the worst terrorist actions in the region. The mastermind of 9/11, Khalid Sheikh
Mohammed, was taken into U.S. custody from a house in Rawalpindi,
the home of Pakistan's army, that belonged to a member of the religious party Jamaat-e-Islami and whose relatives were serving military
officers. Two of the suicide bombers responsible for the hits on the

London transport system on 7/7 in 2005 had met with a leading figure of Jaish-e-Mohammad in the Pakistani city of Faisalabad during a
trip there two months before the attacks. Rashid Rauf, the chief suspect in an al Qaeda plot ordered by Zawahiri to blow up planes over
the Atlantic Ocean, was a member of Jaish-e-Mohammad and related
by marriage to its leader. Pakistani authorities arrested Rauf in 2006
but never handed him over to British police despite repeated requests,
probably because he knew too much of the depths of the links. The
list goes on. Even after the Red Mosque siege in 2007, Musharraf and
Kayani still thought they could control the militants and turn them
to good use. Government policy was to control and use them while
cracking down on the wayward ones, and above all hiding the depth of
the connections. Bin Laden was an intrinsic part of that plan.

There were also occasional visitors to Abbottabad who should have
caused security officials to do a more careful search of the environs.
Abu Faraj al-Libi, an important operational commander, often described as the third in command of al Qaeda, had been behind the two
assassination attempts on General Musharraf in 2003. He lodged in
Abbottabad occasionally before his capture in 2005. One of his associates had rented no less than three houses in Abbottabad for al-Libi's
use, according to Musharraf, who recounts the details in his book, *In
the Line of Fire.*[12] As police closed in on one house, al-Libi, who was
staying in another, managed to escape. That alone should have made
Pakistani law enforcement scrutinize real estate records in towns like
Abbottabad more methodically.

One visitor to Abbottabad who clearly did reach bin Laden was his
third wife, Khairiah, a woman of over sixty who had spent most of the
decade in Iran separated from bin Laden. She had been with a group
of bin Laden's family members that had traveled to Iran after 9/11 and
been detained under house arrest by the Iranian authorities. Iran was
anti-America but had no love for bin Laden. Some of the group were
released in exchange for the Iranian diplomat Heshmatollah Attarza-
deh, who was kidnapped in Pakistan in 2008 and held hostage in the

tribal areas for sixteen months, according to Pakistani intelligence officials. Angry at the deal, Pakistani officials briefed one of my Pakistani
journalist colleagues about it at the time. The story was impossible to
verify then, but some of bin Laden's children were allowed to leave
Iran. Khairiah traveled to Pakistan to rejoin her husband along the
smuggling routes that militant groups have long used to evade border
controls. According to Pakistan's official Commission of Inquiry into
the event, she arrived in Abbottabad in early 2011.

The Abbottabad raid caused shock waves that reverberated through all
layers of Pakistani society: Shock that bin Laden was hiding in such a
small, bucolic town, when Pakistanis had been told for years by their
leaders that he was either in a cave in Afghanistan or dead. Shock that
the U.S. commandos slipped under Pakistan's radar, raided a house,
and escaped unhindered, even stopping to refuel inside Pakistan.
There was little anger, however, at the fact that bin Laden had been
killed. Public reaction was limited to a few small demonstrations by
religious parties, with none of the violence that raged on the streets
after the deaths of Benazir Bhutto in 2007 or the Baluch tribal leader
Nawab Akbar Bugti, shot by the Pakistani army in 2006. Revenge attacks from militant groups would come later, but the general public
did not rise up. Bin Laden was not popular within Pakistan. What did
rise was criticism against the military and the intelligence services for
their evident failures. Shock turned to resentment within the military,
especially when CIA chief Leon Panetta said that the United States had
decided not to work with Pakistan in hunting for bin Laden because of
fears that leaks might alert the target.

The media, especially prominent television talk-show hosts, exploded with outrage and astonishment at the ineffectiveness of the
military, and suspicion that it had been playing a double game and
hiding bin Laden all along. Jokes began circulating by text message
and social media among the English-speaking elite. The favorite one
was a poke at the failure of Pakistan's air defenses to detect the U.S. helicopter raid: "Pakistan radar system for sale: $99.99. Buy one, get one
free (can't detect U.S helicopters but can receive Star Plus)," a reference

to an Indian satellite channel. Others tweaked the army's pride in its service: "Public Service Message from the Army: 'Stay Alert. Don't rely on us. Don't honk. Cantonment area.'" And, "Brave, honest and dedicated 'bloody' civilians for protection of our delicate armed forces." More angry comments circulated about the generals' appropriating much of the country's wealth with investments in vast real estate developments, shopping centers, farms, factories, and banks, instead of guarding Pakistan's borders.

The military was dumbfounded and made no immediate public comment. The first government statement came from the office of President Asif Ali Zardari, the widower of Benazir Bhutto who had succeeded Musharraf as president after her death. He welcomed the death of bin Laden. For General Kayani, however, it was the bad dream as described years earlier to General Helmly. Kayani had an internal crisis on his hands as feelings of humiliation within the army swelled into a backlash against the United States. He was quick to distance himself from the relationship with the United States and asked that the U.S. administration not announce that Pakistan had cooperated in the raid. He announced he was withdrawing military cooperation with the American troops serving in Pakistan's training facilities, and he warned that another such affront to Pakistan's sovereignty would force Pakistan to review its overall cooperation with the United States.

Then the army chief set off around the country, visiting six garrisons in a week to dispel doubts about the state of the army and his leadership. The top brass was alarmed that the raid had revealed the weaknesses of Pakistan's armed forces, which might inspire its rival, India. Internally, the strain in the army was showing. After ten years, the military's dual policy of supporting the United States in the war on terror while trying to keep Taliban and Kashmiri militants in the wings and loyal had confused and angered many in the lower ranks of the army. They were fighting, and dying, in campaigns against Islamist militants, apparently at the request of America, but at the same time they were being fed a constant flow of anti-American and pro-Taliban propaganda, peddled by the military, which considered the Islamist

forces as critical to Pakistan's strategic interests. Those years of propaganda were showing results. Junior officers increasingly questioned
Pakistan's alliance with the United States in the war on terror and saw
the raid on Abbottabad as the action of an aggressor.

Three weeks after the bin Laden raid, the armed forces suffered a
further embarrassment. Pakistani militants armed with suicide vests
and rocket-propelled grenades breached the perimeter of Pakistani
Naval Station–Mehran outside Karachi, blowing up two highly valuable P-3C Orion surveillance planes bought from the United States.
Fitted with banks of computers, listening equipment, and cameras,
these planes are the sort used to intercept pirates in the Indian Ocean,
militants in the tribal areas, and bin Laden in Abbottabad. At least ten
servicemen were killed. There were undoubtedly sympathizers inside
the naval base who had helped to plan the attack.

In the aftermath, American officials pushed for greater cooperation
from Pakistan to prove its loyalty in the war on terror. They wanted
the government to move against other militant leaders in Pakistan,
including Mullah Omar and Sirajuddin Haqqani. General Pasha was
forced to consider the idea in the days after bin Laden's death. But the
anger and embarrassment over the raid was too great. It drove Pakistani military leaders to take a more nationalistic stance. The nation's
media outlets were told by the ISI's chief, Major General Athar Abbas,
to focus on the violation of Pakistani sovereignty by U.S. forces, rather
than the presence of bin Laden in Pakistan and the failings of Pakistani
military and intelligence.

U.S.-Pakistani relations had already reached a breaking point by
May 2010. A few months earlier, a CIA contractor, Raymond Davis,
had shot dead two petty thieves in broad daylight at a busy intersection in the city of Lahore. He was arrested by police — and saved
from a near lynching by the crowd — but his case turned into an angry wrangle between the U.S. and Pakistani governments. Pakistan
was unhappy about the United States' growing network of CIA spies
who were working independently of Pakistani institutions, especially
the ISI. The United States had developed its own web of agents and

informers in the tribal areas to track militant leaders and pinpoint targets for drone strikes. The strategy had improved the accuracy of drone strikes but infuriated the ISI, which was losing control of the program.

Raymond Davis's behavior encapsulated everything Pakistanis hated about the overbearing American behavior toward them. Yet Pakistani military and intelligence chiefs were more worried that they were no longer directing the fight against militancy inside Pakistan nor able to keep particular protégés safe. The bin Laden raid showed America's determination to work alone when it had to.

So Pakistan decided to make its own way.

Someone, almost certainly from the ISI, leaked the name of the American CIA station chief in Islamabad to the Pakistani media one week after the Abbottabad raid. The ISI had done the same thing a year earlier, forcing the then CIA station chief to be pulled out of the country. Then on May 29, in a particularly ugly suppression of the truth, a journalist for the *Asia Times* Online, Saleem Shahzad, was abducted and killed by ISI agents in Islamabad. His badly beaten body was found in an irrigation stream miles from the city. Admiral Michael Mullen, chairman of the U.S. Joint Chiefs of Staff, told American reporters that Shahzad had been killed on the orders of the two most powerful men in the Pakistani army, Generals Kayani and Pasha.[13] The ISI vehemently denied any involvement in Shahzad's abduction, but the United States had intercepted another revealing phone conversation.

Far from pursuing other Taliban or al Qaeda members, Pakistan continued to back the Taliban and let militancy flourish in Afghanistan. On June 28, eight gunmen sent by the Haqqani network stormed the Inter-Continental Hotel in Kabul, a landmark built in the 1970s in the heyday of Afghan development. It featured a swimming pool and popular restaurant on the top of a wooded hill overlooking the city. The gunmen battled Afghan commandos for hours through the night, killing eleven civilians and two policemen. NATO helicopters ended the siege, striking the last gunmen when they reached the hotel rooftop. They were in constant cell phone contact with Badruddin

Haqqani, the younger brother of Sirajuddin, who had become the operational manager of most of the complex attacks in Afghanistan. He repeatedly urged them on from his safe haven in Pakistan.

A few months later in September came two of the worst complex attacks by Haqqani fighters up to that point. A massive truck bomb barreled into an American base in Wardak province, south of Kabul, on September 10, killing five Afghans and wounding ninety-six people, seventy-seven of them American soldiers. Three days later, gunmen seized a tall building under construction on the edge of the diplomatic area of Kabul, and laid siege to the U.S. embassy and several other embassies around it for nineteen hours. It was the most serious armed assault they had ever mounted in the capital. Mortars and rocket-propelled grenades rained down on the embassy and surrounding areas. Visitors to the U.S. consulate on the south side of the compound were hit by the missiles. Sixteen people, including six children, died in the attack. The U.S. ambassador, Ryan Crocker, was pinned down in a bunker, along with all his staff, for twenty-four hours.

Pakistan's continued support and protection for the Haqqanis exasperated the Obama administration. On September 20, the veteran mujahideen leader and former president Burhanuddin Rabbani, who was heading Afghanistan's High Peace Council and pursuing Karzai's aim to woo the Taliban to make peace with Kabul and join the government, was killed by a suicide bomber who carried a bomb in his turban. The man had claimed to be carrying a special message from the Taliban leadership, and Karzai had urged Rabbani to see him. Afghan investigators suspected the ISI of being behind the attack. They caught the bomber's Afghan accomplice in Kabul before he could escape. Under interrogation, he revealed that two Pakistani men in Quetta, whom he knew only as Mahmoud and Ahmed, had plotted the attack and sent him in with the suicide bomber. "Almost certainly they were ISI. They proposed this plan," a senior Afghan security official told me.

For Admiral Mullen, the string of attacks by Haqqani fighters, culminating in the assault on the U.S. embassy in Kabul, was the last straw. Mullen, despite dedicating many hours and air-miles on his relationship with Kayani, realized that the army chief had no intention of reining in Pakistan's proxies and had been deceiving him all the way. About to retire, Mullen decided to speak frankly in testimony before a U.S. Senate panel. Pakistan was aiding terrorism and deserved sanction. He described the Haqqani network as "a veritable arm" of the ISI.[14] Pakistan was supporting the Quetta shura and Haqqani network, he said. "The actions by the Pakistani government to support them — actively and passively — represent a growing problem that is undermining U.S. interests and may violate international norms, potentially warranting sanction.

"They may believe that by using these proxies, they are hedging their bets or redressing what they feel is an imbalance in regional power," he continued. "But in reality, they have already lost that bet. By exporting violence, they've eroded their internal security and their position in the region. They have undermined their international credibility and threatened their economic well-being."

"Mike said what everybody else was thinking," a retired senior official told me.[15] It was the most damning critique yet of Pakistan's behavior.

Pasha and Kayani carried on regardless. They continued pushing back against their critics and against the United States. In November, when U.S. airstrikes killed twenty-four Pakistani soldiers manning posts on the Afghan-Pakistan border — U.S. forces say they struck militant firing positions — Pakistan closed its borders to NATO supply convoys. Pakistan had blocked the border on short occasions before, in protest of U.S. military actions, but this time it did so for seven months, costing the United States and NATO millions of dollars by forcing them to reroute supplies through northern Afghanistan. A Pakistani journalist told me that the generals' whole behavior since the bin Laden raid was typical of his compatriots. Caught doing something wrong, their attitude was "Screw you," he told me.

The government of President Zardari, members of which were only too happy for bin Laden to have been caught and killed, acted carefully in the aftermath. The military was like an angry animal that could easily bite its owner. In a scandal known as Memogate, a memorandum written to Admiral Mullen asking for U.S. intervention to prevent a military coup in Pakistan after the bin Laden raid was leaked to the press. The Pakistani ambassador to the United States, Husain Haqqani, was accused of composing the memo. He came under formal investigation and was indicted for treason. The case later collapsed, but Haqqani was forced to resign amid considerable threats to his person. He had long irked the military, opposed ISI control of foreign policy, and argued for cooperation with the United States.

It took more than a year for the anger over the bin Laden raid to subside enough for cooperative relations to resume between the United States and Pakistan. For some in the region, there was relief that Pakistan's subterfuge was finally revealed. The Afghans felt vindicated, their constant warnings proved true. Admiral Mullen said he had always told General Kayani that if they had intelligence on bin Laden, the United States would act on it. The Americans, it seemed, had finally drawn a line.

Yet vis-à-vis Afghanistan, nothing much changed. Pakistan remained obdurate in its support of its proxies, which continued to conduct high-profile attacks on the Afghan capital. The U.S. government, if more circumspect now about Pakistan's motives, fell back into its mode of careful diplomacy, mollifying Pakistani leaders in public and keeping any stronger talk private. "Everybody now is kind of walking on eggs and hoping that ultimately the relationship can become stabilized," the former official told me.[16]

The Pakistani military was weakened, battered from all sides. For the first time ever, senior generals were arraigned in court for corruption. Politicians appeared bolder, demanding to inspect the military budget, previously secret. They also pushed back on the military's meddling in politics. Nawaz Sharif, victim of the military coup in 1999, won the 2013 election, vowing among other things to impose civilian control over the military. His first six months in office witnessed a spasm of violence, however. Pakistan's militants, and their masters, the military, seemed to be warning him or testing his resolve. His plans to improve relations with India and Afghanistan, and to curb the military, were going to be mammoth tasks, even with Sharif's strong political mandate.

A month after Sharif took office, someone leaked the report of the Pakistani Commission of Inquiry into the Abbottabad raid to Al Jazeera television. The commission did not offer any new evidence of Pakistani complicity in hiding bin Laden, but it did not rule it out. Overall, it blamed incompetence rather than complicity, often the excuse Pakistani officials fall back on, but it added that key government officials had not always provided satisfactory testimony and questions remained unanswered. It was blisteringly critical of almost every institution involved: the police, intelligence agencies, armed forces, and civilian government. It reserved its harshest comments for the ISI, which it found both overbearing in its usurpation of authority and incompetent. Individual security lapses were understandable, but "taken together suggested the possibility of something more sinister," the report said.[17]

General Musharraf meanwhile refused to go quietly. He had gone into exile in London after stepping down as president in 2008 but kept busy with speech tours and television interviews. In 2013, he chose to return to Pakistan to gather political support and run for parliament. He miscalculated, however, and was barred from running for office because of pending court cases charging him with complicity in the murder of Benazir Bhutto and treason for violating the constitution and ordering the arrest of judges during the 2007 state of emergency. Within days he was ordered to appear in court and arrested. He was allowed to remain under house arrest at his spacious farmhouse villa, yet his star, and that of the Pakistani army, had been brought to a new low.

If allowed to proceed, the court cases may unravel some of the remaining mysteries of the Musharraf era. One day as he sat at home in Islamabad, the retired general Talat Masood was watching an interview with Musharraf on television. Masood was struck by something the general said. Musharraf was talking about bin Laden and, as was often the case, he was talking too much. It dawned on Masood that the former army chief had known about bin Laden and where he was hiding. "It was a statement he made in the interview," he told me. "I got a feeling that he knew."

Springtime in Zangabad

"They are finished. Finished. You are witnessing yourself.
This was ungoverned territory, and now the whole area
is full of Afghan flags."

— *Abdul Wudood, leader of a popular uprising against*
the Taliban in Zangabad

February 2013. It happened one day of its own accord. The people of Panjwayi, Afghanistan, stood up and turned against the Taliban. Residents joined police to run them out of a small cluster of villages in Zangabad. Their success set off a popular uprising that spread through dozens of villages. Within days, hundreds of villagers rallied to support the government, and Afghan flags were flying from rooftops across the district. As security forces closed in on the last Taliban bases on the edge of the desert, villagers came forward with information, vowing to keep the Taliban out and offering their sons for a local defense force. It was the most significant popular turning against the insurgents in years of fighting, and it happened right in the Taliban heartland, where the movement had first begun nearly twenty years earlier.

At first there was little reporting of it. So in mid-February, ten days after the uprising began, I went out with the Afghan police to Zangabad to see for myself. We drove in an armored Humvee donated by the U.S. government, along the new, asphalt road built by Canadian troops, and dipped south on a dirt track for a mile or so to the village of Pishin Gan Sayedan. We headed to the home of Abdul Wudood, a former mujahideen commander and farmer who had led the uprising. This had long been hostile territory. Zangabad had been a base of Taliban operations for most of the last decade, and even since the surge was still a hotbed of the insurgency. The previous year, an American soldier had walked out of a special forces base near this village and massacred sixteen Afghan civilians in their homes. The Afghan intelligence chief Asadullah Khaled was attacked by the Taliban when he visited the scene of the massacre to offer condolences to the victims' families. One Afghan soldier was killed in that attack.

Yet I was not too worried about my safety. I had learned that the safest way to visit a village in Afghanistan is with people from the area, and the local police were accompanying us. It flashed through my mind that the local police had been the main culprits in numerous insider attacks, turning their guns on their American mentors or their own Afghan colleagues. But police chief Sultan Mohammad had confidence in them and dispatched us with a few swift orders. The men turned out to be relatives of the police chief. The driver stopped on the way to greet an elder standing by the road, his uncle.

It was a warm, sunny day, one to lift the spirits. The fields and trees were still bare from the winter, but a pale pink blur of almond blossom, the first herald of spring in Afghanistan, brought a hint of color to the muddy brown landscape. The Afghan flag flew above two raisin barns on the edge of the village where police manned positions overlooking the serried banks of the vineyards. Wudood was waiting for us and took us into his guesthouse.

He sent word around the village, and soon fifty or more elders downed tools and congregated at his house. They were poor farmers with weather-beaten faces and gnarled hands. They slipped off their muddied galoshes and sat cross-legged on the floor of a deep verandah, sipping green tea as Wudood recounted his story of the uprising. As I looked around at the gathering of elders, I realized what I was witnessing: the end of the road for the Taliban in this area. Some of these men, perhaps most of them, had long given support to the Taliban.

They had given them shelter and food, and tipped them off with information, whether willingly or under duress. But now they had switched sides, en masse, and there was no turning back once you declared the Taliban your enemy. If the people of Zangabad had turned, the Taliban would struggle throughout Kandahar.

"First it was only us and two other villages, and now more people are joining," Wudood said. "The whole area was fed up with the Taliban and now you see all the people are supporting me and we are together." With the villagers against them, the Taliban would not be able to come back. "They are finished. Finished. You are witnessing yourself. This was ungoverned territory, and now the whole area is full of Afghan flags."

It began one day when the Taliban came knocking at Wudood's door. They were not just ordinary Taliban. It was the shadow district governor, Mullah Noor Mohammad, a thirty-five-year-old commander who was in charge of the insurgency for the entire district of Panjwayi. He posted two men behind the house to catch anyone trying to escape and came to the front door with an armed guard. The man they were looking for, Wudood, was a veteran guerrilla fighter, a sixty-year-old farmer with eight grown sons. He had fought the Soviets in the 1980s from his village, resisting repeated Russian assaults. He was proud that he had never been driven from his home — not by the Soviets, not by the chaos of mujahideen rule, not by the seven years of Taliban government, and not through ten years on the frontline between Taliban insurgents and American and NATO forces.

Alerted that the Taliban were at his door, Wudood sent his eldest son to the gate to talk to them while he slipped through a side door, into the inner family compound, with Abdul Hanan, his twenty-one-year-old second youngest son. At the gate, the Taliban commander announced that he was looking for two of Wudood's sons. One of them was Abdul Hanan. "They are spies for the government," the Talib said. Everyone knew the Taliban's punishment for spying for the government was death.

"They wanted to slaughter my sons," Wudood told me. "They wanted to take them to the desert where they had a court and a base. They wanted to kill them there."[1]

His eldest son told them no one was at home, and the Taliban left empty-handed. But Wudood knew they would return soon. He told me his sons had not had any contact with the government, but there was talk that Hanan had joined a local police force. Talk was enough, and once accused by the Taliban, Wudood knew their fate was sealed and the whole family would be in trouble. Just refusing to give Taliban fighters food could lead to being branded a traitor and government spy, so he knew his sons were in mortal danger. He made a call to the district governor and set off later that night for the district center to seek help.

Few villagers in Zangabad would have turned to the government for help in past years. This was the heart of Panjwayi, the birthplace of the Taliban, where the movement had held sway almost without interruption for eighteen years since its formation in 1994. It was in Zangabad that the old judge Maulavi Pasanai had run his Islamic court and first worked with Mullah Omar to curb the criminal gangs in western Kandahar. Even after the fall of their government in 2001, members of the Taliban were only gone from the area for two years. Zangabad was one of the first places to which they returned in 2003 to start their insurgency.

The group of villages lies close to Registan, the red-sand desert that stretches south to the border with Pakistan. It provided infiltration routes into Afghanistan and a springboard for insurgents into Kandahar city and regions beyond. There were enough people in the community who had prospered under the Taliban to form a base of support. The others in the community had to tolerate them. "They came by force. We could not say anything to them," Wudood told me. "We did not have weapons. They were living on our rooftops." Zangabad became the rear base of the Taliban through seven years of the insurgency against Canadian and coalition forces. As the Russians had before them, NATO forces made forays into the densely cultivated patchwork of vineyards and orchards, and then pulled back to their bases. The Taliban moved with the flow. Even when thousands of extra U.S. and Afghan troops were brought in in 2010 as part of the surge, the insurgents never fully relinquished Zangabad. U.S. special forces established a base in the nearby village of Belambai and began recruiting local police, but progress was slow in gaining the trust of the population.

More than two years had passed since the surge, and Zangabad had remained stubbornly resistant to efforts by the government and U.S. forces to encourage them to cooperate. Then, on the night of March 11, 2012, an American staff sergeant, Robert Bales, committed the single worst atrocity of the war. Stalking from house to house, he killed sixteen civilians as they slept. Three of the victims were women, nine of them children. If anything more was needed to alienate the population of Zangabad, that senseless crime was it. The massacre seemed to encapsulate everything that was wrong with the U.S. presence in Afghanistan: For Afghans, it was yet another example of American soldiers killing innocent Afghans instead of the real culprits of the war, the Taliban. At home in the United States, the massacre rammed home the futility of pursuing such a damaging, long, drawn-out war. It reminded some of the My Lai massacre in Vietnam, when American soldiers, strung out by the relentless battle against an elusive guerrilla force, took revenge on innocent villagers. The specter of Vietnam hung over Afghanistan in the months after.

But in January 2013, a new police chief transferred into Panjwayi district. He was a tough, thickset former mujahideen commander named Sultan Mohammad, a native of Zangabad. His men were also from the area. For the last ten years, they had been working in the border police and had not been able to visit home because of the Taliban presence there. Sultan Mohammad's predecessor had made little headway in this conservative, rural district where no one liked or trusted the government and people were in thrall to the Taliban. But tribal ties made all the difference. Everyone knew Sultan Mohammad since the days of the jihad against the Soviets, and in keeping with tradition, hundreds of elders and villagers from Zangabad called on the new police chief to congratulate him on his posting and to welcome him home.

In those first meetings, they told the police chief they were tired of the Taliban. They wanted security and they wanted police in their villages. For Wudood, the ties were even closer. Sultan Mohammad was family. The two men were from the same tribe, the Achakzai, and they were related by marriage. He knew he could count on the police chief.

Everyone in the district also knew that the police chief had strong backing. Sultan Mohammad had been drafted in by Abdul Razziq, the hard-hitting chief of the Border Guards who had spearheaded much of the fighting during the surge, and had since been promoted to brigadier general and made police chief of Kandahar province. Razziq was also from the Achakzai tribe. For the men of Zangabad, the government for once was represented by men they could trust.

Resentment of the Taliban was already brewing in the village of Pishin Gan Sayedan. When villagers had begun their yearly collective task of cleaning the irrigation canal, digging out the silt and clearing the undergrowth along the sloping banks, the Taliban commander Mullah Noor Mohammad turned up with a group of fighters and ordered them to stop. The undergrowth provided the Taliban with good cover for ambushes, he told them. The villagers answered back that they needed the water to flow for their crops. They continued working. These Taliban were outsiders, and the villagers were fed up with them. The Taliban caused trouble by laying mines everywhere and staging ambushes in the village. Now they were threatening the villagers' livelihood by disrupting the irrigation supply. "The Taliban were saying we don't care if your fields die, or if you die, so the people said: 'Then you can die,'" one resident told me.

The Taliban resorted to force. They waded in with their rifle butts, cracking several people on the head and breaking the arms of two of the farmers. They detained the village elder in charge of the canal cleaning and took him off to their base in the desert.

Just a few days later, the Taliban returned, looking for Wudood and his sons. By now the mood in the village was boiling. Villagers who had lost relatives to the Taliban offered their support to Wudood. When he met with the police chief, they hatched a plan. Sultan Mohammad immediately sent a posse of fifteen men to guard Wudood's house in case the Taliban came back. After three days of waiting, they decided to spring an attack on Taliban positions in the nearby village of Kakaran. The place was an operational base where the Taliban were making bombs and explosives, and where they believed the Taliban commander stayed since the approaches were heavily mined. The police gathered a force of local and national police and intelligence officers, and attacked from two sides. Thirty to forty unarmed villagers accompanied the police, guiding them through the land mines and acting as lookouts. In a short firefight, they shot three members of the Taliban and seized control of the village. The Taliban commander, Mullah Noor Mohammad, escaped with ten others. The police knew his radio code name, Rahmani, and were able to follow his movements on the radio. The three wounded Talibs died as they retreated south.

Villagers from all around, delighted that the Taliban had been sent packing, now came forward to give their support to Wudood. They thronged his courtyard and pledged to stand with him. His group of thirty supporters grew to hundreds, from thirty different villages. Overnight the whole of Zangabad turned against the Taliban. Four days later, the police and army mounted an operation against the Taliban's hideouts near the desert, routing the remaining insurgents and seizing their bases. In Kakaran, the police recovered mounds of explosives and bomb-making materials, and dug up forty mines sown around the base.

The uprising had in fact been building for months. Life in Zangabad under the Taliban had become unbearable. The Taliban had enforced a nightly curfew, only allowing villagers to emerge from their homes in the morning when the Taliban gave the order, often because they had laid mines and booby traps right in gateways and doorways. They restricted which fields farmers could work and when, and prevented them from visiting other villages and congregating with fellow tribesmen. The mines and improvised explosive devices took a terrible toll on the population. Sixty villagers, including many children, had died because of mines and improvised bombs in the last six months in Zangabad.

The same pattern was seen across Panjwayi, the district governor, Haji Fazel Mohammad, told me. He sat cross-legged on the floor of his office with neat handwritten notes laid out on the rug before him. There had been up to four hundred civilian casualties in the district from mines and bombs laid by the Taliban in the last six months. "A lot of people died and a lot were amputated." The men planting the mines would often get killed or arrested, and then no one knew where the mines were and villagers would step on them. "They were laying mines in farms and pathways, in the orchards, everywhere," he said. "They cannot come up to the main road, but they put them wherever they spent the previous night."

As the 2010 surge increased the pressure on the Taliban, the more senior commanders had withdrawn to Pakistan, leaving younger, less experienced commanders in charge. They were often vicious and unpredictable, and their grip over the community began to fray.

The Taliban were losing the moral high ground. "The reputation and power that the Taliban once had is gone, and so the people don't like them. People hate them," Fazel Mohammad told me. "The most difficult thing was we were trapped with the Taliban on one side and the foreigners and the government forces on the other," said Haji Mohammad Ibrahim, an elder in a black silk turban, in Pishin Gan Sayedan.

"We just want to have a safe place to live and a good life," Mohammad Gul, a farmer in gray working clothes, added. "My feeling is that no one is listening to us, they are deciding things elsewhere." I had heard these complaints so many times before. I had known for a long time that people were fed up with the Taliban — yet they had not acted until now.

What had changed in Panjwayi was the shift in the balance of power. The surge had routed the Taliban in much of Kandahar province in 2010, and it had taken another two years for the secondary and tertiary phases of the counterinsurgency strategy, the "hold and build" stages to keep the Taliban out and build a security and administrative system in the area, to take effect. A watershed moment came in 2012 in neighboring Zhare district, according to the American commander in southern Afghanistan in that period, Major General Robert

B. Abrams.[2] The Taliban had declared their intention to regain lost territory in Zhare in 2012 but failed to do so. Instead, they had steadily ceded ground and by 2013, had fallen back across the river, making southern Panjwayi their last stronghold.

They were forced to retreat because of the newfound strength of the Afghan security forces, people told me. The surge had not only flooded the southern provinces with thousands of American troops, but also with twice their number of Afghan soldiers and police. By 2013, there were 17,000 American and coalition troops in the four provinces of Regional Command South, as well as 52,000 Afghans across various agencies of police, army, and intelligence. Kandahar had two Afghan army brigades and 10,000 police manning checkpoints on virtually every road in the province, and another 2,000 local police in the villages. When I heard those numbers, I remembered with pain how provincial governors had pleaded with President Karzai for two hundred police for each district in 2006. Their request had never been met. It had just been a fraction — roughly a fifth — of the forces that were ultimately needed to do the job six years later. Concerted action to strengthen security forces in 2006 could have saved much of the hardship of the six years that followed.

So long disliked for their ill-disciplined and predatory ways, the police were slowly shaping into a better-trained, more responsible force, the district governor, the governor, and others told me. Stories abounded of Abdul Razziq's ruthless leadership, but people were glad to see a firm hand even if the justice was rough. Villagers even spoke approvingly of how he had executed one of his own men for murdering a villager and stealing a motorbike. More important, Razziq represented an Afghan force, one that could conceivably remain in charge after the departure of the American forces in 2014.

I visited Razziq in his new base on the edge of town, a large, barricaded American-style compound with prefabricated offices set behind Hesco barriers, the huge, dirt-filled gabions that fronted virtually every office in Afghanistan to protect against bombs. We passed through security checks and tramped across acres of gravel to reach his office. American minders and an Afghan-American translator joined us for the interview. I noticed Razziq's hands were red from the burns he received when his car had been blown up by a massive roadside bomb six months earlier. Yet he still had his boyish vigor. He answered questions peremptorily and then gave a big grin when I asked him about the uprising in Panjwayi. Having security forces strong enough to protect them had encouraged the people to turn against the Taliban, General Razziq said.

"The people in the villages were under the hands of the Taliban and the Taliban were merciless, but now the people realize the government is with them. They have enough forces, they have police, they have the army, and so that is why they are rising up, they trust the government," he told me. "This is not only in Zangabad, we are expecting more places to rise up. In Kandahar and other provinces," he continued. "We are encouraging the people to protect their own villages by themselves. We are telling them: 'Give your sons to protect the village and guard reconstruction sites, and let the schools be opened. We will secure the areas outside the villages and you can secure your own villages,'" he concluded.

By the end of February, fifty men from Zangabad had joined the local police program. Villages further along the horn of Panjwayi had come over to the government and were asking for local police, Sultan Mohammad, the police chief, told me. "It is not thirty, not fifty, it is hundreds of villages."

The Afghan Local Police program, begun by Generals McChrystal and Petraeus two years earlier, was a game changer in Kandahar. Compared to the Sons of Iraq program, which brought the Sunni tribes in Iraq together to stand against al Qaeda, the Afghan Local Police program in the same way aimed to use young, unemployed men in the districts to mobilize communities against the Taliban and serve as force multipliers for the coalition and Afghan government.

In Afghanistan, the program took off slowly. It had many detractors, especially those who remembered the lawlessness of the 1990s. Opponents feared the local militias would abuse their power, and cases of criminal behavior by the new forces or other rival militias started emerging. Karzai also mistrusted the program, fearing it would create warlords or militia bosses who would grow powerful enough to challenge his power. U.S. forces tried several ad hoc substitutes of local police to speed up the program, but Karzai shut down most of those efforts in 2012.

Other critics, including experienced administrators and analysts, advised that Afghan society was too divided, the tribal structures too weak, and government too mistrusted for the local police or local uprisings to take hold. The people could not and would not stand against the Taliban, they said. General Petraeus patiently reworked the program so that the local police would come under Interior Ministry control, and increased the number of special forces soldiers to mentor them. It took a year to recruit, train, and mentor a local police force, but in the south, tribal elders and aid workers started telling me that they liked the program because it provided a local solution to security. There was every sign that the Taliban felt threatened by the local police. An Afghan elder who lived in Quetta and knew many members of the Taliban in his neighborhood told me that the insurgent fighters were more scared of the local police than the NATO forces and all their firepower. "Forty-two countries have come here with all their high-tech equipment, but the Taliban are not as scared of their technology as they are of the local police."

In Zhare, the local police turned the tables on the Taliban. Drawn from the villages, trained and mentored by U.S. special forces, they were largely responsible for preventing the Taliban from regaining a foothold in the district in 2012, and the population swung behind them, residents told us. The local police were rough, and were demanding money from the population, but they were doing the job since, more than anyone, they knew who were Taliban and how they operated, a landowner from Sangesar told us. "Most of them were working with the Taliban, or they have the attitude of the Taliban, but I hope with interaction with the government they will improve," he said.

By the spring of 2013, the program was taking hold in Kandahar, with 2,000 villagers under arms and approval for police to sign up another 1,200. By the summer, Panjwayi district had 400. Countrywide, the program was reaching 20,000 men with plans for it to expand to 30,000. Petraeus's original plan for 45,000 was put aside.

Change elsewhere was piecemeal. I had always found each province was like a different country, and Afghanistan provided examples for both optimists and pessimists.

An earlier, spontaneous uprising had taken both the government and Taliban by surprise. In the summer of 2012, a group of four or five young graduates in Andar district in the central province of Ghazni complained to the local Taliban commander about his men's harsh treatment of the community. They demanded that the Taliban reopen the schools and allow reconstruction projects. They also complained that Pakistani Taliban were harassing villagers, checking IDs even though they could read neither Pashtu nor Dari. The commander told them to join his group and put up with it or leave the area. He gave them thirty minutes to leave. Instead the men turned on the Taliban, killing some and chasing the others out.

This little band was led by a tall, hook-nosed engineering graduate, Lutfullah Kamran, who had become disillusioned with the Taliban's strictures. In interviews, he described taking the university entrance exams in the provincial capital of Ghazni and seeing scores of ethnic Shiite Hazaras but virtually no Pashtuns, who are the majority in his province. With schools banned in the Taliban-held areas, the Pashtuns were largely illiterate and falling behind, he realized. The Taliban leadership was slow to counter the breakaway group. Kamran meanwhile sought assistance elsewhere. He had approached the Hesbe-Islami Party in Pakistan for support the previous year without luck. He wanted to keep both American and Taliban forces out of the area, but he needed money, weapons, radios, and general support. So the group approached a fellow Pashtun from Ghazni in the Karzai government, Asadullah Khaled, who was then the minister for tribal affairs. Khaled met their representative in his Kabul office but warned them that they would have to stop their opposition to American forces if he was to help them. He gave them money to treat their wounded, and then he persuaded President Karzai to let him nurture the uprising.

The American commander in Afghanistan, General John R. Allen, understood the importance of the uprising too, Khaled said.[3] Kamran's Andar group expanded, gaining support from surrounding villages and pushing the Taliban out of an area of some six square miles. "When the Taliban recognized they had made a mistake it was too late, a lot of people had joined the uprising," Khaled told me.

By September 2012, spontaneous uprisings against Taliban forces had occurred in half a dozen places around the country including Ghazni, Nuristan, Wardak, Ghor, Faryab, and Logar provinces. Each uprising had occurred for different reasons, and the government's responses varied. In one case, in Paktika, the government told people to wait, warning them that it could not provide them with protection from a Taliban backlash. General Allen compared the uprisings to the Sunni awakening against al Qaeda in Anbar province in Iraq. "This is a really important moment for this campaign because the brutality of the Taliban and the desire for local communities to have security has become so, so prominent — as it was in Anbar — that they're willing to take the situation into their own hands to do this," he said in an interview with *Foreign Policy* magazine.[4] Not all were well intentioned. Some participants were opportunists, and some were criminals, preying on the communities they pretended to want to protect. A number used the chance to turn their guns on the foreign soldiers training them. But there were also genuine movements to kick out the Taliban.

In Kamdesh in Nuristan, local tribesmen fought for months against a determined Taliban and al Qaeda force. At one point the government and the United States flew in supplies and commandos to assist them. A senior Afghan intelligence official warned that it was not enough and the government was going to lose the moment. Kamdesh remained cut off by road, and the government was doing nothing to clear the route, the official told me. Karzai was issuing orders, but the ministry responsible was not acting. Nevertheless the tribesmen hung on.

As he entered his last year in office — Karzai was due to step down in 2014 as he completed his second term — the Afghan president still had reservations about the U.S. military campaign against the Taliban.

He continued to apply the brakes to the local police program, denying or only grudgingly approving each incremental increase. He also kept a close grip over the reconciliation program, both the high-level peace talks with the Taliban leadership and the lower-level program to induce Taliban fighters off the battlefield. Karzai insisted on maintaining Afghan control over the programs, and that meant presidential control. Neither program really advanced at all.

The local police program offered the best chance for communities to secure their villages and the government to expand its authority, but it was stuttering along, an example of Karzai's lack of leadership.

As spring unfurled into the summer of 2013, there was no doubt that Kandahar was a changed place. I had always believed that the Afghans in southern Afghanistan did not want the Taliban and one day would stand up against them. The Taliban's supporters were a minority. The remainder stuck with the Taliban for so long because they lacked a decent alternative. The people neither liked the foreign forces nor expected them to stay, and they did not trust the Karzai government to deliver.

By 2013, the fear that had kept many Kandaharis on the sidelines had ebbed. At first it was not obvious. I flew into Kandahar on a civilian flight from Kabul in mid-February. A trusted taxi driver was waiting to pick me up. Scared to be seen driving a foreigner, he urged me to cover my face and head in a shawl. He wrapped his own head in a scarf so he could not be recognized by anyone he knew. He lived in a suburb and feared that if a neighbor saw him working with a foreigner, word would get back to the Taliban. Translators and local reporters were also nervous to be seen collaborating with foreigners. We had long given up street interviews in Kandahar because of the risks, but even two years after the surge, local reporters said that it was too dangerous for them to go to districts such as Zhare and Panjwayi.

Yet I found that many others were able to work and were pushing the boundaries. A campaign of assassinations had decimated the provincial and tribal leadership, from the mayor, religious and tribal leaders, and provincial and district council members, to ministry employees, including several women. Still, there were now more ministry and government officials working than before. Villagers were daring to approach government offices. Even women were coming forward to the district office in Panjwayi.

Two hundred madrassas in the province had newly registered with the authorities, compared with only five a couple of years earlier. Fifty clerics had joined the provincial Ulema Shura, the Council of Clerics. Being a member of the Ulema had been one of the most dangerous jobs in Kandahar since the council had gathered hundreds of clerics from twenty provinces in 2005 to divest Mullah Omar of his title of Leader of the Faithful. The leader of the council was assassinated by the Taliban soon afterward, as were several members of the family that guarded the Shrine of the Blessed Cloak. So many religious figures had been assassinated in the five years that followed that only fifteen clerics were left on the council in 2010, and they worked undercover. By 2013, however, improved security had broken the fear. The clerics were appearing on television and radio, and traveling out to the districts.

Tooryalai Wesa, Kandahar's governor, told me that the surge had not only expelled the Taliban; it had changed people's demands. "Before I was going to the districts everyone was complaining about security: 'We don't have enough guns, our guns are Hungarian, we don't want Hungarian guns, we want German guns, or American guns,'" Wesa said. "Now they say: 'We don't have a clinic,' and some say: 'We do have a clinic but we don't have a female doctor.'" Businessmen were no longer talking about security but about the economy, he added.

It was not just the Taliban who had been pushed back. The most powerful figure of all, Ahmed Wali Karzai, the brother of the president and his omnipotent representative in the south, had departed from the scene. A trusted bodyguard and commander had turned on Ahmed Wali and shot him dead inside his own home in July 2011. He left a vacuum of power. He had wielded immense influence, controlling virtually every government appointment in southern Afghanistan, overseeing security issues, and muscling in on nearly all commercial deals, legal or illegal. He told David Petraeus once that President Karzai kept him in Kandahar because he could deliver the vote for his brother across five southern provinces. Western generals found him useful for the influence he wielded with his brother, yet he had exercised a stranglehold on provincial life and tribal dynamics. Eighteen months after his death, the Karzai monopoly on power had splintered. For Kandahar, that was not a bad thing.

The 2014 deadline for the withdrawal of foreign forces loomed large. Skilled survivors that they were, Afghans were moving with events. As the foreigners withdrew, so the support for the Taliban would drop, some villagers predicted. One elder at the gathering in Wudood's house in Zangabad told me that villagers could see the shift in power and so were supporting the government as it grew stronger and the Taliban grew weaker. "People applaud everyone who seizes power," he said. "People were applauding the Taliban too."

And yet, "a single bloom does not make spring," an Afghan friend warned me. He said the Taliban would be maddened at losing Zangabad and would redouble efforts to regain their influence there. The Karzai government could still bungle things and lose the initiative, he added.

The Taliban struck quickly. In mid-March, a month after my visit, two workers from a construction firm were kidnapped and killed in Panjwayi. The company made metal grates to be fixed over culverts to prevent the Taliban from planting bombs under the road, and these men were monitoring the work. Their booby-trapped bodies were found hanging in different villages near the desert where Taliban fighters still had a presence, police officials told me.

Villagers and government officials warned that the uprising had to be supported or it would falter under pressure from the Taliban. "It all depends on what the government does with these people. If they support them and equip them, it will be a revolution," said Haji Agha Lalai, a member of Kandahar's provincial council from Panjwayi.

Few had much faith that the central government would deliver timely support. "The government is very weak and if the foreigners take their hands from their shoulders, the government will collapse

like a wet wall," said the landowner from Sangesar. It was a good anal-
ogy. In the villages, Afghans make walls from packed mud and straw.
While the wall is fresh and wet it can easily collapse, but once dry, it
can withstand a tank round. "If the foreigners continue their support,
the government will slowly get more powerful," the elder told me.

The police chief Sultan Mohammad exuded toughness as a new
fighting season loomed with the onset of the spring. "If you think because the leaves are sprouting, the Taliban will start to fight, I will tell
you I can also fight well in Zangabad when the leaves grow," he said.
Six months later, he was even more confident. Despite continued casualties from Taliban IEDs, he had expanded government authority
throughout the district and established police posts on the desert's
edge, he told us.[5]

We called Wudood to see how he was faring. He had received repeated death threats but brushed them off. His son had been ambushed
but survived. "I don't have any worries for the future," he said. "The
time to die is in God's hands, and when it is time, I will go." His faith
in the uprising was unshaken. "This time it is not only me. There are
thousands of us in Zangabad and in Sperwan. They cannot eliminate
us all," he continued. "We are the true owners of this land and the men
who are attacking us are coming from outside, and we are not scared.
We will defend our land."

Yet the threat from Pakistan was real and showed no sign of diminishing. Young Taliban graduates were continuing to arrive back in Afghanistan from years of study in Pakistan, preaching jihad and starting
up bands of Taliban. I had come across several cases of new arrivals in
2012. They were all graduates of the Haqqania madrassa at Attock in
Pakistan. They arrived flush with cash and began recruiting and training followers.

In January 2013, I decided to visit the Haqqania madrassa in Pakistan to ask some of the senior clerics about the graduates they were
dispatching to Afghanistan. They denied sending out extremists. They
gave the usual patter that it was every person's individual choice to
fight jihad, and that they could not influence their students who were

set on going. "Our job is not to force religion on people," said Maulana
Imam Mohammad, a politician and deputy to Maulana Sami-ul-Haq,
the founder of the madrassa. "Governments fear us because we have
strength from the people." The mullahs, however, revealed a fanatical
support for the Taliban. "Those who are against the Taliban, they are
the liberals and they only represent 5 percent of Afghans. We are experts on the Taliban and the majority of the people still support them,"
Syed Mohammad Yousuf Shah, the spokesman for the madrassa, told
me. He and his fellow clerics were set on a military victory for the Taliban in Afghanistan. "We would prefer the Taliban to win militarily in
Afghanistan. America's presence in Afghanistan is a threat to stability,"
he said. "A parliamentary democracy cannot work in Afghanistan," he
continued. "Afghanistan is a weapons culture, a tribal culture, and they
have been a monarchy for a long time. So a dictatorship is the only system for them." Moreover, "it is a political fact that one day the Taliban
will take power," he concluded. "The white flag of the Taliban will fly
again over Kabul, inshallah."

These clerics seemed madly in love with the Taliban and, I felt, were
out of touch with the reality on the ground in Afghanistan, but they
almost certainly reflected broader thinking within the ISI and the military establishment. They had always been an important conduit of ISI
influence on the Taliban.

It would be easy to dismiss their comments as so many dreams of
fanatics. Yet Pakistani security officials, political analysts, journalists,
and parliamentarians warned of the same thing. Pakistan was still set
on domination of Afghanistan and was still determined to use the
Taliban to exert influence now that the United States was pulling out.
Kathy Gannon of the Associated Press reported in September 2013 that
Punjabi militants were massing in the tribal areas to join the Taliban
and train ahead of an anticipated offensive into Afghanistan in 2014. In
Punjab, mainstream religious parties and banned militant groups were
openly expanding their operations, building larger establishments and
recruiting hundreds of students for jihad. Dozens of young men had
been dispatched by militant groups to Syria to fight jihad there, and
dozens more dead were being returned to madrassas in the Punjab, a

former legislator told me. "They are the same jihadi groups, they are not 100 percent under control, but still the military protects them."[6]

The United States was neither speaking out against Pakistan nor changing its policy toward a government that was exporting terrorism, the legislator lamented: "How many people have to die before they get it? They are standing by a military that protects, aids, and abets people who are going against the U.S. and Western mission in Afghanistan, in Syria, everywhere."[7]

In Afghanistan, even General Razziq said that the Afghans would not be able to hold on long unless the United States maintained strong support for the Afghan security forces and put pressure on Pakistan to cease its support for the Taliban. "If they leave Afghanistan as we are now in present conditions, and if they do not put pressure on Pakistan and Iran, which are openly supporting the opposition, where they have training, where they have safe havens and everything, then I think the government will not be able to resist for long against the opposition," he said. "Pakistanis are very clever and smart. They duped the world community by giving them false information." Pakistan had been imprisoning those Taliban who supported negotiations with Kabul and was pushing others to keep fighting, he said. "They have been playing these tricks for the past ten years.

"We need strong support," he continued. "The war is not in Afghanistan, it is not in our villages and districts, the war is being imposed on us." Furthermore, Razziq warned, "Pakistan is playing a double game. On the one hand they are supporting the Qatar negotiations [peace talks between the Karzai government and Taliban leaders], on the other hand they are telling the Taliban to prepare their leadership and appoint their leaders for the period after 2014," he told me. "Pakistan can hand over fifty big Taliban commanders but on the other hand they can do something else, they can make five hundred more," he said.

A number of senior Afghan officials offered the same warning. While the Taliban pursued its campaign of assassinations, targeting in particular former Northern Alliance leaders, Pakistan began diplomatic overtures to leaders of all the northern ethnic groups. Pakistan's ambassador announced a new policy of broader relations with Afghans of all factions, and, at the same time, began a campaign to savage Karzai's reputation. It was a new way of showing they intended to play a role in deciding Afghanistan's future. Apparently as part of that diplomatic offensive, an ISI official paid a visit to a senior Northern Alliance official in Kabul in August 2012. The ISI man gave him a veiled warning. The ISI controlled every Taliban and Haqqani group operating in the country, and the Northern Alliance would do well to make peace with the Taliban or suffer the consequences. "You have to extend the hand of friendship," he was told.

Pakistan's Afghan proxies were showing strain, however. There were signs of divisions within the Taliban leadership, which the U.S. forces and Kabul were clearly trying to exploit. The repeated calls for peace talks from the Afghan government had been resonating through the rural communities and the ranks of the Taliban for several years. Afghan officials insisted that many Taliban leaders did want peace but were prevented from entering into negotiations by Pakistan. Field commanders, who bore the brunt of the fighting, often complained about their leaders, and had begun to question why they were fighting, if their leaders were making peace. People who met with Taliban members described divisions within the Taliban. Some Taliban were exhausted, worn down by the night raids and ready for peace, yet there were still plenty of young firebrands who showed no desire to stop fighting. "These people don't care about their own head. If someone does not care about his head, how can you stop that person," an Afghan elder from Quetta told me.

Yet under the pressure of the surge and the drone war, the fight had become particularly grim, and I sensed the Taliban movement was rotting at the core. The ISI had maintained an iron grip on the Taliban, but in order to do so, had had to detain scores of mid-level and senior members who showed dissent, or were found to have cultivated ties with Kabul. Such harsh treatment of senior Taliban members, in particular the detention of Mullah Abdul Ghani Baradar in 2010 and the deaths of Mullahs Obaidullah and Yassar in detention, angered many in the ranks. The ISI's refusal to hand over their bodies to their families was an added callousness that won no supporters.

Then came a spate of assassinations of senior Taliban figures in Quetta and the surrounding areas in the first months of 2013. Thirteen were killed in typical Taliban style: gunned down by two men on a motorbike. The man behind the assassinations was caught when one of his victims survived. He was a senior Taliban commander himself, named Mastana, a former favorite of Mullah Omar. He admitted to conducting the assassinations for the Afghan government before he and his son were executed. The Taliban slaughtered his son like a sheep, slitting his throat on the grave of one of the assassinated clerics. The Taliban rounded up forty of Mastana's followers after that. They were all Achakzai tribesmen. The Taliban now had serious tribal divisions within its ranks.

The U.S. added pressure by killing one of Pakistan's loyal Pakistani Taliban commanders, Mullah Nazir, an important supporter of the insurgents fighting in Afghanistan, in a drone strike in January.

The collapse of the Taliban from within had long been an aim of the U.S. military. General Petraeus's rejection of peace talks early on made sense by 2013, since all along he had never intended to give in to the Taliban or to Pakistan. Despite talk of peace, the bloodletting promised to continue, at least from the Taliban side, the elder from Quetta said. "They are so used to killing. For them killing a human is the same as killing a pigeon."

NATO countries, weary of the high cost of the campaign in blood and treasure, had agreed to hand over security to Afghan forces in 2014 and to withdraw NATO troops. In another example of Western bureaucratic miscalculation, Afghanistan now faced a perfect storm of difficult transitions all in the same year: the election of a new president and appointment of a new government (which last time had taken months to resolve), the handover of security to Afghan forces, and the withdrawal of tens of thousands of NATO forces in the middle of the summer fighting season. It is a punctuation mark that closes a chapter in Afghanistan's bloody history — and it closes this book. But what will remain?

When I remember the beleaguered state of Afghanistan in 2001, I marvel at the changes the American intervention has wrought: the rebuilding, the modernity, the bright graduates in every office. Yet after thirteen years, a trillion dollars spent, 120,000 foreign troops deployed at the height, and tens of thousands of lives lost, the fundamentals of Afghanistan's predicament remain the same: a weak state, prey to the ambitions of its neighbors and extremist Islamists. The United States and its NATO allies are departing with the job only half done. Counterinsurgency is slow work. A comprehensive effort to turn things around only began in 2010. The fruits were only starting to show in 2013, and progress remains fragile.

Meanwhile the real enemy remains at large. The Taliban and al Qaeda will certainly seek to regain bases and territory in Afghanistan upon the departure of Western troops. Few Afghans believe that their government and security forces can keep the Taliban at bay. I believe they can, but they will need long-term financial and military support.

The cost in lives to reach this unfinished state had been painfully high. There is no complete count of how many Afghans have died since the American intervention began in October 2001. My own rough estimate places it between 50,000 and 70,000 Afghans. By the end of 2013, over 3,400 foreign soldiers have died in the campaign, 2,301 of them American.

Civilian deaths in the war had been running between two and three thousand a year since 2006.[7] Casualties among Afghan security forces have been between one and two thousand a year, and rising, as their forces have grown and they have taken up the frontline fighting.[8] Thousands of young Afghan and Pakistani men have died in the ranks of the Taliban, too, many of them villagers and madrassa students, used as so much cheap cannon fodder. They are referred to as "potato soldiers" by their Pakistani recruiters.

The toll in the rural districts of Afghanistan has been disastrous. In

Panjwayi district, in just the six months prior to January 2013, three hundred people were killed and four hundred wounded by mines and bombs laid by the Taliban. Assassinations and targeted killings have been an increasing danger too for Afghans who were working for or connected with the government and anyone near them. Nearly seven hundred civilians died in 2012 in targeted killings by insurgents, according to United Nations figures.

A tribal elder in just one small district of Kandahar, Zhare, told me that forty-two council members were killed in the last six years by Taliban insurgents. The men had worked variously on the district council, the development council, and the peace council. They were targeted for their collaboration with the government. The Taliban tried to eliminate local Afghan leadership in a systematic drive to control the populace. They struck at community leaders across the country, including women working in the governmental department of women's affairs; police; mujahideen commanders, elders, and clerics working on the peace council; senators; schoolteachers; and interpreters. A dozen influential Northern Alliance figures, men who had fought against the Taliban and retained powerful positions in the government and their communities, were killed in suicide bombings.

Kandahar suffered heavily too, with an estimated three hundred tribal elders killed since 2001. Some of those killed undoubtedly had their own enemies and were victims of local power struggles, or of Ahmed Wali Karzai's desire for political dominance. But the Taliban were behind most of the bloodletting as they pursued a strategy to remove any resistance to their aims. I thought of the Taliban commander's explanation to me a year earlier: "We just have to kill two people, and the village is in our hands." Even as the Taliban lost territory in the surge, it demonstrated an urgent desire to wipe out all potential opponents ahead of 2014.

The cost of the last twelve years of fighting has not just been in lives. The disruption, dislocation, and damage to the soul of the Afghans have been incalculable. While the ten-year Soviet occupation was far more catastrophic for the population — an estimated one million

Afghans died, and five million fled the country—by the time of the American intervention, Afghans were in their third decade of continuous war and were that much more vulnerable, impoverished, fearful, and disillusioned.

Two years after the surge in Zhare, for example, even after American troops had cleared the area and compensated people for the destruction, villagers were too destitute to move back home. "The village is still all destroyed. People are too poor to go back," councillor Mohammad Sarwar told me. "People are living on the edge of the city, and in the desert. Some are in tents." The majority had not been able to rebuild their homes because the compensation had been inadequate. In some cases, the Taliban had seized the money from the villagers. "The people feel that nothing has improved in ten years. Their houses and gardens have been destroyed, and they don't have money to send their children to school. They cannot afford to buy them notebooks. It is because we used these ten years like this." The man who led the uprising in Zangabad, Abdul Wudood, noted bitterly that with almost twenty years of consecutive Taliban rule in his village, not one of his eight sons had been to school.

These men wanted to see a strong continued U.S. commitment to Afghanistan, not necessarily with troops on the ground but with assistance, training, and security support. They warned that the United States and NATO were withdrawing their forces too early, before Afghan communities had been able to gather their strength and before Afghan forces could consolidate. Even opponents of the foreign forces said they should not leave hastily, as the Russians had, and allow the country to collapse under internal and external strains.

For me it seemed America was turning its back on Afghanistan because it was tired but also because it saw Afghanistan as a lost war. As one former diplomat put it: the war was essentially unwinnable, and that win, lose, or draw, Afghanistan was not worth the effort.[9] That is the wrong way to look at the problem. Militant Islamism is a juggernaut that cannot be turned off or turned away from. Pakistan is still exporting militant Islamism and terrorism, and will not stop once foreign forces leave its borders. The repercussions of the U.S. pullout are already inspiring Islamists, who are comparing it to the withdrawal of the Soviet Union after its ten-year debilitating war in Afghanistan. They are the real enemy in this war and they have not finished fighting. They fully intend to reclaim Afghanistan and have set their sights on horizons beyond. The United States has already paid heavily in blood, treasure, and prestige over a decade and more. Yet it is not in danger of collapsing as the Soviet Union did after that war, as al Qaeda leaders frequently predict. And it still has much work to do before leaving to bring Afghanistan and Pakistan into better shape to resist the tyranny of militant Islamism, or be responsible for even more blood and destruction. Pakistan, for its part, has to stand up to its responsibilities as a nuclear power and one of the world's largest Muslim countries and stop spreading terrorism and fanaticism around the world. The United States and its NATO allies cannot walk away until that is ensured.

Afterword

2014 was a bruising year for Afghanistan. Through an incredible lack of foresight, the nation faced a perfect storm of difficult transitions all in one year. U.S. and NATO troops were set to end combat operations and withdraw, handing over security to Afghan forces, while at the same time the country was holding presidential elections and inaugurating a new president and government.

Hamid Karzai had completed two terms as president and under the constitution had to step down, which he did, giving the country its first ever democratic transfer of power. But the election proved messy — even more fraudulent than that of 2009 — and threatened to plunge the country into factional violence. Thousands were being laid off from the closing military bases and contracting companies, and assistance programs were shrinking, all amid a continuing roll of high-profile attacks by the Taliban. Confidence wavered, businessmen moved their money abroad, and Afghans began to recall the dark days under the Taliban and even the fraught times of the civil war.

The Taliban returned to the offensive, and 2014 proved the bloodiest year for Afghan forces since the American intervention. The Afghan National Army mostly held its ground, but casualties reached an all-time high — more than 4,600 Afghan security personnel killed in ten months — a rate that the deputy American commander in Afghanistan described as unsustainable.[1] The Taliban were pulling out all the stops: attacking outposts, overrunning remote district centers, encouraging insider attacks, and reaching right into Kabul with suicide bombers seeking maximum publicity by gunning down foreigners and blowing themselves up in the heart of the capital.

Pakistan, after declining for years to move against the hub of militant groups in the tribal areas, finally began a military offensive into North Waziristan in June. It was a sweeping and serious campaign, with bombers and artillery gutting the towns of Mir Ali and Miranshah and emptying the whole Tochi River Valley almost to the Afghan border. The army busted open bomb factories, training camps, and torture cells, but at the cost of displacing almost the whole population. More than a million and a half people fled from the tribal areas down to Peshawar, and a quarter of a million of them into Afghanistan.

In July I was on an Afghan-piloted helicopter powering over the familiar terrain of Afghanistan's eastern mountains: jagged peaks and bare brown slopes that dropped away to narrow, winding river valleys; a sudden flash of green terraced fields and a mud-walled farmhouse hiding in the folds of a mountain. We were flying southeast from Kabul, over Logar province, and into Paktia and then Paktika, much of the land below us Taliban territory, stretching toward the Pakistani border.

The landscape flattened out into broad fields of golden stubble. The wheat was already harvested and piled in high hayricks, the grain, winnowed by hand, swept into neat mounds. This was the town of Orgun, in Paktika province, a day's drive from the border with Pakistan and a frontline base in the battle against the Taliban and al Qaeda for the past dozen years.

The reason for our visit was a grim one. A huge car bomb driven by a young suicide bomber had blown up the day before in the center of the bazaar in Orgun, demolishing shops and part of a madrassa. The death toll was staggering — as many as seventy-two dead and many more wounded, the police chief told us. The journey down to Orgun was long and dangerous, and Afghan journalists had pressed Afghanistan's intelligence agency, the National Directorate of Security, to fly some of us down to the scene. We spent only a few hours on the ground, but it was enough time to visit the site and talk to the towns-people and officials.

The bomb had gouged a crater four yards across in the street. Twisted wrecks of a dozen cars were flung aside. Rows of shops on both sides of the street had collapsed, and trees were splintered to blackened stubs. Shopkeepers said they saw the black SUV barrel through the police barrier at the end of the street. It was mid-morning and the street was full of shoppers, students attending the madrassa, and patients from the countryside visiting a health clinic. The police commander at the checkpoint ran shouting after the car, shooting at its tires. When the car came level with the madrassa, a truck blocked its way. The driver stopped and set off the explosion.

"It was very, very huge," said a bystander, Baz Mohammad.

"There were no cars, no ambulances, people were just lying wounded here on the ground and everyone was trying to help," Amin Gul, told me, standing in the wreckage of his pharmacy.

He pointed across the street at the rubble of the shops. Most were family-run businesses, and ten families had each lost five or six people. Four brothers and a cousin who decorated cars with flowers and rib-bons for weddings were killed inside their shop. Next to them a family of four brothers who sold car tires had died.

It was the second suicide bombing in the town in as many weeks. The first bombing had badly wounded a popular special forces com-mander, Azzizullah Karwan, and killed several police. The townspeo-ple were shaken and angry.

"Day by day, the security situation is becoming really bad," Amin Gul said. At that moment the crowd gathered to talk to the journal-ists began to shout abuse at the local officials. The police chief and the district governor had escorted our group to the bomb site and the townspeople began raining curses down on them. "We do not believe in the governor. He is a thief," Amin Gul said as he watched the com-motion from his shop.

An upright old man in a turban was among those berating the of-ficials. Haji Mohammadullah was an uncle of the five people slain in their wedding shop. "The police were so incapable they did not even help us pull the people from the rubble," he said.

The townspeople did not waste their breath ranting against the Taliban, who had caused the bombing. What they wanted to see was a strong defense of the town by the government, to keep the Taliban out, and they feared things were slipping.

It was not only the townspeople who were rattled. Commanders of the security and intelligence forces in Paktika told me that the Taliban and foreign militants had moved into the province as American forces had pulled out. Over the past two years the Central Intelligence Agency had closed down three bases and three combat outposts along the border in Paktika that it had used to watch over Pakistan's tribal areas and prevent infiltration by al Qaeda and the Taliban into Afghanistan.

The CIA had offered to continue paying the costs for two years so that the Afghan forces they had trained could maintain the bases and continue operations along the border. President Karzai, by this time alienated and angry about the behavior of U.S. specialist units in Afghanistan, refused the offer. The Afghan units were disbanded, and the Taliban quickly seized control of two American bases, at Lwara and Marga. The National Directorate of Security realized the mistake and later absorbed some of the CIA-trained units into its own forces, but officials told me that they had already lost ground.

"Lwara is flying a Taliban flag," the CIA-trained commander in Orgun told me. He was a Waziri tribesman and wore his hair down to his shoulders, the same style favored by the Taliban, but his sunglasses, fatigues, and accent were all American. Marga had become a base for Taliban and foreign militants inside Afghanistan, as important as their base in Pakistan, he said. "Marga is like Miranshah."

An Afghan legislator, Juma Din, told me that his home district of Gayan, which stretches from Orgun to the Pakistani border, had been under Taliban control for the past four years and was too dangerous for him to visit. The few Afghan army outposts on the border were surrounded, and the soldiers there could barely venture out a few hundred yards from their posts. Two other districts had been under Taliban control for six to eight years. These areas are remote and sparsely populated, and in the grand scheme of things may seem not worth the struggle to keep them clear of insurgents, yet Juma Din knew they would provide the Taliban with a base and springboard for attacks, such as the one in Orgun.

When he had learned two years earlier that the American forces were pulling out, he had urged the Afghan defense minister and chief of staff to post Afghan army units at Lwara. He warned them that the Taliban would take over the base and use it to infiltrate deeper into Afghanistan. "That is what happened," he told me. "They did not listen."

"That is a very strategic location, and daily now twenty pickups come from Pakistan bringing Taliban, and from there they set out to go to other districts," he said. "I told the Americans, if you leave, you are opening the gate."

A month before our conversation, Pakistan had at last made a decision to move against the foreign and Taliban militant groups active in North Waziristan and to establish military control of the area. For thirteen years the foreign fighters had enjoyed sanctuary there following their flight from Afghanistan in 2001. Pakistan had harbored them and used them to destabilize Afghanistan and undermine the U.S. and NATO mission there. Over time they had recruited more people, radicalized much of the local population, and even become a menace to the Pakistani state. Now, with the U.S. and NATO forces leaving Afghanistan, the foreign fighters were no longer of use to Pakistan. They were advised it was time to move on, I learned. Hundreds of foreign fighters began to move away from the area. Chechens, Uzbeks, Turks, Iraqis, and Chinese Muslims left for Syria, traveling down to the Pakistani town of Quetta and on to the Gulf countries, or on smuggling routes to Iraq. Fighters said that Qatar was providing documents for them to travel to Turkey, another way into Syria. The militants were to provide a sharp injection to al Qaeda's spinoff in Iraq, ISIS.

Some of the foreign fighters chose to stay and crossed into Afghanistan. An Afghan intelligence official who lives at the border was so worried he traveled up to the capital to talk to me. Hundreds of Taliban and ninety foreign fighters with their families had arrived in the border area in recent weeks, apparently escaping the Pakistani offensive in North Waziristan. Many of the lower-level fighters had settled inside Afghanistan in the guise of refugees, he said. There were Turkmens and Uzbeks from Central Asia, but also Punjabis from Pakistan. Their commanders were living just inside Pakistan and were still being provided sanctuary, he said.

"Our soldiers and police are very scared," he told me. "Pakistan is controlling them, and when they want, they will push them and they will seize control of the area. Afghanistan is going to have problems with its neighbors, and without international support we will not have the strength to defend ourselves."

Even while it was mounting an offensive against them, Pakistan was selective in which groups it targeted. The military pursued the Taliban and foreign fighters that had broken from its control and opposed the state. Some of those groups pulled back to Shawal, a remote valley near Afghanistan, and heavy fighting continued there through the fall. But Pakistan protected the groups that complied with its interests. Arab al Qaeda fighters had moved to South Waziristan, where they lived undisturbed by the Pakistani military. The top Taliban leaders, including Mullah Omar, remained at large in Quetta and Karachi while inflicting a terrible war on Afghanistan. The Haqqani network decamped to the next-door Kurram tribal area, a move that could not have been made without the knowledge and sanction of the Pakistani military. The Haqqani network remains the most potent strain of the Taliban, according to a Pentagon report, committed to expelling U.S. and coalition forces from Afghanistan, destabilizing the Afghan government, and reestablishing the Islamic Emirate of Afghanistan, all while still enjoying sanctuary in Pakistan.[2]

Despite the persistent threat from the Taliban, the country was distracted for much of 2014 by politics. Karzai was finally stepping down, and presidential elections went ahead in April. From a field of twenty-seven, two candidates emerged as the front-runners: former foreign minister Abdullah Abdullah, longtime member of the resistance and aide to guerrilla leader Ahmed Shah Massoud, and Ashraf Ghani, a former finance minister, anthropologist, and academic who had spent much of his career in the World Bank. They represented the two sides of the main cleavage in Afghan politics: Abdullah stood for the northern, mainly Tajik bloc (although his father was Pashtun, his long association with the Northern Alliance meant he was seen as a northerner), Ghani the Pashtun south. The two advanced to a runoff in June.

The first round had been a vibrant and largely democratic event, but the second round was marred by massive fraud. I visited Afghanistan just after the election and found that an array of government and election officials from the president down had helped tilt the scales dramatically away from Abdullah — who was well ahead in the first round — and turned the election in favor of Ghani. As when he himself ran for president, Karzai was determined not to betray the Pashtun vote. His own Pashtuns made up the largest ethnic group and had ruled Afghanistan for centuries, but because of the insurgency many would not or could not vote. Karzai saw the meddling as correcting an unfair imbalance. But the north, mainly populated by Tajiks and other minorities, was growing impatient for change.

Weeks of legal wrangling followed. Abdullah was sure that he had won, and accused the election commission of orchestrating the fraud. When he was ignored, his supporters took to the streets. When the election commission pressed ahead and announced preliminary figures showing that Ghani had won, Abdullah's supporters threatened to march on the presidential palace and seize control of the government. The country was close to civil war, Abdullah later admitted. He held his supporters in check with the promise that U.S. Secretary of State John Kerry was on his way to mediate.

Kerry once again was flying in to paper over the results of a fraudulent election. In 2009 he had persuaded Abdullah to back out and let Karzai claim victory. This time he persuaded the two protagonists to share power. Kerry — seemingly out of thin air — proposed an idea for a national unity government under which Ghani would serve as president and Abdullah as chief executive, pending the creation of the post of prime minister. He borrowed heavily from a blueprint written by

Ahmed Wali Massoud, the younger brother of the legendary resistance leader Ahmed Shah Massoud.

Frustrated by the inequities and ineffectiveness of the Karzai presidency, Wali Massoud had written a book laying out his idea for a more consensual system of governance, which would create a prime minister and presidential council of the five or six senior leaders to advise the president, a stronger parliament, and greater devolution of power to the provinces. He handed a précis to Abdullah as he went into negotiations. Kerry had already seen it through his own channels. Ghani and Karzai had always advocated a strong central government and presidential system, but now they were facing a major revolt from the populous north, whose followers made up a large part of the personnel in government and the security forces. The power-sharing deal will depend largely on the skill and cooperation of the two leaders, Ghani and Abdullah, and it may prove unwieldy, but it could serve as an important step toward a more just and stable system of governance for Afghanistan.

The sweeping success of ISIS in Iraq in the summer of 2014 served a sharp lesson about the ambitions of Islamist radical groups. Ranks of black-clad militants from the battlefields of Syria exploded across Iraq, routing the Iraqi army and declaring a Taliban-style caliphate, the Islamic State. The near collapse of the Iraqi army in the face of the onslaught was a warning of what could happen in Afghanistan if it was left to fend for itself. As a wake-up call for the world, it came just in time for the Afghans. In May, President Obama had announced that the American force in Afghanistan would be reduced to a train-and-assist mission of fewer than ten thousand by the end of 2014, and that residual force would be gone by the end of 2016. By November, he had revised that plan to authorize U.S. forces to continue combat missions and provide air support to Afghan forces into 2015.

For the Taliban, the success of ISIS was a huge boost. So too was the release of five senior Taliban officials detained for more than twelve years in Guantánamo Bay, among them Mullah Fazel and Mullah

Noori, whom I had seen surrender in 2001. They were exchanged for the captured American soldier Bowe Bergdahl and sent to live in Qatar. That exchange was supposed to nudge forward peace talks, but the Taliban instead unleashed a furious run of attacks in the weeks after President Ghani was inaugurated on September 29, including another devastating bombing in Paktika province that killed over sixty men and boys at a volleyball game.

The horror that Pakistan had helped unleash rebounded at home on December 16 in one of the most appalling atrocities of the decade, when Pakistani Taliban fighters stormed a military school in Peshawar and shot 147 schoolchildren and teachers in revenge for the operation in North Waziristan. The scale of the killing shocked the nation, and many wondered whether the massacre would bring Pakistan to finally end its policy of fostering terrorist groups. The country was inching towards greater clarity but was not there yet. Afghanistan's struggle with extremism was by no means over, nor was America's longest war.

Many people have wondered why I did not conclude this book with recommendations. My answer is that I am a journalist, not a policymaker. But here follow a few thoughts:

Countering the Islamist extremism of the Taliban and al Qaeda in all their forms and spinoffs, of which ISIS is only one, is going to take a generation or more. Each country will have to find its own way to deal with the threat. What I have learned is that it has to be done by the people themselves; not a foreign army, but also not just a national army. It is only when the people come together and work with the police, when political parties unite, when government, security forces, and civil society are on the same page, that a society can overcome this violent breed of Islamism. That may come only when a society has suffered such atrocities that it rejects the movement, and that may take years. The more vulnerable states need help in building institutions and security forces, as well as protection from outside threats. Afghanistan is actually close to reaching that goal. With Ghani and Abdullah working together, they have the best chance of pulling the population behind them, since the majority of Afghans are opposed to terrorism.

AFTERWORD 299

They have lived under and rejected the Taliban. The difficulty will be fending off Pakistan, and for that they need continued U.S. and international support. Afghanistan will also need solid economic support, to feed its people and to survive as a state for at least another decade. It still is one of the poorest countries in the world.

Pakistan, where politics is divided and the civilian government still at loggerheads with the military, has much further to go in confronting its demons. The military dictates security and foreign policy in Pakistan, and there are some in the military establishment who still think Islamism is the best nation-building and defensive strategy for the country. Successive civilian governments have wanted to end the proxy wars and switch to more cooperative relations with India and Afghanistan, but so far have not been able to override the powerful military. The madrassa education system still promotes violent extremism.

An absolute imperative is that the United States should bring clarity to its relationship with Pakistan. It should have a policy of zero tolerance for terrorism and the use of terrorist groups against another country. That is a fundamental red line under international law, and should be respected anywhere in the world. ISIS and al Qaeda are not tolerated anywhere in the world. Why is Pakistan allowed to protect its Islamist groups which are just as extreme? A failure to draw that red line with Pakistan has allowed the Pakistani military to run terrorist groups into Afghanistan and inflict thousands of casualties on Afghans and U.S. and coalition troops with impunity.

American policy and financial assistance have long bolstered the military in Pakistan. This should be reversed as much as possible, and aid and diplomacy directed to help strengthen the civilian government and civil society.

The United States should use the leverage of its large military assistance to Pakistan and revisit the conditionality of that funding. Military assistance should be made dependent on specific goals in stopping the transfer of IED components, arresting Taliban leaders and al Qaeda remnants living in Pakistan, and ending funding for the Taliban.

The United States should also expose and force Gulf countries to curtail their funding of extremist groups and madrassas in Pakistan. This has long been a well-kept secret in Pakistan, but it must be exposed and controlled. Pakistanis deserve to know the truth about where the extremism is coming from, and transparency — and turning off the taps of the funding — is the first step.

The American government and the international community should also consider smart sanctions against members of the Pakistani military and intelligence who continue to support the Taliban and foreign Islamist groups operating out of Pakistan. And it should support Pakistanis under threat from the military: journalists, politicians, and activists require protection so they can write and educate people at home and abroad to combat the narrow and dangerous policies of the military.

In the end, until the Pakistani military ceases to use the Taliban as an instrument of its strategic aims, Afghanistan's long war will continue.

ACKNOWLEDGMENTS

I hardly ever worked or traveled alone in Afghanistan and Pakistan, and so this book, and all my reporting from the region, comes thanks to many collaborators along the way: translators, local reporters, photographers, fixers, and drivers who shared many of these events with me. When I write "we," it is often because a translator or local reporter was relaying the conversation or there were several of us traveling and reporting together in a team. In some cases, Afghan and Pakistani reporters would elicit more information than I could as a foreigner. Some of them have to remain anonymous because of continued threats, but they know who they are and my special thanks goes to them for their bravery and integrity.

All those who helped me over more than a decade are too numerous to mention, and I will forget some, so forgive me for that. Extra special thanks goes to Ruhullah Khapalwak, translator and reporter in southern Afghanistan for the *New York Times*, who guided me indefatigably through the Pashtun heartlands for the most part of a decade, ultimately at great personal risk. His work is present on almost every page of this book. Another longtime collaborator at the *New York Times* was Abdul Waheed Wafa, the most tenacious of reporters with a sharp political brain, who helped me with interviews for this book. I was lucky over the years to have many terrific partners at the *New York Times* Kabul and Islamabad bureaus: Sultan Munadi first among equals; Sangar Rahimi, whose humor lightened some hard times, including the horror of Azizabad; Taimoor Shah, who never faltered in reporting a litany of sorrows in southern Afghanistan; Aziz Gulbahari; Arif Afzalzada; and Shafiq and Saboor, early companions who kept me safe in northern Afghanistan in 2001. Thanks in Pakistan go to Salman Masood, our anchor in Islamabad who has ridden through many ups and downs; Ismail Khan, who saw early on danger brewing in the tribal areas; Pir Zubair Shah, who dug deep under the Pakistani Taliban and its ISI connections; Ihsanullah Tipu, who is following his standard; in Lahore, Waqar Gillani for his energy for a story; Najam Sethi and Ahmed Rashid for wise counsel; Mubasher Bukhari for his good company and principled reporting; Shahzada Zulfikar for some memorable journeys. The Quetta journalists and photographer remain nameless for their own safety, but they should be proud of their work. So too Baluch and Karachi journalists who worked with me.

Afghans and Pakistanis are world-famous for their hospitality, and the list is long of all those who opened their homes and their hearts to me over more than two decades. Many of the interviewees in this book gave me hours and hours of their time; many more, not mentioned, went to great pains to help me understand events past and present, and the spirit and sensibility of the people of the region. My first contacts came through my father, who brought Afghanistan into our family life in the 1980s and set up a charity for disabled Afghans. The assistance Afghans showed me was often in respect for my father, so I am doubly indebted. Some I have known for thirty years, since I was a student and they were refugees in London from the Russian invasion: the Gailani family and their best ambassador and spokeswoman, Fatima Gailani; the brothers of Ahmed Shah Massoud, Ahmed Wali, Yahya, and Zia Massoud; Naser Saberi; and the late Noor Akbari, killed by the Taliban in 2013, whose brother Yunus, Afghanistan's first nuclear physicist, was killed at the beginning of it all by the Communists. Valuable instructors since my first trips to Peshawar and Afghanistan have been Massoud Khalili, Rustam Shah Mohmand, Amir Shah at AP, Sayed Salahuddin, Abdullah Abdullah, Muslem Hayat, Hashem, as well as Nancy Dupree, Anders Fange, Jolyon Leslie, Peter Jouvenal — all honorary Afghans for their expertise. During my twelve years' reporting in Afghanistan, special thanks for their willingness to explain: Engineer Amin, Mir Wali, Mohammad Ayub, Faiz Mohammad and family, Nader Nadery, Jawed Ludin, Khaleeq Ahmad, Amrullah Saleh, Rahmat Nabil, Asadullah Khaled, Mullah Rocketi, Hanif Atmar, Hafizullah Khan, Mohammad Lal and family, and many more. Thanks to Rahim Faiez at AP for his casualty lists; ambassadors Francesc Vendrell, Christopher Alexander, Sherard Cowper-Coles, Ronald E. Neumann, William B. Wood, Anne Patterson, generals Dan McNeill, Ron Helmly, Karl Eikenberry, David Petraeus, David Richards, Nick Carter, and Mick Nicholson and Afghan experts Vali Nasr, Rina Amiri, Reto Stocker, Michael Semple, Barnett Rubin, and Tom Gregg for making extra time for me. In Pakistan, special thanks to Siraj ul Mulk and his venerable late father Colonel Kush, and Reza and Ali Kuli Khan, whose gracious hospitality and friendship made me love Pakistan. As a reporter I found stalwart collaborators and colleagues: Ishaq Khakwani, General Talat Masood, Afrasiab Khattak, Brigadier Mahmood Shah, Farah Ispahani, Husain Haqqani, Omar Waraich, Declan Walsh, Bard Wilkinson, and Kathy Gannon. Thanks to Commander Zafar for always taking my calls. Thanks to Ministers Tariq Azeem and Sherry Rehman for unscrambling things for me. There are many more I have missed.

I would never have managed to put this book together without the golden opportunity of a fellowship at the Nieman Foundation at Harvard; thanks to Bob Giles and Ann Marie Lipinski, curators old and new, and their staff, for offering both a respite and a stimulating sabbatical; and my editors at the *New York Times* who gave me leave of absence to take up the fellowship and then another to write the book. Special thanks to Paige Williams, narrative journalism instructor, for encouraging me to write and helping with early chapters, and Nieman fellows of 2012 for their companionship and support.

Thanks to Bruce Nichols, who commissioned and edited this book, and who trusted me to tell the story as I wanted; Gloria Loomis, my agent, for her unswerving patience and guidance; Jane Perlez for matching me up with Gloria; Martin Beiser, a master line editor; and Margaret Hogan, the smoothest of copy editors.

Thanks to Diana Soler and her family for the loan of their house in

Segur de Calafell in Spain; Hiromi Yasui for such a warm welcome at the Silk Road Hotel in Bamiyan and her home in Kabul; Ansa Zafar and her family for beautiful, reflective days in Gulberg, Lahore; Sima Natiq and family, friends for so many years in Peshawar and Kabul. Thanks, too, to Sabrina Tavernise and Rory MacFarquhar for welcoming me so often in Washington, D.C., and for being the most enthusiastic supporters when this book was only an idea; Thomas de Waal and Georgina Wilson also for their hospitality and encouragement; and Gretchen Peters for making space for me in her house and giving me enough ideas to write a whole second book.

Good colleagues in difficult times: Chris Chivers, Tyler Hicks, David Rohde, Pamela Constable, and Hiromi Yasui.

To the many photographers, good companions all, who followed this story with me and shared their photos.

Special admiration and love to my colleague, photographer Joao Silva, and his wife, Viv, and children, for their courage and determination to pull through Joao's injuries. Joao, more than anyone, reminded me to keep following the Afghan story.

Finally, thanks to my family for their combined love of Afghanistan: my parents for their unfailing belief that I had a book in me that was worth reading; my sisters, Fiona and Michaela, always willing to discuss Afghanistan, who read and advised on the manuscript and photos; my brother-in-law, Dr. Philippe Bonhoure, for his *solidarité* and cuisine, and all the staff and supporters at Sandy Gall's Afghanistan Appeal, who became like a second family.

And to all my Afghan friends, too many to mention, and sadly too many departed, for their incomparable dignity and generosity of spirit.

NOTES

All quotations that are not specifically cited are drawn from my interviews with the people quoted.

PROLOGUE

1. Elizabeth Rubin, *Roots of Impunity: Pakistan's Endangered Press and the Perilous Web of Militancy, Security and Politics,* special report for the Committee to Protect Journalists, May 2013, p. 19, http://www.cpj.org/reports/CPJ.Pakistan.Roots.of.Impunity.pdf.
2. Bob Dietz, Introduction, ibid., p. 6.

1. THE TALIBAN SURRENDER

1. Officially called the United National Islamic Front for the Salvation of Afghanistan (or Jabha-yi Muttahid-i Islami-yi Milli bara-yi Nijat-i Afghanistan), the front was formed in 1996 after the Taliban seized power in Kabul.
2. Interview with Amrullah Saleh, chief of Afghan National Directorate of Security, 2002 to 2010, Kabul, September 30, 2012.
3. Summarized Sworn Detainee Statement, Combatant Status Review Tribunal Transcripts, Guantánamo Bay Detention Facility, p. 3, http://projects.nytimes.com/guantanamo/detainees/7-mullah-mohammad-fazl/documents/4.
4. Interviews with Amrullah Saleh, September 30, 2012, and Arif Sarwari, head of intelligence for the Northern Alliance in 2001, Kabul, November 2012.
5. Interview with Mohammad Mohaqiq, Kabul, October 4, 2012.
6. Interview with Shams-ul-Haq Naseri, one of the mediators, Balkh, Afghanistan, December 2001.
7. Interviews with Northern Alliance officials who had intelligence from inside Kunduz at the time, Mazar-i-Sharif, December 2001, and Kabul, April 2013.
8. Interviews with Colonel Imam, Islamabad, May 2, 2009, and Rawalpindi, February 15, 2010.

2. THE PEOPLE TURN

1. The four were Karzai and three former mujahideen commanders from Kandahar: Hafizullah Khan, Haji Mand, and Haji Mohammad Shah Kako. Interviews with Hafizullah Khan, Kabul, November 2012.

2. Interviews with Mohammad Lal, Kabul, 2002 and October 2, 2012.

3. The four commanders were Bari Gul, a young and energetic commander; Muallem Qader; Mullah Jailani Akhundzada; and Ibrahim Akhundzada. Interviews with Mohammad Lal, his son Abdul Bari, and Mohammad Rahim, Durji, May 2002, and Kabul, October 2012.

4. Karzai has always claimed that he was evacuated to an airfield inside Afghanistan. This was clearly for political reasons so as not to be seen as having fled the country. In fact, he spent ten days in Jacobabad Airbase in Pakistan and only returned to Afghanistan after Kabul had fallen. Mohammad Lal and Hafizullah Khan spent five days with him in Jacobabad, and then were flown back to Uruzgan where they dispersed. In my view, it was a mistake by the Americans to break up the group since Karzai needed heavyweight tribal figures with him as well as fighters. Interviews with Mohammad Lal and Hafizullah Khan, Kabul, 2002 and 2012.

5. Interviews with Habib Ahmadzai, Kabul, 2005 and 2012.

6. Interview with Haji Din Mohammad, Kabul, October 3, 2012.

7. Abdul Razzaq was a notoriously vicious official from the Pakistani border town of Chaman. He is also accused of being behind the execution of former president Najibullah and his brother in Kabul in 1996.

8. The former Taliban minister, the late Mullah Khaksar, explained that the Taliban saw Abdul Haq as a potential leader and so a threat. See Lucy Morgan Edwards, *The Afghan Solution: The Inside Story of Abdul Haq, the CIA and How Western Hubris Lost Afghanistan* (London: Bactria Press, 2011).

9. A fragment of a speech of October 6, 2001, contained in an unreleased book written in 2004 by Amir Khan Mottaqi, a senior Taliban commander and former minister in the Taliban government, as reported by Carlo Franco in Antonio Giustozzi, ed., *Decoding the New Taliban: Insights from the Afghan Field* (London: Hurst, 2009), p. 272.

10. Recounted to me by a friend who was told this by Haji Bashar.

11. Eric Blehm, *The Only Thing Worth Dying For: How Eleven Green Berets Forged a New Afghanistan* (New York: HarperCollins, 2010), p. 91.

12. Interviews with Abdul Waheed Baghrani, Kandahar, May 2005, and Kabul, July 15, 2009.

13. Interview with Western diplomat, Kabul, December 2012. A member of the Taliban delegation involved in peace negotiations with Karzai in 2012 told this to the diplomat.

14. Interviews with Hafizullah Khan, Kabul, October and November 2012. Hafizullah Khan is now a senior diplomat in Afghanistan's foreign ministry and remains a

close friend of the president. He joined Karzai in Kandahar soon after the fall of the Taliban and learned of Mullah Omar's letter from Karzai himself. The Western diplomat involved in peace negotiations confirmed that the Taliban are now denying the existence of the letter.

15. Interviews with Abdul Waheed Baghrani, Kandahar, May 2005, and Kabul, 2010.
16. Some officials in Pakistan believe that bin Laden headed north through Kunar and then crossed over to the northern part of Pakistan's tribal areas. But that would have involved returning to Jalalabad from Tora Bora, which would have been hard to do undetected. Gulbuddin Hekmatyar has claimed that his group helped bin Laden into Kunar, although his assertions are often dubious. The more obvious route for bin Laden's escape was toward North Waziristan.
17. Bin Laden's words are paraphrased by Dalton Fury, *Kill Bin Laden: A Delta Force Commander's Account of the Hunt for the World's Most Wanted Man* (New York: St. Martin's Press, 2008), p. 233.
18. Interviews with villagers in Shkin and Bormol, January 2003.
19. One U.S. estimate is that ten thousand Taliban fighters were killed.

3. PAKISTAN'S PROTÉGÉS

1. Faizullah was aligned to Jamaat-e-Islami and then later Harakat-i-Inqilab-i-Islami, the mujahideen party led by Mohammad Nabi Mohammadi from which many Taliban came. When Mullah Omar broke away from Faizullah, he remained with Harakat.
2. Telephone interview with Mohammad Nabi, December 25, 2012. Mohammad Nabi is not his real name. The commander asked not to be identified by his real name to avoid trouble from the Taliban.
3. Telephone interview with Mohammad Nabi, December 25, 2012.
4. Interview with Hafizullah Khan, Kabul, October 24, 2012.
5. Interview with Hafizullah Khan, Kabul, October 24, 2012. The Taliban always claimed legitimacy for their actions by citing atrocities committed by the warlords and militias. In particular, they popularized a tale that Mullah Omar first moved against a checkpoint commander after two girls from Sangesar were abducted and raped at the checkpoint. The tale was untrue, according to Hafizullah Khan, whose own men were present on the raids. Most of the checkpoint commanders were thieves and stole cars and extorted money, but the Taliban exaggerated their crimes in order to justify their own usurping of power, he said.
6. Interview with Ustad Aleem, mujahideen commander in Kandahar and contemporary of Mullah Omar's, Kandahar, February 11, 2013.
7. Abdul Salam Zaeef, *My Life with the Taliban* (New York: Columbia University Press, 2010), p. 65.
8. Interviews with Colonel Imam, Islamabad, May 2, 2009, and Rawalpindi, February 15, 2010.

9. Shahzada Zulfiqar, a reporter with Agence France Presse in Quetta, was one of those reporters.

10. Interviews with Colonel Imam, Islamabad, May 2, 2009, and Rawalpindi, February 15, 2010.

11. Interview with Mansour's nephew Brigadier General Abdul Razziq, police chief of Kandahar, Kandahar, February 16, 2013.

12. For one of the best accounts of Pakistan's military assistance to the Taliban campaign, see Anthony Davis, "How the Taliban Became a Military Force," *Fundamentalism Reborn? Afghanistan and the Taliban,* ed. William Maley (New York: New York University Press, 1998), p. 43.

13. Interview with a source who knew the family involved.

14. Alex Strick van Linschoten and Felix Kuehn, *An Enemy We Created: The Myth of the Taliban/Al Qaeda Merger in Afghanistan 1970–2010* (London: Hurst, 2012), pp. 131–33. The authors suggest that there were questions about his leadership within the Taliban movement.

15. Interview with a journalist, Washington, D.C., June 22, 2012. The journalist requested not to be named for fear of repercussions from the ISI.

16. Interview with Abdul Waheed Wafa, Kabul, summer 2012. Waheed was at the time a student in Kabul. He worked at the *New York Times*'s Kabul bureau as a reporter from 2001 to 2011.

17. Rustam Shah Mohmand conducted his shuttle diplomacy in 1997 and 1999, on the request of then–prime minister of Pakistan Nawaz Sharif.

18. Interview with Rustam Shah Mohmand, Peshawar, December 3, 2012.

19. Interview with Jehangir Karamat, Lahore, November 26, 2012. General Karamat served as chief of army staff from 1996 to 1998.

20. Interview with Amrullah Saleh, Kabul, September 30, 2012.

21. Interview with Ziauddin Butt, Lahore, November 29, 2012.

22. Najwa bin Laden, Omar bin Laden, and Jean Sasson, *Growing Up Bin Laden: Osama's Wife and Son Take Us Inside Their Secret World* (New York: St. Martin's Press, 2009), p. 247.

23. Gretchen Peters, *Seeds of Terror: How Heroin Is Bankrolling the Taliban and al Qaeda* (New York: St. Martin's Press, 2009), p. 87.

24. Interview with Robert L. Grenier, Washington, D.C., June 22, 2012.

25. Ahmed Shah Massoud, *A Message to the People of the United States of America,* 1998, http://www.afghan-web.com/documents/let-masood.html. The numbers are higher than most diplomats' estimates, yet Massoud's intelligence gathering during the Soviet invasion and the Taliban era was often impressively accurate.

26. Reports by Kate Clark, *The Independent,* September 7, 2002, http://www.commondreams.org/headlines02/0907-08.htm, and the British Broadcasting Company, September 7, 2002, http://news.bbc.co.uk/2/hi/south_asia/2242594.stm.

27. From the transcript of an interview with Mullah Omar by Spozhmai Maiwandi, Voice of America, September 21, 2001.

28. Interview with Colonel Imam, Islamabad, May 2, 2009.
29. Interview with Talat Masood, Islamabad, November 24, 2012.
30. Interview with Colonel Imam, Islamabad, May 2, 2009.

4. THE TALIBAN IN EXILE

1. The Taliban would also gather at two other squares in Quetta, Nawai Ada and Chalu Bowri. By 2013, the Thursday gatherings were far bigger and the Taliban much more self-confident.
2. Bruce Riedel, *Deadly Embrace: Pakistan, America and the Future of the Global Jihad* (Washington, D.C.: Brookings Institution Press, 2011), p. 65.
3. Interview with Talat Masood, Islamabad, November 24, 2012.
4. Interview with Qazi Hussain Ahmad, Peshawar, December 4, 2012, shortly before his death.
5. Interview with a senior politician, Peshawar.
6. The statement was received and reported by the Peshawar-based news agency Afghan Islamic Press, as reported by various newspapers and agencies, February 17, 2003.
7. This account is according to Red Cross officials who spoke on condition of anonymity, Kandahar and Kabul, 2003.
8. Interview with Mullah Dadullah by Mirwais Afghan, BBC Pashtu Service reporter, Kandahar, March 28, 2003; Carlotta Gall, "As Rockets Strike, U.S. Hunts for Taliban Tied to Ambush," *New York Times,* March 31, 2003, http://www.nytimes.com/2003/03/31/world/nation-war-afghanistan-rockets-strike-us-hunts-for-taliban-tied-ambush.html.
9. Interview with Gul Agha Shirzai, Kandahar, April 2003.
10. As reported in the Pakistani daily newspaper *The News,* June 2003. Among those named were the former Taliban defense minister, Mullah Obaidullah; Mullah Dadullah; and Mullah Akhtar Mohammad Usmani.
11. Interview with Zalmai Khalilzad on Aina Television, Kabul, *Reuters,* June 18, 2005.
12. Interview with a senior retired ISI officer who served in positions in the tribal areas and the North West Frontier province, Islamabad, January 24, 2013.
13. Interview with Talatbek Masadykov, Kandahar, April 9, 2003, and Kabul, December 2012.
14. Interview with Robert L. Grenier, Washington, D.C., June 22, 2012.
15. Interview with Habib Jalib Baloch, Quetta, May 2003.

5. AL QAEDA REGROUPS

1. Chechens were often named as protagonists in the fighting, but the term seemed frequently to be used to include a variety of Russian-speaking Central Asians, Muslims from Russian republics such as Tartarstan and the republics of the North Cau-

casus, and even Chinese Uighurs. In 2001, I interviewed a Tartar who had fought in Chechnya, and a fighter from Kabardino-Balkaria, a republic in the Caucasus, among survivors at Qala-i-Janghi, but no Chechens.

2. Press conference by Colonel Rodney Davis, U.S. military spokesman, Bagram Airbase, October 29, 2003.

3. Briefing by Brigadier Amjad Rauf at the National Crisis Management Center, Ministry of Interior, Islamabad, September 13, 2006, at which I was present. Of the 709 foreigners apprehended and suspected of being members of al Qaeda, 542 were extradited, 123 were released, and 44 remained in custody in Pakistan. Some were given to the United States and sent to Guantánamo with their home countries' consent.

4. Interview with Mahmood Khan Achakzai, Quetta, May 2003.

5. Interview with a former senior ISI official, Islamabad, January 24, 2013. The official spoke on condition of anonymity in accordance with the rules of his organization.

6. Zahid Hussain, *The Scorpion's Tail: The Relentless Rise of Islamic Militants in Pakistan — and How It Threatens America* (New York: Free Press, 2010), p. 71.

7. Interview with Talat Masood, Islamabad, November 24, 2012.

8. Robin Wright and Peter Baker, "Musharraf: Bin Laden's Location Is Unknown," *Washington Post,* December 5, 2004, http://www.washingtonpost.com/wp-dyn/articles/A35711-2004Dec4.html.

6. THE WRONG ENEMY IN THE WRONG COUNTRY

1. Interview with Abdul Rahim, Deh Rawud, Afghanistan, July 2002.

2. Interview with foreign aid coordinator, October 2002.

3. Carlotta Gall, "Evidence of Air Strike in Afghanistan Seems to Rebut U.S. Account," *New York Times,* September 8, 2008, http://www.nytimes.com/2008/09/08/world/asia/08iht-afghan.1.15972217.html.

4. Carlotta Gall, "Afghan Leader Criticizes U.S. on Conduct of War," *New York Times,* April 26, 2008, http://www.nytimes.com/2008/04/26/world/asia/26afghan.html.

5. Some of those involved in the mistreatment of Dilawar and Habibullah (see pp. 107–111) were charged and found guilty of lying to investigators.

6. Interview with Abdul Jabar, Zazi Maidan, Khost province, Afghanistan, February 6, 2003.

7. Interview with Hakim Shah, Spyworzai village, Khost province, Afghanistan, February 6, 2003.

8. Reporting by David Rohde; Carlotta Gall and David Rohde, "Afghan Abuse Charges Raise New Questions on Authority," *New York Times,* September 17, 2004, http://www.nytimes.com/2004/09/17/international/asia/17afghan.html.

9. The death certificate was shown to me by Shahpoor at Yakubi, February 4, 2003. Under "Mode of Death" there were four boxes listing "natural," "accident," "suicide," and "homicide." "Homicide" was marked with a capital X. A photograph of the

medical certificate was later taken by Keith Bedford for the *New York Times;* see http://keithbedford.photoshelter.com/gallery-image/AFGHAN-MAN-KILLED -IN-U-S-CUSTODY/GoooovFzilmAmyho/Iooo07vNyyyFCt1Q.

10. U.S. military spokesman Colonel Rodney King confirmed that Habibullah's death certificate indicated his death as a homicide to a *New York Times* colleague, Amy Waldman, in March 2003.

11. Carlotta Gall, "U.S. Military Investigating Death of Afghan in Custody," *New York Times,* March 4, 2003, http://www.nytimes.com/2003/03/04/international /asia/04AFGH.html.

12. President George W. Bush, State of the Union speech, Washington, D.C., January 28, 2003, http://georgewbush-whitehouse.archives.gov/news/releases/2003/01 /20030128-19.html.

13. Two years after their deaths, the army's confidential investigative reports were leaked to Human Rights Watch and shown to colleagues at the *New York Times.* The papers confirmed the Afghans' accounts of the treatment at Bagram, and gave shocking detail of the behavior of U.S. military police and interrogators.

14. An Afghan government delegation visited the Guantánamo Bay prison in May– June 2006 and said that after interviewing the ninety-four Afghans still being held, roughly half of them were not guilty of serious crimes and should be released.

15. Interview with John W. Nicholson Jr., Washington, D.C., June 22, 2012.

16. Neil Sheehan, *A Bright Shining Lie: John Paul Vann and America in Vietnam* (New York: Random House, 1998).

7. THE TALIBAN RETURN

1. Abdul Rauf was released in 2008 and resumed a prominent role in the Taliban insurgency. A number of senior Taliban figures were released as a result of poor coordination between investigators in Guantánamo Bay and Kabul. Officials in southern Afghanistan, who knew how dangerous the men were, complained that they were never consulted.

2. Interviews with Abdul Razziq, Kajaki, July 23, 2007, and by telephone, October 15, 2012.

3. A flier found in a mosque in Zangabad in February 2006 was shown to me by a villager. Translated from Pashtu into English, it read as follows:

> *Announcement of the Islamic Emirate of Afghanistan.*
> *This is our message to all Muslim brothers:*
> *Today jihad is an obligation for all Muslim men and women; an*
> *obligation upon them, upon their wealth, and upon their sons. These infidels*
> *came to our country to destroy our Islam. If you call yourself a Muslim, come*
> *and work for Islam.*
> *The infidels are lying to you when they say they are giving you assistance.*

Be sure, they are never truthful in what they say. Never believe them. They are the sons of Satan. If anyone helps these infidels in any way, that person is an infidel, and that person will be given the death sentence.

Quickly withdraw your hand of support for the government. If anyone does not withdraw their support, they will be sentenced under Sharia law.

Do not go to school. If anyone goes to school they will be sentenced under Sharia law. If anyone shaves their beards, or cuts it shorter than Sharia rules, and if anyone goes to a dog fight, or if a driver takes them to a dog fight, they will face a very strong sentence.

You must grow opium; this is a jihad against the infidels, and be sure that no one can eradicate your fields.

Government members should be beheaded, and their property should be looted.

4. The three Anglo-Afghan wars occurred in 1839–1842, 1878–1880, and 1919.
5. Interview with a journalist from South Waziristan who spoke with me on condition that his name not be used. See also Syed Saleem Shahzad, *Inside Al-Qaeda and the Taliban: Beyond Bin Laden and 9/11* (London: Pluto Press, 2011), p. 24.
6. Interview with American diplomat, Washington D.C., June 2012. The diplomat spoke on condition of anonymity in accordance with standard diplomatic practice.
7. Karzai's own account at a press conference on February 18, 2006, in Kabul on his return from Islamabad.
8. Interview with Amrullah Saleh, Kabul, September 30, 2012.
9. The resident, well known to me, requested that his name not be used for fear of retribution from the Taliban. Interview with Ruhullah Khapalwak, Kandahar, April 2006.
10. American officials estimated that armed Taliban in the province numbered from 300 to 1,000 men. The governor estimated that there were 300 armed insurgents in each of the six districts, making 1,800 in all.
11. Carlotta Gall, "In a Remote Corner, an Afghan Army Evolves from Fantasy to Slightly Ragged Reality," *New York Times,* January 25, 2003, http://www.nytimes .com/2003/01/25/world/threats-responses-rebuilding-afghanistan-remote-corner -afghan-army-evolves.html.
12. Interview with Lieutenant General David Barno, commander of U.S. forces in Afghanistan, Kabul, April 19, 2004.
13. Thanks to colleague David Rohde for his work on the failures of police training; see James Glanz and David Rohde, "Panel Faults U.S.-Trained Afghan Police," *New York Times,* December 4, 2006, http://www.nytimes.com/2006/12/04/world /asia/04police.html.
14. Zhare district was created out of Maiwand and Panjwayi districts after 2001.
15. First reports said sixteen civilians were killed, but a joint Afghan-ISAF investigation concluded that thirty-five civilians were killed.

16. Interview with Western diplomat, Kandahar, May 2006.
17. Carlotta Gall, "Taliban Surges Reduces as U.S. Reduces Afghan Mission," *New York Times*, June 6, 2006, http://www.nytimes.com/2006/06/11/world/asia/11afghan.html.
18. Al Jazeera's enterprising bureau chief in Afghanistan, Palestinian journalist Samer Allawi, took a taxi and drove into Panjwayi looking for the Taliban. Taped interview filmed by Al Jazeera, Panjwayi, August 27, 2006, viewed by me in Kabul, September 2006.
19. Interview with Canadian military official, Pashmul, Afghanistan, September 22, 2006. This Mullah Abdul Rauf said he was from Spin Boldak. He was no relation to the Abdul Rauf of Kajaki.
20. Email correspondence with Gary Bowman, January 22, 2013.
21. Interview with Staff Sergeant Gregory C. Robinson, FOB Wilson, Zhare, Kandahar province, Afghanistan, January 24, 2011.
22. Sergeant Robinson returned to active duty and was deployed to FOB Wilson again as part of the surge in 2010, one of a dozen amputees back in theater in Afghanistan.
23. The Manley Panel report was released in 2008. A web version is available at http://www.afghanistan.gc.ca/canada-afghanistan/assets/pdfs/Afghan_Report_web_e.pdf, accessed January 14, 2013.

8. THE SUICIDE BOMB FACTORY

1. Interviews with intelligence officials, Kandahar, February 2006, http://www.nytimes.com/2006/02/15/international/asia/15afghan.html.
2. I was allowed to interview Daoud Shah in an anteroom at the National Directorate of Security jail in Kabul in the presence of intelligence officials, October 2006.
3. Interviews with Daoud Shah and Afghan intelligence officials, Kabul, and with Daoud Shah's father, Hekmat Shah, and Maulavi Khairpuri, Karachi, October 2006.
4. Interview with Afghan intelligence officer, Kabul, October 10, 2006. The official spoke on condition that his name and rank not be used in keeping with the rules of his organization.
5. Bruce Riedel, *Deadly Embrace: Pakistan, America and the Future of the Global Jihad* (Washington, D.C.: Brookings Institution Press, 2011), p. 65; interview with Talat Masood, Islamabad, November 2012.
6. Husain Haqqani, *Pakistan: Between Mosque and Military* (Washington, D.C.: Carnegie Endowment for International Peace, 2005), p. 306.
7. Interview with madrassa student, Islamabad, January 12, 2013.
8. Interview with Pakistani police officer, Lahore, November 2012.
9. This was told to me in strictest confidence so I have withheld the name of the village, the elder who took part in the meeting, and my acquaintance who relayed to me the story, for their own safety.

10. Interview with Western diplomat, London, August 2012. The former diplomat asked to speak on condition of anonymity in accordance with the rules of his office.

11. Interview with former interior minister and peace negotiator Rustam Shah Mohmand, Peshawar, December 3, 2012.

12. Interview with the official, United States, September 2013. The official agreed to talk to me on condition of anonymity in keeping with the rules of his organization.

9. MILITANCY EXPLODES IN PAKISTAN

1. Thanks to my *New York Times* colleague Salman Masood for his frontline reporting with me that day, July 3, 2007.

2. For the transcript of his video statement, see http://azelin.files.wordpress.com /2010/08/dr-ayman-al-zawahiri-the-aggression-against-lal-masjid1.pdf.

3. Interview with former Pakistani cabinet minister, Islamabad, December 2012.

4. Interview with former Pakistani cabinet minister, Lahore, December 1, 2012.

5. Interview (by me and *New York Times* colleague David Rohde) with former Pakistani senior intelligence officer, Islamabad, December 2007.

6. Mujahid Hussain, *Punjabi Taliban: Driving Extremism in Pakistan* (Delhi: Pentagon Press, 2012), p. 85.

7. Among the militant leaders brought in to intercede were Fazlur Rehman Khalil, the leader of the banned group Harakat-ul-Mujahideen, who had helped in negotiations at the Red Mosque; Abdul Rauf Azhar, brother of the leader of Jaish-e-Mohammad, who spoke to the militants on the phone; and Commander Jabar, the deputy of Jaish-e-Mohammad and one of the most infamous militants who has been accused of attacks on Christian churches and schools after 9/11.

8. Malik Ishaq was released from jail in July 2011 after he was acquitted of some cases against him and given bail for others as part of the deal made in 2009. He was detained again in March 2013 after one of the worst campaigns of sectarian violence, blamed on Lashkar-e-Jhangvi, against Shiites in Quetta.

9. Thanks for extra input from a Pakistani reporter on this incident. I am not naming the reporter for their own safety. A spokesman for the ISI confirmed that on some occasions, the military has negotiated with armed militants in order to win the release of hostages. He denied, however, any nefarious intentions on this occasion or others. "War is something in which you have to try everything," he told me. Interview, Islamabad, January 2013.

10. Bhutto was speaking at a press conference in Dubai at which I was present, October 17, 2007.

11. Interview with Ejaz Shah, Lahore, December 1, 2012.

12. Interview with Syed Mohammad Yousuf Shah, Akora Khattak, Pakistan, January 12, 2013.

13. A UN Commission of Inquiry that investigated the circumstances of her death found the security arrangements provided by the government "fatally insufficient and inef-

fective." Bhutto faced threats from multiple sources, Taliban, al Qaeda, local jihadi groups, and potentially from elements in the military establishment, it said. See http://www.un.org/News/dh/infocus/Pakistan/UN_Bhutto_Report_15April2010 .pdf.
14. Interview with Chaudhry Zulfiqar Ali, Islamabad, January 23, 2013.
15. Interview with senior Afghan security official, Kabul, October 2012.

10. THE TALIBAN CLOSE THEIR GRIP

1. Press conference on the investigation into the April 7, 2009, attack on the national parade, Kabul, April 30, 2009.
2. Interview with a senior Afghan intelligence official, Kabul, 2008.
3. The strategy is laid out by Brigadier Muhammad Yousaf who headed the Afghan bureau of the ISI in the 1980s. Muhammad Yousaf and Mark Adken, *The Bear Trap: Afghanistan's Untold Story* (London: Leo Cooper, 1992), pp. 1, 151.
4. General Kayani said this to a group of Pakistani journalists when he was head of the ISI. American officials have quoted him as saying the same, apparently overhearing it through electronic intercepts. See David E. Sanger, *The Inheritance: The World Obama Confronts and the Challenges to American Power* (New York: Random House, 2009), ch. 8.
5. Interview with Nuristani elder, Kabul, 2008. The elder requested his name be withheld for security reasons.
6. Interview with farmer by a *New York Times* colleague, Taimoor Shah, Kandahar, August 2009.
7. Interview with Haji Abdul Majid, Kandahar, August 2009.
8. Interview with Samad Zazai, Kabul, October 6, 2012.
9. Interview with Mohammad Haq Jenabi, Kandahar, August 2009.

11. KARZAI'S TURN

1. Sabrina Tavernise, Mark Landler, and Helene Cooper, "With New Afghan Vote, Path to Stability Is Unclear," *New York Times,* October 21, 2009, p. A12, http://www .nytimes.com/2009/10/21/world/asia/21afghan.html.
2. The cables were later released by Wikileaks; see http://documents.nytimes.com /eikenberry-s-memos-on-the-strategy-in-afghanistan.
3. House of Commons, oral evidence taken before the Foreign Affairs Committee, "The UK's Foreign Policy towards Afghanistan and Pakistan," November 9, 2010. Corrected transcript posted online at http://www.publications.parliament.uk/pa /cm201011/cmselect/cmfaff/c514-iii/c51401.htm.
4. Interview with former cabinet minister, Kabul, April 24, 2013.
5. Telephone interview with Simar Samar, Kabul, April 25, 2013.
6. Interview with Richard C. Holbrooke, Kabul, August 2009.

7. Telephone interview with Sayed Tayeb Jawad, June 13, 2012.

8. Interviews with General David Richards, Kabul and Kandahar, September 2006.

9. For details of President Karzai's handling of the Kabul Bank crisis, see reporting by Matthew Rosenberg, "Political Meddling Hampers Inquiry into Kabul Bank Debacle," *New York Times*, November 28, 2012, http://www.nytimes.com/2012/11/28 /world/asia/inquiry-into-kabul-bank-fraud-hits-snags.html.

10. Interview with Umar Daudzai, Afghan ambassador to Pakistan and former presidential chief of staff, Islamabad, January 29, 2013.

11. Interview with a Western diplomat, Kabul, 2006.

12. Alissa Rubin, "Karzai's Words Leave Few Choices for the West," *New York Times*, April 5, 2010, http://www.nytimes.com/2010/04/05/world/asia/05karzai.html.

13. Sherard Cowper-Coles, *Cables from Kabul: The Inside Story of the West's Afghanistan Campaign* (London: HarperPress, 2011), p. 58.

12. OBAMA'S SURGE

1. Commander's Initial Assessment, Commander, NATO International Security Assistance Force, Afghanistan, U.S. Forces Afghanistan, August 30, 2009.

2. Interview with Abdul Razziq, Kandahar, February 16, 2013.

3. Interview with Lieutenant General Nick Carter, deputy commander of HQ ISAF, Kabul, March 1, 2013.

13. OSAMA'S SAFE HAVEN

1. For a detailed account of bin Laden's family life, see bin Laden, bin Laden, and Sasson, *Growing up Bin Laden*.

2. Pakistani officials gave conflicting accounts as to how many women and children were in the compound and taken into custody. This is my tally from various sources and may not be complete.

3. I have withheld further details regarding the source in order to protect those involved. I have not been able to confirm this account with a second source, but two former senior U.S. government officials told me that the report was consistent with their own conclusions.

4. Interview with former U.S. official, United States, September 2013.

5. Interviews with ISI spokesmen, Islamabad, 2011 and 2013.

6. Carlotta Gall, Pir Zubair Shah, and Eric Schmitt, "Seized Phone Offers Clues to Bin Laden's Pakistani Links," *New York Times*, June 23, 2011, http://www.nytimes .com/2011/06/24/world/asia/24pakistan.html.

7. Thanks to reporting from colleague Pir Zubair Shah; see ibid.

8. Mark Mazzetti, "Signs That Bin Laden Weighed Seeking Pakistani Protection," *New York Times*, May 26, 2011, http://www.nytimes.com/2011/05/27/world/ middleeast/27binladen.html.

9. Account of Maryam, widow of Ibrahim, *Report of the Commission of Inquiry into the Abbottabad Incident of May 2, 2011*, p. 44, note 55. The report was not made public but was leaked to Al Jazeera and posted on its website in July 2013; see http://www.aljazeera.com/news/asia/2013/07/20137813412615531.html.

10. Both episodes, according to a Pakistani intelligence source.

11. Special Correspondent, "Qaeda Plans to Trap U.S. in Afghanistan beyond 2011," *The Daily Times*, July 5, 2010, http://dailytimes.com.pk/default.asp?page=2010%5C07%5C05%5Cstory_5-7-2010_pg1_6. The newspaper report states that the meeting occurred in the Afghan border region, but a senior Pakistani official confirmed that the meeting actually took place in Kohat, inside Pakistan.

12. Pervez Musharraf, *In the Line of Fire: A Memoir* (New York: Simon and Schuster, 2006), p. 259.

13. Elizabeth Rubin, *Roots of Impunity: Pakistan's Endangered Press and the Perilous Web of Militancy, Security, and Politics*, a special report of the Committee to Protect Journalists, May 2013.

14. Senate Armed Services Committee Hearing on Iraq and Afghanistan, Washington, D.C., September 22, 2011, http://www.jcs.mil/speech.aspx?ID=1651.

15. Interview with former senior U.S. official, United States, September 2013.

16. Interview with former senior U.S. official, United States, September 2013.

17. See *Report of the Commission of Inquiry*, http://www.aljazeera.com/news/asia/2013/07/20137813412615531.html.

14. SPRINGTIME IN ZANGABAD

1. Interview with Abdul Wudood, Pishin Gan Sayedan, Kandahar province, Afghanistan, February 16, 2013.

2. Telephone interview with Major General Robert B. Abrams, March 19, 2013. He also gave an interview to a group of Pentagon reporters, March 13, 2013, http://www.defense.gov/transcripts/transcript.aspx?transcriptid=5204.

3. Interview with Asadullah Khaled, head of the National Directorate of Security, Kabul, October 13, 2012.

4. Interview by Gordon Lubold with General John Allen, "Are We Winning in Afghanistan?" *Foreign Policy*, September 5, 2012, http://www.foreignpolicy.com/articles/2012/09/05/are_we_winning_in_afghanistan.

5. Telephone interviews with Sultan Mohammad, April and September 2013.

6. Interview with former Pakistani legislator, Washington D.C., September 2013.

7. The United Nations reports that in the six years from 2006 to 2012, 14,728 civilians were killed. *Afghanistan Annual Report 2012: Protection of Civilians in Armed Conflict*, United Nations Assistance Mission in Afghanistan, p. 1, http://unama.unmissions.org/LinkClick.aspx?fileticket=KoB5RL2XYcU=.

Afghan police and army deaths were tallied at around 1,000 in 2007 and 3,400 in 2012. Total deaths from 2007 to 2012 came to nearly 10,000. Afghanistan Index,

Brookings Institute, http://www.brookings.edu/about/programs/foreign-policy/afghanistan-index.

8. Interview with Zhare elder, Kandahar, February 10, 2013.
9. Thomas McAdams Deford, "Leaving Afghanistan–Now the Hard Part," *The Free Press*, May 23, 2012; http://www.freepressonline.com/main.asp?SectionID=50&SubSectionID=72&ArticleID=19483

AFTERWORD

1. Members of the Afghan police and army killed in action reached 4,634 by November 2014, higher than the total for 2013 of 4,350. Missy Ryan, "Afghan Forces' Casualties 'Not Sustainable,' U.S. Commander Says," *Washington Post*, November 5, 2014, http://www.washingtonpost.com/world/national-security/afghan-forces-casualties-not-sustainable-us-commander-says/2014/11/05/a3df595a-6514-11e4-bb14-4cfea1e742d5_story.html.
2. *Progress Towards Security and Stability in Afghanistan*, Department of Defense, October 2014, p. 14, http://www.defense.gov/pubs/Oct2014_Report_Final.pdf.

INDEX

security. *See* Inter-Services Intelligence
Seeds of Terror (Peters), 51
Serena Hotel attack, 186, 187–88
Shah, Daoud, 148–49
Shah, Ejaz, 175, 246, 249–50
Shah, Hakim, 109
Shah, Mohammad, 94–97
Shah, Mohammad Zahir, 24, 205
Shah, Pir Zubair, 162
Shah, Syed Mohammad Yousuf, 282
Shah Wali Kot, Afghanistan, 33, 72
Shahikot, Afghanistan, 37
Shahzad, Saleem, xix, 259
Shahzada, Mullah, 58
Shamshatu, Pakistan, 149
Sharif, Abdul Malik, 93–96
Sharif, Mohammad, 93–96
Sharif, Nawaz
    election of, 177, 262–63
    in exile, 66
Shawal Valley, Pakistan, 295
Sheehan, Neil, 117
Shiberghan, Afghanistan, 18
Shirzai, Gul Agha, 72, 212–13
Shkin, Afghanistan, 78–82
Shomali Plain, Afghanistan, 46, 49–50
Shrine of the Blessed Cloak, 48, 279
Silva, Joao, 231–32
Siya Sang, Afghanistan, 97
Sohail, Mohammed, 150
Sons of Iraq, 274
Soviet Union, in Afghanistan, xii–xiii, 40,
    120–21, 204, 299n1
Spann, Johnny Micheal, 12
Spanta, Rangin Dadfar, 211
Special Services Group (SSG), 167,
    169–70
Spin Boldak, Afghanistan, 43, 69, 226–27
Spinpul suicide ambush and homicide,
    115–17
SSG. *See* Special Services Group
Status of Forces Agreement, 112

Steiner, Michael, 221
students. *See* madrassas
suicide bombing. *See also* 9/11
    for Bhutto, Benazir, 176–77, 178–79
    casualties, 12, 68, 115, 144–46
    families of, 153–57
    goal of, 151–52
    Haqqania madrassa, 177–78
    investigations, 147–62, 187–89
    ISI involvement in, 149, 151, 170,
        187–89
    in Kabul, 149, 185–89
    Kandahar, 143–46
    Karachi, 176
    London (7/7), 255
    Mehran Naval Station, 258
    middlemen, 155–56
    NATO and, 149, 189
    organizations, 151, 155, 187
    Orgun, 291–94
    of Pakistan's military, 169–73, 178–79,
        253, 258
    Pakistan's strategy of, 147–59, 178,
        187–90
    Paktika, 298
    Pashtunabad, 157–58
    principles of, 33
    of Rabbani, Burhanuddin, 260
    Rawalpindi, 171–73, 178–79, 253
    recruitment, 147–50, 154–59
    rise of, 143
    Spinpul, 115–17
    training, 154
    Waziristan, 169
surge. *See* insurgency
surveillance, NSA, 159–60
Swat Valley, Pakistan, 64, 253

Tablighi Jamaat, 153
Taj, Nadeem, 250
Tajiks, 2, 46
Takht-e-Pul, Afghanistan, 44